RELIGION, AGENCY,

Religion, Agency, Restitution

The Wilde Lectures in Natural Religion 1999

ROLAND LITTLEWOOD

OXFORD

UNIVERSITY PRESS

OXFORD

UNIVERSITY PRESS

Great Clarendon Street, Oxford OX2 6DP

Oxford University Press is a department of the University of Oxford.
It furthers the University's objective of excellence in research, scholarship,
and education by publishing worldwide in

Oxford New York

Athens Auckland Bangkok Bogotá Buenos Aires Calcutta
Cape Town Chennai Dar es Salaam Delhi Florence Hong Kong Istanbul
Karachi Kuala Lumpur Madrid Melbourne Mexico City Mumbai
Nairobi Paris São Paulo Shanghai Singapore Taipei Tokyo Toronto Warsaw

with associated companies in Berlin Ibadan

Oxford is a registered trade mark of Oxford University Press
in the UK and in certain other countries

Published in the United States
by Oxford University Press Inc., New York

British Library Cataloguing in Publication Data

Data applied for

Library of Congress Cataloging in Publication Data

Data available

ISBN 0–19–924197–X
ISBN 0–19–924675–0 (pbk)

1 3 5 7 9 10 8 6 4 2

Typeset by J&L Composition Ltd, Filey, North Yorkshire

Printed in Great Britain
on acid-free paper by
T.J. International Ltd., Padstow, Cornwall

ACKNOWLEDGEMENTS

I owe a particular debt of gratitude to the Wilde Electors, to All Souls College and its warden, Dr John Davis, for inimitable hospitality during the period I gave the Wilde Lectures, and also to Professor David Parkin for his generosity and the invitation to join him in teaching at the Institute of Social and Cultural Anthropology. To both of them, my sincere thanks. I am also grateful to publishers and editors for kindly allowing me to publish argument, and in some cases text, which has previously appeared in the following publications of mine: *British Journal of Medical Psychology*, 53 (1980), 213–25; *Social Science and Medicine*, 19 (1984), 705–15; (with Simon Dein) *Culture, Medicine and Psychiatry*, 19 (1995), 339–83; *Anthropology Today*, 14/2 (1998), 5–14; Royal Anthropological Institute Occasional Paper 43 (1996). My original fieldwork in Trinidad was supported by the Social Science Research Council.

I owe much to my student and colleague Dr Simon Dein, not least for permission to use here some of his splendid field material in Lectures 5 and 6; and also to my other graduate students, particularly for their contributions to seminars where some of these lectures were presented in a more tentative form. The original oral style of my presentations has been partly revised here. My thanks for secretarial and editing work to Mary Bamber, Gloria Jones, and my Oxford University Press editors.

CONTENTS

And I shall behold God through my flesh
(Job 19: 26)

Introduction

While these lectures draw in part on my clinical work as a psychiatrist with patients from religious movements in the West, they are primarily based on earlier anthropological fieldwork with a new African Caribbean religion in Trinidad (which has provided the first detailed day-to-day account of the genesis of a new religious cosmology) and more recently with ethical transformations in the older Caribbean cults (shango, vodu), and among the ultra-Orthodox Jewish Hasidim. There is a close relationship between the explanations of misfortune (which are hardly arbitrary), reconciliation, and restitution in the historical—and other—religions and in therapeutics. I think that cosmological and redemptive assumptions exist in any type of healing, whether physical or psychological. Spiritual and healing conceptualizations interpenetrate in a number of surprising ways, and I examine the religious turn in systems of therapeutics as well as the appearance of healing practices within social institutions which are more generally regarded as religious.

Running through all of this is the question of how and why human cognition may attribute agency and purpose to the natural world; the pragmatic limitations of doing so; and, beyond that, our customary distinction between what we may term the naturalistic and personalistic modes of thought, the scientific and the humanistic, and how both healing and religion may proceed from one to the other.

The physical origins of religious experience and belief have been debated since the eighteenth century. To what extent may cosmologies and their moral order be derived from—or modelled on—natural phenomena? May we argue that they originate in human experience of the physical world, whether through appreciation of that world or more directly through psychophysiology? Or should we look rather at cultural and historical evidence for the sources of 'religion' as do most social scientists and critics? How could we reconcile these rather different approaches?

To develop a phenomenology of religion grounded in our physical experience is not to reduce vital cultural meanings to biology or even to pathology, but rather to suggest a jointly biosocial understanding of what have been called our 'intuitive notions'[1] concerning ultrahuman agency, invidia, suffering, and restitution. And these primary representations, says William James,[2] may certainly be more evident in what we take as 'extreme' situations.

Outline of the Lectures

How does physical experience become a plausible model for the divine? There is a (particularly psychoanalytical) Western tradition, briefly summarized in the first lecture, which equates all religious innovation and experience with psychological abnormality. While this may be faulted for its hypothetical psychohistory and implausible psychodynamic assumptions, its main problem is its equation of the original process of innovation with that of everyday continuing religious experience in the new group: what has been termed the 'genetic fallacy'. Yet we cannot exclude the possibility that religious innovation may on occasion originate in extreme (psychopathological, if you will) experiences. The likely conditions under which this may occur are outlined in the first lecture, with particular emphasis on the likely process of the reception of new ideas by others. Instances are provided by Sabbatai Sevi, the seventeenth-century Jewish messianic figure (discussed in the first lecture); Mother Earth, the founder of a new religion in the Caribbean (in the second and third lectures); the Canadian Dukhobors. This is rather different from the usual consideration of the biology of religion:[3] in other words how religious precept and membership contribute to an individual's Darwinian fitness. The reverse direction in fact.

Explicit parallels between the human body and the cosmos are commonplace in comparative studies of religion, yet academic interest tends to emphasize the physical body simply as shared discipline and knowledge: there appear no 'natural symbols' unmediated by any social cognitions. Without attributing ontological primacy to either physical body or religious world-view, to individual experience or collective practice, we can note, however, the deployment of novel cosmological idioms which are derived directly from engagement in, for example, sexual relations and childbirth (Mother Earth, Ann Lee (the originator of the American Shakers), Margery Kemp, and Joanna Southcott) or from ex-

---

[1] Boyer (1997).   [2] James (1958: 24).   [3] Reynolds and Tanner (1983).

perience in physical space (Sabbatai Sevi). My argument is not conventionally psychological here, except inasmuch as we accept Marcel Mauss's idea of 'psychological facts as connecting cogs and not as causes, except in moments of creation or reform'.[4] Both childbearing and bodily movement in a gravitational field (discussed in the second lecture) provide the ground (or 'base model' in Lakoff's[5] terms) for complex figurings of origin, divine agency, and theodicy: and in which followers themselves resonate with these bodily idioms. Without making too extravagant and universal claims, we might consider whether idioms of spiritual flight and creation at a distance do not appear more congenial to men, idioms of experienced penetration and cosmological unfolding more accessible to women.

The personal life and radical physical experiences of a contemporary African Caribbean prophet, Mother Earth, are considered in some detail, including the process by which these experiences were interpreted by her and others to provide the cosmological charter for a new religious community known as the Earth People, in which everyday contingency and the natural order are invested with something like human agency. The prophet's own formal narrative of her life, as found in her teaching, is intended simultaneously as her personal biography and as the new cosmological order; and the structure of her group realizes the personal sentiments the members hold for her as refracted through this cosmogony. The subsequent development and history of the group is briefly described, along with the limitations of pathomimesis for a religious community, together with a refutation of the biographical fallacy. Only partly tongue-in-cheek I conclude by recommending her own account of Western institutions and knowledge (in which to an extent she anticipates the later ecofeminism of the United States) as an incestuous mimicry of our conjectured origins as being perhaps no less unreasonable than empirical science's claim to mirror an external reality. 'Religion' may be argued as rather more an epistemology than a metaphysics.

While proposing (in the fourth lecture) some renewed interest in currently unfashionable aspects of religion—pathological sources and euhemerism—I am not, unlike the Durkheim of *The Elementary Forms of the Religious Life*,[6] proposing a general explanation of religion as a shared experience but only for the founders: and for a small proportion of them

---

[4] Mauss (1979*b*: 121).   [5] Lakoff (1987).   [6] Durkheim (1976).

at that.[7] I am not of course concerned with the plausible origins of 'religions' but only with certain dramatic revisions within a continuing tradition. One might, however, perceive certain affinities between my accounts of Mother Earth and Sabbatai Sevi and the affective theories of religious origin proposed by Robert Marett.[8] But, again, this is not to declare that origin and continuation share the same affective state.[9]

While Western monotheisms radically distinguish the sensible world from its ultrahuman reality, an explicit image of healing has been common to both the restoration of the body to health and safety, and the deliverance of a wounded spirit, or indeed the redemption and protection of a whole community. Prophets and the founders of new religious dispensations commonly engage in, or are regarded by later hagiographers as having employed, miracles of healing. They assert a double register, mundane versus sacred, embodiment versus representation, usually enhancing the very separation, yet at the same time they show that it may be mediated by certain individuals. Indeed their own moral authority appears to be justified through tapping higher realities to heal sickness and insanity. The expectations on a prophet to reconcile the two worlds through healing—and his occasional resistance to these—are well demonstrated for the Baal Shem Tov (the founder of Jewish Hasidism) and for Jesus (Matthew 4: 23; Mark 5: 25), together with the use of an idiom such as healing for an increased turning to the spiritual, through confession and absolution with conversion of sick soul (and body) to a fundamentally new perspective. The fifth and sixth lectures develop through more detailed accounts of the relationship between bodily experience in religious conversion and in healing: possession and catharsis, the illocutionary act of *kvitl* (petitioning) among Hasidim, and the dispersal of invidia in folk healing and Western medicine. The limits of a shared mechanism of restitution in religious and physical healing are considered, emphasizing how physical idioms of catharsis and balance may be shared to a certain extent between the two; and how an idiom of pathology may reconfigure suffering, misfortune, and sin. Conversely, the influence of recent Pentecostalist moral dualism on African Caribbean religions (shango, vodu) shifts their pragmatic healing into a more absolute ethical position.

---

[7] At the same time, my stay with the Earth People has permitted certain speculative conceits on the early life of Christianity: say, on how the chance encounter of two disciples with a stranger on the road to Emmaus became translated into an appearance of the recently executed prophet (Luke 24: 13–35).

[8] Marett (1909).   [9] Evans-Pritchard (1977: 44–6).

The last two lectures consider the introduction into purely naturalistic (here generally biomedical) accounts of bodily experience of what we can gloss as religious (personalistic) phenomena. In both, we are concerned not only with personal experience and the purely intellectual possibilities made available, but with the organization of a particular interpretation in a social group with its own political processes. The first instance is that of the progression from nineteenth-century hysteria and its treatment, hypothesis, to spiritualism, Christian Science, and the animism (as they called it) of psychologists such as Myers, McDougall, and William James. The second traces the religious turn in such Western cults of affliction as Alcoholics Anonymous and other 'twelve step' therapeutic programmes. In both, ascription of diminished agency and accountability is converted into an accommodation of suffering, a cognition recalling that of certain African and South Asian possession cults. The recent appearance in America and Europe of something like spirit possession as multiple personality disorder increasingly pictures the alternative self as an intrusive spiritual power (such as a vengeful aborted foetus—compare the sar cults of Somalia and the Sudan). Not surprisingly, new figurings of self and other, self and divinity, reflect current preoccupations with our physical and moral experience (rape, pregnancy, abortion, trauma, managerial self-realization). The attribution of agency and restitution are considered here in relation to contemporary public ideas on child sexual abuse and the recent popularity of the idiom of therapy as one of moral restitution in the 'human potential movement'. The empirical and cultural suppositions that have structured these as intrusive extraterrestrial aliens (at one well-known United States medical school clinic) or as Satanic child abductors (in both Britain and America) is considered in the context of a recent social and political turn in the West to the personalistic. The consideration of altered locations of the self and agency in cyberspace (contemporary computer use and virtual reality) returns us to our original starting-point: how embodied experience can be cognized in a way that allows humans to perceive agency, purpose, and rule-governed justice in accidents and natural phenomena; and how these may be recognized as divine, or at least as ultrahuman.

The last is a generally more theoretical lecture, systematizing and commenting on the evidence of the earlier ones. Following Kant and others, I would propose that we understand ourselves and the world in two fundamentally different ways: either as a consequence of cause and effect relationships, generally independent of, but potentially accessible to, human awareness (the naturalistic mode of thought); or we can understand the same matters personalistically—as motivated action, volition, purpose, representation, suffering, self-awareness, intersubjectivity, and identification. While Europeans and European Americans conventionally allocate a particular area of interest to one or the other, we can apply either mode to any phenomenon. The experiencing self may be objectified; the nature (or divine) world may be personified. Human suffering may be translated into a disease entity, or the reverse. Neither mode can be demonstrated as either true or false: we always live with the two options, and while we can pass from one to the other, only one is plausible at any one time. Such a dichotomy can itself be explained both from neuropsychology and evolutionary psychology, but also from cultural history. Examples are drawn from recent experimental work by psychologists on the attribution of agency, from the comparative ethnography of emotions and suffering as *passiones*[10] sent by a deity, and from ethnographic material on the collective attribution of justice and on the direction of invidia.

[10] Lienhardt (1961: 151).

1

Extreme Experiences and
Religious Cognitions

Insanity and Extreme Experience

In these lectures I propose to deal with certain associations between personal physical experience and established religious cosmologies, looking at how each reflects on the other and how we might go about considering this relationship. How 'natural' is religion? Could it be derived from our bodily experience? Let me start with an apparently easy—and once fashionable—question: may extreme personal experiences like insanity contribute to new religious formations? First a quotation from W. H. R. Rivers, the early twentieth-century anthropologist and psychiatrist (who has recently obtained popular fame through a series of novels about his treatment of shell-shock in the First World War):

We have, I think, reason to believe that the person who has attained perfection of balance in the control of his instinctive tendencies, in whom the processes of suppression and sublimation have become wholly effective, may thereby become completely adapted to his environment and attain a highly peaceful and stable existence. Such existence is not, however, the condition of exceptional accomplishment, for which there would seem to be necessary a certain degree of instability. I believe that we may look to this instability as the source of energy from which we may expect great accomplishments in art and science. It may be also that, through this instability, new strength will be given to those movements which under the most varied guise express the deep craving for religion which seems to be universal among Mankind.[1]

The Innovator Dismissed as Mad

Innovators and leaders of new social and religious movements are of course frequently dismissed by us as mad: particularly when their

[1] Rivers (1920: 158).

innovations are unacceptable or based on premises at odds with those of their critics. To denigrate them as mad is to deny them rationality. It is to mock their followers, for only the credulous and simple-minded could take the mad seriously. This use of 'mad' or 'crazy' or their analogues to imply unrestrained or unreasonable actions is of course common to most, perhaps all, societies. For a journalist to describe a community torn between two options as 'schizophrenic' may be a metaphor currently fashionable. The journalist may permit himself further licence: the former prime minister of Grenada (who was famed for his speeches to the United Nations on the subject of flying saucers) has been characterized as 'a street-corner eccentric, a mystical maniac'.[2] To explain the origins of war as the conspiracy of a mad dictator may be a commonplace conceit, but how seriously are we to take the ethnographer who suggests that St Paul, 'another vatic with inchoate ego boundaries', was epileptic, or the psychologist who confidently asserts that Tiberius and Calvin were schizophrenics, and Stalin 'a paranoiac'?[3]

The idiom of disease is a powerful political metaphor[4] and we take it as such when our journalist tells us that the doctrine of the Peoples Temple in Guyana was 'infected with disease'.[5] It is perhaps a metaphor when Alfred Kroeber calls magic 'the pathology of culture' or Weston La Barre, another American anthropologist, dismisses snake-handling sects as 'zany' or 'crazy'.[6] But when ethnographers explain shamanism as the very specific consequence of 'epilepsy, hysteria, fear neurosis [and] veritable idiocy'[7] or the psychoanalyst characterizes the shaman as psychotic and his religion as 'organised schizophrenia',[8] one may be permitted to wonder about the explanatory value of such designifications. The ancient Hebrews attempted to discredit their more embarrassing prophets by suggesting they were insane,[9] and the anthropologist who talks of the 'authentic schizoid component' of the members of the religious movement he is studying is clearly not a potential recruit.[10]

Since the aftermath of the French revolution (which was regarded by some doctors as a veritable epidemic, while others dwelt on the psychopathology of the hereditary monarch[11]) the medical profession has not scrupled to use clinical diagnosis to interpret history. The professor

---

[2] Naipaul (1980: 17).   [3] La Barre (1970: 348, 603, 607). Wolman (1973: 95).
[4] Sontag (1979).   [5] Naipaul (1980: 134).
[6] Kroeber, cited in Lifton (1974); La Barre (1969: viii, 109).
[7] Cited by Ackernecht (1943).   [8] Devereux (1956).   [9] Rosen (1968: 21–70).
[10] La Barre (1969).   [11] Rosen (1968). Ackernecht (1943).

of medicine at Makerere University, fleeing Idi Amin, offered this diagnosis of his former president: 'grandiose paranoia, hypomania, probably
schizophrenic, hypomanic paranoia, possibly GPI [general paralysis of
the insane] and the Jekyll and Hyde syndrome'.[12] American psychiatrists
in a well-publicized report suggested that Senator Barry Goldwater, then
a candidate for the presidency, was mentally unstable, and as a consequence were very nearly sued.[13] In their attempt to understand society
and social change, psychiatry and psychoanalysis have formulated interpretations couched primarily in psychopathology. Freud suggested that
religion is essentially a codification of individual neuroses, particularly
when it took the form of innovation.[14] While sociologists following
Durkheim's well-known dictum not to explain the social through psychology have at times been able to dispense with purely psychological or
psychopathological interpretations of existing institutions, they appear to
have near universal recourse to them when describing social change, particularly when it takes a dramatic or chiliastic form.

It may be that functionalist steady-state theorists of society always have
difficulty with the problem of innovation and rely on a psychological
idiom which lies outside the social domain and which can initiate the necessary changes.[15] Certainly, when faced with millennial movements, particularly those Linton has characterized as 'nativist',[16] not merely do
social scientists frequently describe them in psychological terms, but they
appear to regard them as somehow *more psychological* in nature than the
social institutions of quieter times: millennial movements are considered
more 'affectively laden' and they operate at 'high intensity'.[17] The Oxford
sociologist Bryan Wilson, conceptually far removed from the psychoanalytic anthropologists of the United States, nevertheless describes
'affected members . . . uttering gibberish [in] outbursts of frenzy' and
suggests that the social organization of millennial groups is hampered by
their 'affectivity'.[18] Similarly, the 'dancing mania' of Madagascar and the
'Vaihala madness' of Papua are described as 'spontaneous and stimulated
frenzy':[19] i.e. they are either pathology or passive manipulation, in either
case outside normal psychological and social functioning. The contemporary use of the term 'charisma' unites the two—the disordered prophet
with his suggestible flock.

[12] Association of Psychiatrists in Training (1977).   [13] Ballard (1973: 69–74).
[14] Freud (1928).   [15] Kenniston (1974).   [16] Linton (1943).
[17] Beckford (1975).   [18] B. Wilson (1973: 317–19).
[19] Williams (1934). He describes the movement as 'an epidemic', 'antics [which] origi-
nated in delusions'.

The visions of millennial leaders have been described by scholars as insane even when regarded as relatively normative by their contemporaries: Hung Xiuquan, the leader of the Taiping rebellion; Te Ua, the founder of the Maori Hau Hau; Jim Jones of the People's Temple; Evara of the Vaihala madness; Counselheiro, leader of the Canudos uprising; Britain's Joanna Southcott.[20] Theory aside, colonial and national authorities have frequently interned chiliastic sectarians in psychiatric hospitals: Richard Brothers, George Turner, and William Courtenay, nineteenth-century British sectarians; Ne Loiag, a leader of the 1943 Jonfrum movement in the New Hebrides; Rice Kamanga, founder of the Barotse Twelve Society; Alexander Bedward, the Jamaican revivalist; Father Divine, who founded the American sect which bears his name; Leonard Howell, the Rastafarian.[21] In Canada Dukhobors who demonstrated naked were put in the local asylum, as were Jehovah's Witnesses in Germany in the 1930s, and Baptists and Pentecostalists in the declining years of the Soviet Union.[22]

Popular perception of madness leads to official denigration: 'The wider [Jamaican] society associated Rastafarianism with madness', says the Jamaican sociologist Rex Nettleford, and leaders were 'taken to gaol on sedition or to the asylum for lunacy . . . The process of becoming a Rastafarian is still regarded by the wider society as one of mental deterioration and the more modern embrace of the creed by young educated high school and university graduates is seen as an urgent matter for the psychiatrist.'[23]

To employ the idiom of insanity in order to discredit implies the prior recognition of a distinct sphere of psychopathology, one that is characterized by a defect, either a disorder of the individual mind analogous to physical disease or a physical disturbance of the brain itself. The small-scale non-industrialized societies with whom anthropologists have been largely concerned may have such a separate domain of psychopathology, or they may regard what the psychiatrist terms 'mental illness' as the secondary and unnamed consequence of unsuccessful interaction with mystical forces.

---

[20] La Barre (1970: 233–94); B. Wilson (1973: 135); Yap (1954); Williams (1934: 372); Da Cunha (1947: 87, 96, 176, 213).
[21] Armytage (1961: 282); Worsley (1970: 168–9); B. Wilson (1973: 42); Simpson (1955); Nettleford (1970, ch. 2).
[22] Woodcock and Avakumaic (1968: 59); Beckford (1975: 34); Bloch and Reddaway (1977).   [23] Nettleford (1970: 56–7).

Insanity as a Creative Force

There has, of course, been an alternative tradition in the West which, while certainly accepting the existence of a separate domain of psychopathology, nevertheless refuses to denigrate it or divorce it from the possibility of active meaning. This tradition asserts that insanity can be both creative and innovative. In any period it seems likely that both positions—the denial of meaning in madness and the affirmation of meaning—are held by some. The first scholarly Western attempt to assert meaning in psychopathology appears to be that of Plato. While he agreed that madness is a 'disease of the body caused by bodily conditions', he is concerned with meaning, not causation, and meaning can only be ascribed by reason, coming after the illness or from others: 'We only achieve [prophecy] when the power of our understanding is inhibited by sleep or when we are in an abnormal condition owing to disease or divine inspiration . . . It is not the business of any man so long as he is in an irrational state to interpret his own visions and say what good or ill they portend.'[24] In medieval Europe insanity was popularly perceived as a punishment or test sent by God or the Devil; although in itself it was meaningless as a communication, by rational meditation on it by the healthy part of the mind it could become 'a healing agent of penitence'.[25] At the same time there existed a Christian tradition which placed a positive value on the state of 'folly' itself (including foolishness and insanity) for its intimations of childlike innocence: if the world was rational and thus compromised, then the Incarnation, said Erasmus, could only have been an act of folly.[26] Perhaps Jesus himself had been mad (Mark 3; Corinthians 25)?

The shift in moral authority from clergy to medicine in the early modern period deprived psychopathology (now totally shorn of its supernatural origins) of any possibility of conventional meaning: it was merely symptomatic of bodily disease. Scot and Bright daringly asserted that the practice of witchcraft was the consequence of brain disease, and in the eighteenth century Swift and Pope used the presumed physical origin of mental states as the basis for satire: in his *The Mechanical Operation of the Spirit* Swift notes that eloquence is no more than an orgasm without stimulation, and that when the vapours in Louis XIV's head went up he engaged in war, while if they descended Europe was at peace.

---

[24] Plato (1965).   [25] Feder (1980: 106–7).
[26] Erasmus's *In Praise of Folly*; Savonarola's iconoclastic *Feast of the Higher Folly*.

Like Plato, the Romantics accepted the separate existence of psychopathology but divorced its origin from its potential value as a communication; it was natural and elemental and hence a source of creativity. Madness was akin to genius, as it was to the thought of the child or primitive: 'The greater the genius the greater the unsoundness', quoted the psychologist William James.[27] So far from the biological aetiology of madness devaluing its products, abnormal mental states, and hence genius, were artificially cultivated; the mentally ill were regarded as additionally advantaged through being placed outside social constraints, and thus resistant to cultural indoctrination.[28] While a few writers like Lamb (in *The Sanity of True Genius*) deplored the necessary equation of madness and genius, the thesis was to grip the poetic and popular imagination late into the twentieth century. Nietzsche wrote that 'it seems impossible to be an artist without being diseased' and suggested that in ecstatic madness man gave rein to underlying emotions and participated 'in a higher community . . . a collective release of all the symbolic powers'.[29]

In *The Varieties of Religious Experience* William James wondered if the essence of religion might not lie in the 'pattern setters . . . for whom religion exists not as a dull habit but as an acute fever . . . [They] frequently have nervous instability.'[30] He quoted with approval the English psychiatrist Henry Maudsley: 'What right have we to believe Nature under any obligation to do her work by means of complete minds only? She may find an incomplete mind a more suitable instrument for a particular purpose.'[31] Although James says that religious experience should be measured 'by its fruits' rather than its origin, he clearly prefers pathological religion as more authentic. It is probably Lombroso who is still most closely associated with the equation of madness and genius, the latter being 'a system of hereditary degeneration of the epileptoid variety'.[32] If human nature was naturally conservative, then change could only be initiated through abnormality, and he distinguished between 'true genius' (of the epileptoid type) aligned with 'the general course of evolution', and 'pseudogenius' associated with unsuccessful rebellions:[33] Francis Galton, too, postulated a link between madness and eminence, but Havelock Ellis's subsequent report that there was little

---

[27] J. R. Nisbet's *The Insanity of Genius* (1893), cited by James (1958).
[28] Cited by Hayter (1968).
[29] Nietzsche's *The Will to Power*, cited by M. Harrison (1922).
[30] James (1958: 24).　　　[31] Ibid. 36.　　　[32] Kurella (1911).　　　[33] Ibid. 72.

evidence for the hypothesis has been confirmed generally.[34] One recent suggestion is that it is the relatives of schizophrenics who are more creative than the general population,[35] and the common contemporary conclusion by writers on creativity is that while creative people may have more 'psychological conflicts', they are unlikely to be actually insane because they possess 'greater ego strength'.

Be that as it may, the two Romantic axioms, the equation of mad, childlike, primitive, and archaic, and the idea of the artist–genius as an unbalanced prophet without honour, formed the European avant-garde's image of itself. Van Gogh, who experienced epileptic fits and periodic depression, regarded himself as insane: 'For a madman is also a man to whom society did not want to listen and whom it wanted to prevent from uttering unbearable truths . . . It is a man who has preferred to go mad in the sense in which society understands the term, rather than be false to a certain idea of human behaviour.'[36] What Georg Lukács has called 'modernism's obsession with pathological and extreme states' was most clearly seen in Surrealism: André Breton's dictum that the surreal endeavour was 'Dictée de la pensée en l'absence de tout contrôle'[37] returned the artist or poet to the untrammelled primitive core of creativity; the models were the mad, the eccentric, the mediums, the cranks, inventors, and self-publishers. Antonin Artaud observed that 'Delirium is as legitimate, as logical, as any other succession of human ideas or acts.'[38]

The anti-psychiatry movement in Europe and the United States in the 1960s and 1970s similarly decided that 'the boundary between sanity and madness is a false one'.[39] In the writing of R. D. Laing we can note a movement from victimology (the psychotic is formed by a process of social labelling) to one in which he is a hero, the artist who can offer a privileged critique of social reason. The counter-culture, however, failed to establish a situation in which psychopathology could be perceived as a meaningful everyday communication. Mark Vonnegut's autobiography *The Eden Express* describes how the hippie commune in which he lived proved unable to cope with his episode of schizophrenia; after a good deal

---

[34] Storr (1972).
[35] Karlson (1974). From the position of an evolutionary behavioural ecology, Price and Stevens (1996) argue for the value of a tendency to psychosis in population dispersal, and cite Mother Earth.   [36] Trans. from Cabanne (1961).
[37] Breton (1969: 37)   [38] Esslin (1976: 52)   [39] Feder (1980: 242).

of debate they took him to the local mental hospital, where he received electroconvulsive therapy.[40]

The major social science contribution to the question of whether psychopathology can offer a meaningful communication has come from those anthropologists who were influenced by psychoanalysis. For Freud culture was a product of instinctual strivings and social demands, a dynamic conflict whose resolution could include social integration in the form of instinctual sublimation or individual psychopathology. Health was a balance between instinctual strivings and social restraints; if culture was a product of individual conflicts writ large, cultural innovation was only possible through such an individual conflict. As Roheim, the anthropologist who most closely adhered to an unmodified Freudian position, put it, '[Social] change is only the discharge of suppressed emotion.'[41] It is not my intention to review here the vast literature, principally American, which seeks to demonstrate the social role of psychopathology by employing psychodynamic theories. Suffice to say that when Georges Devereux and Weston La Barre[42] suggest that culture may originate in individual psychopathology, their use of terms like 'schizophrenia' are unrecognizable to contemporary descriptive psychiatrists, who would find little to add to Ackernecht's critique in 1943: 'The custom of covering moral judgements with a pseudoscientific psychopathological nomenclature is no advance at all and is equally bad for both morals and science ... When religion is but "organised schizophrenia" [Devereux's expression] then there is no room or necessity for history, sociology, etc. God's earth was, and is, but a gigantic state hospital and pathography becomes the unique and universal science.'[43] Ackernecht suggested that the only possible instances for religious roles being *routinely* proceeded by mental disturbance were the classical Siberian shamans described in the nineteenth century by Sieroszerski and Bogoras.

The social institution of shamanism thus *might* include the mentally ill, those recovered from mental illness, and those incipiently ill.[44] Where

---

[40] Vonnegut (1976).   [41] Roheim (1950).

[42] Devereux (1956); La Barre (1969, 1970).

[43] Ackernecht (1943: 31, 35). This criticism is not taken to include the 'new psychohistorians' (Lifton, Erikson, Kenniston), for they have largely restricted themselves to a consideration of normative psychodynamics and have developed a considerably more sophisticated conceptualization of the relationship between individual personality and the social order. Erikson's 'great man of history' is not the charismatic psychotic of Devereux and La Barre but one who articulates the 'dirty work of his age'.

[44] Following Eliade, no contemporary students of shamanism have claimed that the shaman is invariably psychopathological. What Eliade (1964) terms 'signs of election' have

medical anthropology has been concerned with the major psychoses, it has regarded them as 'natural symbols' upon which social meanings are imposed not as a potentially active social force in their own right. Is there anything which can be salvaged from a debate now confined to studies of the history of anthropological theory?

Five Situations of Acceptance

If we accept the existence of an autonomous domain of psychopathology, closely allied to the popular Western concept of 'insanity', can it actively influence a society's religious cognitions? If it does, under what conditions may the statements of the mad person be taken by his or her contemporaries as valid? As there is no real biological marker of most psychopathology independent of social action, and observers (as we have seen) ascribe psychopathology to normative situations on rather slender grounds, it would be appropriate initially to restrict our search to situations where we find evidence of a biological component in psychopathology, or at least to psychopathology defined on descriptive rather than dynamic grounds. There appear to be, I suggest, five situations under which such an 'imitation of madness' becomes possible.

1. An individual who is already influential becomes insane but is validated for a time by the inertia of the political structure. A limited example of this is what psychiatrists call *folie à deux*, where, in a close but socially isolated family, a dominant member develops delusions which dependent family members then accept; the 'passive' delusions of the dependants rapidly disappear when they are isolated from the dominant originator.[45] Something like this is the idea behind the popular perception of Hitler or Amin as charismatic madmen. While it is probably rare for an influential individual to maintain his influence if actually insane, there are frequent instances of absolute rulers becoming increasingly isolated and suspicious as a result of their situation. If leaders become seriously psychotic, they are probably soon eliminated, as Suetonius suggested in the case of Caligula. Mad rulers are unlikely in the general run of things, for their predisposition is likely to have manifested itself earlier and to have

been recognized as including acute psychosis, along with physical disease or misfortune, but the pattern of shamanism is a conventional pattern superimposed on the psychotic individual and not derived from him. With acculturation, however, increasingly deviant individuals may come to occupy the shamanic role (Murphy 1964).

[45]   Gruenberg (1957).

eliminated them from the power struggle: Idi Amin, for instance, had been head of the Ugandan armed forces for some years before he sought absolute power.

2. Alternatively, the individual may be only periodically insane and in between episodes live in the shared social reality where he can validate his delusions as acceptable communications by explaining them in conventional terms. He may find his previous psychopathological ideas strange, and the quest for their meaning may then be identical with external validation. In his *Journals* George Fox, one of the founders of the Quakers, describes an episode when, passing near Lichfield, he felt impelled to take off his shoes in a field and run through the town shouting 'Woe unto the bloody city of Lichfield'; returning later to retrieve his shoes he was puzzled about the meaning of his act, and appears to have been relieved on discovering later that the town had been the site of Christian martyrdom under Diocletian.[46] I am not suggesting that Fox was actually insane; merely that the instance provides us with a suitable model. Psychopathology, like schizophrenia, which includes widespread personality changes and a lowering of social competence, is unlikely to be subsequently integrated in this way. Early psychosis, isolated psychotic episodes, or phasic reactions like manic-depressive psychosis, are more amenable to re-entry into the shared world, and thus to imitation—what George Devos has termed 'pathomimesis';[47] the episode itself may be less a transformation of existing themes into a new religion than the signal that merely legitimizes a shift which is previously (or subsequently) conceived of in a normative state. If epileptic fits are believed to be of divine origin, then the presence of divinity will be ushered in by fits whether spontaneous, sought, or simulated.[48]

[46] Fox (1952: 71–2).

[47] Devos (1972); Williams (1934: 371–2). Devos derives the term from Schwartz 1976. Herschmann and Lieb (1988) argue that the two phases of manic-depressive psychosis are especially conducive to communication of inspiration. Mania inspires, while depression allows the slow working up of the innovation into a conventional form.

[48] Devos restricts himself to the mimesis of states such as epilepsy, whose imitation Eliade (1964) describes in shamanism, while Radin (1953: 68) wonders if the origins of all religions might not lie in the mimesis of the manifestations of biological brain disease. Field suggests that organic hallucinations perpetuate witchcraft beliefs in rural Ghana (1960: 38–40, 43–6), and indeed may actually initiate them (ibid. 318). La Barre (1970: 316) cites F. E. Williams on Evara of the Vaihala madness spreading 'a stylised epilepsy in his group apparently genuine in him originally'; in fact Williams (1934: 371–2) merely said Evara had 'ecstatic seizures' for some time before the movement began; for a more critical account of the Western Pacific imitation of epilepsy, see Hoskins (1967). The Native American Shakers institutionalized a form of shaking originally 'spontaneous'. Similarly, the manifes-

3. Nietzsche, Strindberg, and Artaud are not automatically discredited by the Western intellectual because they developed, respectively, general paralysis of the insane, paranoia, and schizophrenia, even though it is impossible to separate the later work of each from their psychopathology. Delusions may be isolated from the recognition of pathology: 'He's mad but . . .'. There is a recognition that there is something valid in psychotic statements without denying the primary illness. An instance: In early eighteenth-century North America it was quite acceptable for all whites, including members of the Society of Friends, to own slaves. Two insane inmates of a Friends' asylum independently declared that slave-owning was no longer acceptable for Quakers; the idea spread beyond the asylum walls and within a few years the practice of slavery was incompatible with membership of the Society. The two innovators, however, appear to have remained within their asylum.[49]

4. It is the meaning for the community which determines whether psychotic delusions result in the originator becoming a prophet. In his study of 'charisma'[50] Bryan Wilson points out that

If a man runs naked down the street proclaiming that he alone can save others from impending doom, and if he immediately wins a following, then he is a charismatic leader: a social relationship has come into being. If he does not win a following, then he is simply a lunatic . . . The very content of 'plausibility' is culturally determined. It may be a more than average endowment of energy, determination, fanaticism, and perhaps intelligence. Or it may be an altogether different set of attributes, epilepsy, strangeness, what we should regard as mental disorder, or particularly when children are regarded as prophets, even sheer innocence.

tation of 'madness' may be used to recognize religious experience and the local community then attempt to distinguish 'mundane madness' from 'divine madness' (Morris 1985; McDaniel 1989), problematic where, as in Bengal, divine inspiration is often marked by antinomian acts. Consideration of the local psychology is necessary before we can consider whether terms analogous to 'madness' are being used in an extended sense or else prosaically (in a restricted, 'medical' sense). A similar antinomian attempt to 'provoke salvation' among Tibetan *smyo* monks is known as 'insane' (*smyo*), but the individuals concerned are not necessarily 'mad' in a strong sense (Ardossi and Epstein 1975).

Harner has argued that individual drugs may generate very specific experiences such as 'flying', but Eliade (1964) points out that 'flight' is common to all shamanic contexts and anyway has a universal supramundane significance. Reichel-Dolmatoff has proposed the pharmacological origin (*Banisteriopsis caapi*) of social representations among the Tukano such as those for exogamy. A similar argument has been used by Redgrove and Shuttle to characterize pregnancy visions as the consequences of hormonal changes, by Wasson to look at mythological themes as derived from the experience of *Amanita muscaria*, by Kennedy through *qat*, and by De Martino through the symptoms of tarantula bites.

[49] Davis (1966).   [50] B. Wilson (1975).

If innovation is meaningful it has to respond to certain themes in the audience. At times of crisis solutions are likely to be accepted or sought from those who at other times would be stigmatized as mad: desperate times need desperate remedies.[51] In the 1660s Solomon Eccles wandered about London with a brazier of fire on his head, naked apart from a loin-cloth, proclaiming the imminent destruction of the city: he was largely ignored until the Plague, and then the Fire, made him a fashionable prophet. London was rebuilt while Solomon continued to preach the identical doctrine, and he lapsed back into his former obscurity.[52] If we accept with R. D. Laing that the girl who says she is dangerous because she has an atomic bomb inside her is 'less crazy' than a government prepared to use nuclear weapons, this is because we are so concerned about the possibility of atomic war that we are prepared to modify our conceptions of reason.[53] The cultural psychiatrist Henry Murphy has taken this further: delusions may occur in times of increased stress as if, in reaction to changing conditions, the culture does call on individual members to sacrifice their mental health by the development of individual delusions which relieve communal anxieties.[54]

5. To say a mad individual would have been 'accepted' at another time or in another place is a biographical commonplace: the audience has somehow failed the author. Artaud's biographer suggests that in other epochs he might have been a shaman, a prophet, an alchemist, an oracle, a saint, a gnostic teacher, or indeed the founder of a new religion.[55] If we accept that both the individual and psychopathology itself must be located in a particular society, then this is meaningless, but it is likely that some societies, particularly small-scale pre-literate ones, are always open to a greater variety of idiosyncratic communications than is our own. In other words, there may be societies which do not share our rigorous exclusion of all psychopathology from the possibility of meaning. This is true of the Quakers and the 1960s counter-culture, both open to 'the

---

[51] La Barre suggests *all* cultural innovation takes this route. On the contrary it seems to me that times are seldom so desperate that we seek solutions proposed by the conspicuously deviant. J. E. C. Harrison (1979, ch. 8), attempting to explain the occurrence of the 18th-century British millennialists, calls it a period of 'unprecedented change' but admits it is difficult to say one age is 'more anxious' than another; similarly Beckford (1985, introd.). Whatever our external analysis, 'desperate times' may be seen as such by the individuals concerned: the Dukhobors sought unusual prophets at times of community crisis (H. Hawthorn 1955: 172–5).

[52] Hunter (1959), cited in Rosen (1968).   [53] Laing (1959: 12).

[54] H. B. M. Murphy (1967). How radical we take this to be depends on our interpretation of 'as if'.   [55] Esslin (1976: 116).

workings of the spirit'. It may occur when societies have a more restricted concept of psychopathology than our own. Among the Dukhobors 'A deranged old man, after a week spent fasting at a hill-top graveyard, delivered to an attentive gathering of people irrational, obscene, but mysterious messages, which were submissively accepted as oracular, and which caused many Sons of Freedom families to leave homes and belongings to embark on a brief and futile pilgrimage.'[56] While a majority of tribal societies appear to recognize a state akin to 'insanity', this may be restricted to chronic mental illness; the early stages of what psychiatrists regard as schizophrenia may be conceived of as a potentially meaningful experience. As Kroeber pointed out, 'In general the psychopathologies that are rewarded among primitives are only the mild or transient ones. A markedly deteriorated psychosis . . . would be rated and deplored by them as much as by us.'[57] Murphy suggests that there is a cost: 'Societies which encourage greater contact with unconscious feelings can freely accept the idiosyncratic behaviour and delusions of the mentally ill but they pay a price in economic and social inferiority.'[58] We do not have to accept fully Murphy's understanding of the unconscious to agree that societies which take madness seriously are probably not the most appropriate ones for developing and operating advanced technology. I shall now turn to one specific instance and attempt to see how psychopathology may sometimes provide a model for the religious experiences of others and provide a charter for a common set of cosmological beliefs.

Sabbatai Sevi

The exile of the Jews from Palestine soon after the beginning of the Christian era dispersed a single self-contained community from its own land into a series of complementary relationships with Christian and later Islamic communities. The rabbinical tradition preserved the original culture, elaborated into the Law which defined the boundaries between Jew and non-Jew, and explained the separation from the historic land as a temporary interlude until the messianic redemption. The traditional Messiah was a conquering king who would re-establish the historical kingdom. Alternatively, he was pictured in Isaiah as the suffering and rejected servant who held a message for the Gentiles. For others, the exile was a metaphor for personal alienation from God, and the promised redemption was purely spiritual. One tradition suggested that the Messiah would

---

[56] H. Hawthorn (1955).   [57] Kroeber (1952).   [58] H. B. M. Murphy (1967).

come when the existence of the community was threatened by internal disharmony and external violence, and another, only when man had deliberately entered into the sinful world to release the divine sparks hidden there.

With the development of the modern nation-state, the traditional Jewish accommodation in eastern Europe began to fail. The physical identity of east European Jewry was threatened by assimilation and attrition: massacre and forced conversion accounted for perhaps half a million Polish Jews in the 1640s. Sabbatai Sevi, a devout young rabbi in the Ottoman empire, began to engage in frequent fasts, ritual purifications, and all-night prayer.[59] After two successive marriages were annulled for non-consummation, he commenced increasingly antinomian behaviour— breaking the Law for the value inherent in this act. A cabbalistic tradition had asserted that as the Messiah had to redeem evil he was in some measure evil himself, and Sabbatai offered a new prayer: 'Praised be to Thee O Lord who permits the forbidden.'

Expelled by the local rabbis, Sabbatai was proclaimed Messiah by a follower, and the movement spread rapidly. Sabbatianism was characterized by miracles, prophecies, mass visions, states of possession and ecstatic confession and penance, fasts to death, and self-burials. Sabbatai invented new ceremonies and fantastic titles: days of ritual mournings became days of rejoicing. He married a prostitute and encouraged free love, nudity, and incest: if the messianic age could only be ushered in by sin, the people must sin. Within a year perhaps half Europe's Jews were influenced by his ideas and Sabbatai was arrested by the sultan for sedition, had converted to Islam under pain of death, and was pensioned off under house arrest. Most followers abandoned him in this ultimate rejection of Judaism and returned to traditional rabbinical teachings, but for others his apostasy was the ultimate messianic sacrifice: 'The Lord was but veiled and waiting.' A few followed him to Islam and some converted to Christianity. Many continued as apparently Orthodox Jews but conducted Sabbatian rites in secret. As an organized body of belief the movement soon died away, but in the eighteenth century a Sabbatian, Jacob Frank, proclaimed himself Messiah. The relation of Sabbatian messianism to the subsequent Hasidic movement remains controversial. It has been described as a neutralization of messianic elements into mainstream Judaism, or alternatively as a dialectical synthesis of the two.[60]

---

[59] For the history of Sabbatianism I am considerably indebted to the work of the late Gershom Scholem.   [60] Scholem (1954); Bakan (1958). See Lectures 5 and 6.

Why is this instance of interest? There is a certain amount of evidence that Sabbatai Sevi was what we now know as manic-depressive. He was constantly depressed 'without his being able to say what is the nature of this pain'. Extreme apathy and withdrawal, known to his followers as 'the Hiding of the Face', alternated with periods of 'illumination'; infectious elation and enthusiasm, restlessness and a refusal to eat or sleep, practical jokes, and flights of apparent nonsense. Jewish mystics already used high–low (*aliyah–yerida*) to refer to nearness to or absence from God, and Sabbatai employed this spatial metaphor to explain his moods as religious experience: 'high' was associated with religious ecstasy, 'low' with self-doubt. His followers accepted his explanation of his mood swings and followed them, themselves experiencing episodes of religious exaltation and despair which became normative experiences for many. His psychosis thus provided a natural representation of the cabbalistic doctrine, together with a firm conviction on Sabbatai's part (when 'high') of his messiahship and also a model for explaining the fluctuating relations between God and man, and thus the waxing and waning of the movement. It is likely that the jokes and tricks and inversions of normal behaviour make an individual with periodic manic-depressive psychosis a particularly well-placed person to modify traditional modes of belief and behaviour through antinomian acts.

To what extent does Sabbatianism meet our five possible conditions? Sabbatai was certainly respected as a promising scholar before his antinomian actions, and it is not easy to see how he could have been taken seriously otherwise: he was not, however, so influential that his community would accept any ideas immediately (situation 1). His reputation did establish his acts as antinomian—controlled and motivated contraventions of the Law rather than a simple failure to follow it. His episodes of madness were periodic, enabling him to explain their meaning within the common shared assumptions (2). The audience did not have a restricted concept of psychopathology, nor did they recognize Sabbatai as 'mad but . . .'[61] (3,5). Certainly east European Jews were living in desperate times (4) but the movement was most significant under Ottoman rule, where Jews were more secure than in Christian countries. Sabbatian adherents were as likely to come from the affluent and assimilated sections of the Jewish community as from the pauperized and insecure peasantry. My example is limited by the usual problem of conjectural psychohistory: 'diagnosis' across time based on secondary sources. Our

[61] Granek (1976); Scholem (1973: 54).

assumption of Sabbatai Sevi's manic depression is based on sources compiled by his followers: the fact that his highs and lows were so neatly
coded in cabbalistic terms may lead us to wonder whether the coding was
not prior to the experiences, and merely shaped everyday mood changes.

Religious Innovation Overturning Political Dominance

To conclude, I shall say a little about the mode of religious innovation we
can expect in situations such as those of Sabbatai Sevi. Primarily it is *dramatic*. When we have a tradition of linear intellectual tradition and reciprocal dialogue with the dominant culture, it is perhaps unnecessary. It
seems particularly relevant to those small-scale conservative societies
which principally interest ethnographers, but it is not limited to them—
indeed Sabbatai does not come from anything like a tribal society. He is,
however, a member of a group dominated by another group. It is dramatic
then—often an overturning of the accepted patterns—an *inversion* of
them.[62] As Gershom Scholem, the historian of Jewish mysticism, says
'Sabbatai took over items of Jewish tradition and stood them on their
heads.'

Whatever may be the merits of the anthropological debate on systems
of dual classification,[63] there appears to be a particular situation where
binary oppositions play an important social role: those societies which
have been politically dominated for a considerable period of time by others. We may include here colonies and ex-colonies, including much of the
contemporary Third World, black people in the Americas, and the older
Jewish communities in Europe. Caribbean society, which I shall consider
more in my next lecture, like Jewish society, has been described as dualistic—'us' and 'them'—in this case black and white (for Jews—Jew and
Gentile).

The individual has to attain an identity by personally articulating the
various elements of the two contrasted sets of values: the minority culture itself is defined by its difference from the dominant set of values.
Some groups in society, particularly women, are already in an 'inverted'

[62] I am not suggesting that inversion is the only, or indeed the major, mode of the imitation of madness, but it is the one which appears relevant for my example, characterized by
'gratuitous' obscenities and contravention of norms. It appears the more likely mode in
bipolar affective psychosis. I have continued to use the term 'inversion', in spite of more
recent suggestions (Needham 1980*b*) that 'opposition' might be more appropriate: 'inversion' does not describe the latent possibilities of the system so much as convey the physical
sense of overturning institutions so characteristic of the participants' experience.

[63] Ibid.

symbolic position relative to men. If West Indian middle-class–working-class relations are articulated by 'white–black' values, then the black middle-class man is, in some sense, white. If the relation Jew–non-Jew parallels that of observance of the Law to ignorance of it, it thus also parallels that of male–female, so that the Jewish woman, to a certain extent, takes on Gentile qualities[64] and the black woman is in the same way 'white'.[65]

I am suggesting that certain patterns of extreme experience like psychosis can, as it were, hot up these latent contradictions, both by overt statements and actions, and by inverting the normal schema in certain areas. Symbolic inversions can be regarded as intellectual tools which have the potential to enlarge the conceptual repertoire.[66] Although oppositions may be a dominant mode of symbolic ordering, their inversion provides the basis for change. The apparent paradox is resolved at a 'higher' implicit level in which the opposition is lost: simple oppositions thus may become the means by which a more sophisticated, radical, and universalist conceptualization may be attained.[67] As the original symbolic schema was closely related to the social order, the weakening of this schema in some particular is likely to lead to a greater autonomy of ideology from specific environmental and political determinants and thus perhaps to more 'internalized' values—and maybe to a more general historical trajectory of religious experience. Thus, when Jesus denied that plucking corn on the Sabbath was work, he implied a new dispensation in which the Law was broken in Form to be fulfilled in Spirit. Scholem, to whom I am indebted for his account of Sabbatai Sevi, suggests that Judaism always contained a 'dialectic' between the rabbinical and apocalyptic traditions, what I have termed here the Law and its inversion. Sabbatai Sevi confused the dual classification, calling women to read the Torah, ridiculing the learned, encouraging Gentiles to join the movement, and maintaining that evil could be transformed into good. To follow the traditional Law in the Last Days was, he said, like working on the Sabbath. It has been suggested that the attack on the traditional Law by the Sabbatians both reflected and precipitated the development of modern secular Judaism;[68] freed from traditional constraints, the method of criticism and argument perfected in the ghetto was harnessed to the development of modern rationalism.

[64] Zborowski and Herzog (1962).   [65] Fanon (1952).   [66] V. Turner (1974).
[67] Babcock (1978).   [68] Scholem (1954).

In subsequent lectures I am going to consider how Sabbatai's inversions are consolidated in the group of Hasidim, and how women's bodily experience in particular can become the model for a cosmology. I shall also return to a theme referred to briefly in this lecture—identification of the individual with a messianic or godlike figure.

2

Moments of Creation: Pregnancy and Parturition as Cosmological Idiom

Cosmological Creation and Human Birth

An explicit parallel between the human body and the religious cosmos is commonplace in the findings of comparative religion. Dreaming, excretion, pain, and bodily movement, for instance, have long been argued to make possible quite specific local categories as well as more general understandings of creation, causality and space, illness and agency.[1] Without attributing ontological or epistemological primacy either to the biological body, or to the cosmic or social order, to bodily experience or to cultural practice, we can certainly note the individual deployment of *novel* idioms to figure the cosmic world which may, for instance, draw on

---

[1] Tylor (1904); Douglas (1973); Merleau-Ponty (1962); Lakoff (1987); Johnson (1987). I need not trace here the various critiques of empiricist 'representation' of a natural world which pass under a number of current rubrics—interpretation, Foucauldian historiography, anti-essentialism, anti-objectivism, postmodernism, and so on—except to note that the dilemmas of the representation–embodiment dialectic are hardly avoided in the newer re-deployments of phenomenology (Lectures 5, 6) (Lyon and Barbalet 1994; cf. the variant meanings of 'representation' and 'embodiment') which in their emphasis on subjectivities tend to ethnography rather than social anthropology. Cognitive and psychological approaches which recall 19th-century intellectualism appear to be undergoing a resurgence (Lakoff 1987; Johnson 1987; Boyer 1993, 1997) but have yet to provide a more plausible understanding of a given set of data, and on the whole work from individual experimental psychology rather than a more situational biosociality. What still remains problematic is the value of findings from laboratory psychology; putting it crudely, how does the 'top–down' (culture's embodiment in body technique) encounter the 'bottom–up' (neuropsychology's representation of an apprehended physical world and thus a cosmos)? (And that particular geography rather begs the question.) In the further course of these lectures I shall argue that the two domains are objectified procedures, radically incommensurate modes of thought, both of which we can identify either (personalistically) in Western cultural history or (naturalistically) in the neuropsychological capacity to attribute agency or non-agency to self and others (Littlewood 1993, 1994, 1996; cf. Johnson 1987). And that our analyses, like those of the cabbalist (Lecture 6), must be dual if ironic passages back-and-forth between representation and embodiment.

pregnancy and childbirth as (to use Marcel Mauss's term) 'biological-sociological' phenomena.[2]

Figuring the relationship between cosmos and human in terms of sexuality or parturition appears virtually ubiquitous in our understanding, whether as implicit trope, as conventional analogy, or as some expressly concrete generation. Indeed it is difficult to conceive of any formal set of cosmological ideas which do not in some way eventually evoke or return to our everyday sensory modes. Without making too extravagant claims, we might consider whether idioms of spiritual flight and of creation *de novo* at a distance (by spirit, breath, dream, speech, or gesture) may not appear more congenial to the male imagination; idioms of experienced penetration or of a cosmic unfolding more accessible to women. Compare the encounter with ultrahuman agency for St Augustine and St Teresa of Avila, male and female shamans, or for central and peripheral cults. Nor can we assume any sort of inevitable progression from one to the other: current instances of a reassertion of a 'female mode' of immanent connectedness and inherent obligation may be instanced in Western theology, jurisprudence, philosophy, and science.[3] And the contemporary revival of something like spirit possession in multiple personality disorder among women in North America and Europe increasingly pictures the alternative self less as some psychological potential capacity than as an intrusive alien power such as a vengeful aborted foetus.[4] Not altogether surprisingly, new figurings of self and other, self and cosmos, employ current preoccupations (such as the life versus choice debate in the United States) about the body in a physical world (rape, pregnancy, miscarriage, abortion, childbirth).

Revisions of Christianity by radical women prophets in the English tradition have frequently favoured a repeated unfolding (or entelechy) of immanent creation rather than divine action at a distance.[5] This possibil-

---

[2] Mauss (1979*b*); Durkheim and Mauss (1963). Even if, in the course of the embodiment of social concerns, the limitations and capabilities of the body remained somewhat elusive.

[3] Corea (1988); Weigle (1989); Eilberg-Schwartz (1994); Hogan (1995); Raphael (1996); Gilligan (1982); Baier (1994); Haraway (1989, 1991). A major issue for the embodied view in feminist theology (e.g. Raphael 1996) is whether a view of the sacred derived from women's experience can be said to be equivalent to that of men. Male writers on religion (e.g. Eliade 1965; Otto 1958) have emphasized a more abstracted transcendent perspective for male sacrality. Whether this is *less* body based is, however, open to question.

[4] See Lecture 7. Multiple personality disorder also appropriates existing practices of female self-help and mediumship, resurgent evangelical notions of the final 'rapture', current psychiatric idioms of loss of agency in 'stress' and 'trauma', not to mention American enthusiasms for extraterrestrials.

[5] Weigle (1989); Southcott (1995); Hopkins (1982); Hollywood (1995); Holloway (1966); Lovejoy (1985); Andrews (1953); Adler (1986); Albanese (1990); Corea (1988); Nelson (1979).

ity is exemplified by the founder of the Earth People, an African Caribbean religion which developed in the 1970s. The principal subject of this lecture, a case of a new prophet's formal narrative of her own pregnancy, is intended by her to be read simultaneously as her personal biography and as the cosmological order. And the understandings of the community she establishes are to be identified as her own life. As with such female religious innovators as Margery Kemp, Joanna Southcott, and Ann Lee, the bodily experience (or awareness) of multiple and problematic childbirth becomes objectified and figured into a universal order of female divinity, one which is constantly threatened by an incestuous male power which seeks to gain her power of generation only to produce the mechanical simulacrum of European technology.

The Earth People

Trinidad, the most southerly of the Caribbean islands, lies in the Orinoco delta, eight miles from the South American mainland. A Spanish possession until its capture by the British in 1797, it was largely ignored after the extermination of the Amerindians, although a few French planters from other West Indian islands settled with their slaves and grew sugar in the lower areas in the west. Trinidad's history has been typical of the British Caribbean: the development of sugar plantations; the emancipation of the slaves in 1838 followed by indentured immigration from India in the latter part of the nineteenth century; the collapse of the price of cane sugar, economic stagnation, and imperial neglect; increasing local political participation progressing to internal self-government in the 1950s and independence in 1962. The governing parties since 1956 have been pro-Western and social-democratic, committed to a mixed economy and welfare state, deriving their support predominantly from the African-descended population, and have comfortably maintained power through patronage and regular elections, apart from brief hiccups in 1971, when an army mutiny sparked a short-lived Black Power rebellion, and a failed Islamicist coup in the 1990s.

The oil industry has been exploited since independence, and the standard of living is high, reputedly the third highest in the Americas after the United States and Canada; certain rural areas excepted, concrete houses, electricity, piped water, and metalled roads are standard. Secondary education is compulsory, and the oil revenues have allowed the establishment of a steelworks and large construction and other industries. The labour-intensive agricultural cultivation of sugar, coffee, cocoa, and ground provisions (yam, dasheen, etc.) has been effectively abandoned, and the bulk of 'local' food is brought in from the smaller and poorer islands to the north.

In the north-east the mountains of the Northern range, the geographical continuation of the South America Cordilleras, rise from the sea to 3,000 feet. They were unoccupied until the late nineteenth century, when isolated families established a peasantry of small estates of coffee and cocoa in the lower reaches, growing coconuts and provision in the narrow littoral.

Few Trinidadian people have not heard of the Earth People, a small community established on this coast. In a country familiar with the millennial religious response of the Spiritual (Shouter) Baptists, and with the Rastafari movement, a recent import from Jamaica, the Earth People remain an enigma. Their appearance, from the villages to the capital Port of Spain, causes public outrage to all, for their most outstanding characteristic is that they are naked. Public opinion favours the view that these young men, carrying cutlasses, and with the long matted dreadlocks of the Rastas, are probably crazy: if not the whole group, then Mother Earth, whose visions gave birth to the movement and who leads their marches to town. Every year the group comes from the coast to Port of Spain to pass on their message and gather new recruits from the poorer working-class areas around the capital, areas which appear to have missed out on Trinidad's oil wealth. Communication is hampered by the Earth People's characteristic language, their deliberate and frequent use of obscenities, and Mother Earth's striking doctrines. She announces to Trinidadians, a largely devout if not so churchgoing population, that God does not really exist, and that she is the Mother of Africa and India, Nature Herself.

The Teaching of the Earth Mother

In 1971 Jeanette Baptiste, a 39-year-old woman, left Port of Spain to live on the north coast of the island together with six of her twelve children and her current partner, Cyprian.[6] She recalls being reluctant to move; only the promptings of Cyprian, a minor participant in Trinidad's 1970 Black Power mutiny, persuade her to leave town. The family settle among the remains of one of the now deserted hamlets; initially paid by an

---

[6] I have used pseudonyms here. Jeanette died in 1984 after conflicts in the group and the burning of her settlement, but I retain the present tense for the account she gave me in 1981–2 and for my description of the community at the same time.

absentee overseer to collect copra, by tacit agreement, and after an argument, they continue to squat on the abandoned land. They grow ground
provisions, selling the surplus to the nearest village some twelve miles distant through the bush. Both Jeanette and Cyprian have been somewhat
half-hearted Shouter Baptists—a local Christian group with recognized
'African' themes in their doctrine and practice—and they continue to
'pick along in the Bible', as they put it, fasting in Lent and interpreting
the visionary import of their dreams. From 1975, after the birth of twins
in their wooden hut, until 1976 Jeanette experiences a series of revelations
which become the foundation of the Earth People. She comes to understand that Christian teaching is false, and that our world is the work of a
primordial Mother, whom she identifies with Nature, with the Earth, and
with her own body. Nature gave birth to a race of Black people, but her
rebellious Son (the Christian God) re-entered his Mother's womb to steal
her power of generation and succeeded by producing (or forcing her to
create) White people. The Whites, the Race of the Son, then enslaved the
Blacks and have continued to exploit them. The Way of the Son is that of
Science—of cities, clothes, schools, books, factories, and wage labour.
The Way of the Mother is the Way of Nature—a return to the naked
simplicity of the Beginning, cultivation of the land by hand, and of
gentle and non-exploiting human relationships.[7]

The Son, in his continued quest for the power of generation, has now
succeeded in establishing himself in Black People, and is on the point of
replacing humankind altogether through mechanization, computers, and
robots. His mother, Nature, who has borne all this out of love for the
whole of her creation, has finally lost patience. The current order of the
Son will soon end in a catastrophic drought and famine, or a nuclear war,
a destruction of the Son's world through his own acts. Jeanette herself as
Mother Earth is the primordial Mother in bodily form, but the Mother
will only fully become her at the End. Her task now is to facilitate the
return to the Beginning by organizing the community known as Hell
Valley, and to 'put out' the Life to her people, the Black Nation, the
Mother's Children. She has to combat the teaching of the churches,
which place the Son over the Mother, and to correct the distorted teaching of the Bible, where she is represented as the Devil. She embodies Life
and Nature, in opposition to the Christian God, who is her rebellious
Son, the principle of Science and Death. As the Devil she is opposed to

---

[7] Capitalization thus of the (functionally illiterate) Earth People's recurrent idioms and
cosmology is of course mine.

churches and prisons, education and money, contemporary morals and fashionable opinions. Because God is 'right', Mother Earth teaches the Left, and the Earth People invert various conventional oppositions: 'left' for 'right'; 'evil' or 'bad' for 'good', and so on. What others now take as obscenities are only Natural words, for she herself is the Cunt, the source of all life. Her community does not 'force the end'—to use Martin Buber's phrase: the exact timing of the End is uncertain, but it will come in Jeanette's physical lifetime. Then Time will end, Sickness will be healed, and the Nation will speak its one language. The Son will be exiled to his planet, the Sun, currently hidden by Fire placed there by the Mother: Fire which will eventually return to where it belongs, back to the heart of the nurturing Earth.

In her Message to the World,[8] Mother Earth describes our origins:

In the Beginning was Nothing. Nothing was Life. Nothing formed herself into the elements. The elements resolve itself as Life. So Life formed herself: the Fire, the Water, the Earth, Dirt, Slime and Salt, and revolving herself, with the womb in the middle—the Moon. And there were all the planets for and against the Mother inside her . . . A Son she bring forth. The Son was inside the Womb: Death. So then Life and Death together once, not in the form as it is now but, as the people say, 'in the spirit'. Death revolving itself in the womb, in the Earth, Slime and Salt, Fire and Water. Well, she give him his own planet (everything carry its own planet by the name) so the Son carry his planet which is the planet Sun which we have up there, covered over with heat.

He left his planet. The reason for the heat around the planet is by him leaving his planet and enter the Earth. He wanted to have life, to bring forth like The Mother so he enter . . . When he entered, pain entered the Earth. So he enter the Earth and the Earth change. It keep changing, changing until she put out flesh. And the first Flesh on the Earth were mothers which we were in a form. Not in this form of flesh: what we call the prick and the cunt was one form of Flesh which were the mothers . . . The Flesh keep changing because he keep interfering until I divide myself in half and give him half. So the Son call himself Man but it is still The Mother. So now we carry bones and we become weaker. Bones were formed by The Mother but in his shape and form . . . Time is he, Time is bones. Always jealous because he said

---

[8] I stayed with the Earth People, on and off, over a period of eighteen months between 1981 and 1982, and more briefly in 1987 and 1991. When not in their valley I was in the nearest village twelve miles distant studying bush medicines. As with any prolonged stay in a millennial community, my status was ambiguous—neither neophyte, casual passer-by, nor reporter. I went naked as they did and, at their request, did not bring notepads, camera, or other equipment. When my departure to Britain became imminent, however, I was requested to bring a tape recorder for Mother Earth's formal Message to The World (in English not Creole), from which the quotes here are extracts. Her daily addresses in the valley had frequently anticipated it word for word.

'I am jealous God'. Well, that is still jealousy, covetousness, all these things, pain, sickness, disease, shame and pride, age, time, all belongs to him. This is why we have these changes, that is why we have so much corruption on the earth. He have his share: the White people is really the Race of the Son because that was the Flesh that Mother prepared for the Son in the Beginning. And she had hers which is the Black Race. You could say all races come from the Black Race because we are the beginning of all races. And now all Flesh mix up and we are living the Life of the Son, not of the Black Race. You is all half Son. The Fire belongs to the Earth, which is the heat. The Sun is coming nearer and nearer. So that the heat will return to the Earth, and the planet shall be free once more. He has to return; the Spirit of The Mother will remain, which that belongs to the Earth.

In the Beginning when Flesh was placed upon the Earth, through the inter-ruption of the Spirit of the Son enter in Earth, Mother had was [*sic*] to put out Flesh. And when she put out Flesh, she put out her Spirits which they were all mothers on the earth . . . So when they say you die, you don't really die. When the Flesh grow old it is weak in all the Spirit—the Spirit comes out—and you come again in a new birth as a baby again. That Spirit come back. So then you always live it. You keep going and coming to meet to this stage here—what I call the Beginning. So when they talk about ancestors and these spirits guard you, I am seeing it as yourself spirit, not really a spirit of ancestors, who are they say depart for so much years. It is you yourself. Your ancestor is you!

The Spirit that is in the Flesh is the Spirit of Death, which is the Spirit of the Son, which we call—even we call it—God . . . So that Spirit is what using Flesh so your [Natural] Spirit is still there too but it guards the Flesh while a next spirit is using it. So when you talk about 'the guarding of the Flesh', it's your own self that was also there from the beginning. You keep going and coming, going and coming, so yourself always there to guard you.

We become a robot for him, a machine. They can't really push him out com-pletely: that is for when the hour come. The Mother allow him to do it because of her love. It is love she have. And she know all that he can never win. So she allow him to do what he wants until his time is up to return back to his Planet. Even though it is suffering for the Flesh and pain for the Flesh, they have to bear it . . . All [the Son] does is to put out material: the wars and the fights, the bombs and the [planes], trying to make human, trying to change them, some a mother to a son, change a son to a mother. All these are his experiment, trying to take over. He know everything about Life but not this—not the power to bring forth. That is what he really wants, the power of love. The onliest thing the Son has is machines and chemical. He has to use Science. He gains Science by interfering with Nature. Must he even have to use the oil of the Earth too, which is the Mother, take the oil out, pulling substance from the Earth. It becomes a cripsy.[9] The oil is the blood of the earth.

[9] 'Cripsy': local metathesis. Compare 'flim' (film, cinema).

Many of these figurings are of course common to earlier oppositional movements originating in Christianity: the communality of all; the Christian deity as subordinate but interfering demiurge; church and society as immoral and compromised; the return to the Edenic past and the abandonment of mechanized technology along with formal education and clothes; the indwelling of divine power; redemption in the near future on this earth; a divine or semi-divine identity for the prophet and others. Some recall anti-colonial interpretations of European expansion such as cargo cults: an explanation of political defeat as spiritual betrayal; the identification of the colonized as the chosen people; the Whites' appropriation of the Bible; identification of the Whites with cosmic disharmony; the return to an idealized pre-colonial past after an apocalyptic destruction. Two unusual themes stand out: the identification of the prophet herself with the primordial processes of the world, and thence an idiom of divine creation as likened to her own human history of childbearing.

Nudity and Eccentricity

Since her revelations, which initiated the Beginning of the End in 1975, Mother Earth's immediate family have been joined by numbers of Trinidadians, usually young men who bring their partners and children. The community has a high turnover and, while over fifty people have been associated with the Earth People, when I stayed with them, there were twenty-two staying naked in the valley with perhaps a similar number of committed sympathizers in town. Once a year the group march into town and present their teachings in the central streets, particularly in Woodford Square, the popular site for political demonstrations next to the Parliament. After a few weeks of 'putting out the Life' and visits to friends and relatives, they return to their valley and 'plant for the Nation'. The authorities have responded with raids on the community by police and nurses, with short prison sentences or incarceration in the psychiatric hospital, and sarcastic leading articles in the press.[10]

---

[10] 'Nuisance From the Earth People. We notice that the so-called Earth People, a troupe of nude or semi-nude adults and children, have again been visiting the capital city. This time they are said to have come in furtherance of some petition of the Government for land with which to carve out a large food garden to help feed the nation. They hope to hold talks with the Prime Minister. While we may appreciate their willingness to help the nation in this particular problem, we believe their obvious rejection of society, their lack of any serious skill or experience in farming and their disorganised and undisciplined lifestyle would disqualify them for that kind of Government assistance ... We should not permit a continuation of this nuisance' (editorial, *Trinidad Guardian*, 9 Jan. 1982).

Some of the younger men in the villages along the coast demonstrate an allegiance to Rastafari and say they remain in the country to pursue a 'natural' life. They express sympathy for the Earth People and would actually join the group if it were not for the nudity, Mother Earth's repudiation of Haile Selassie (the late Ethiopian emperor revered by Rastas as God), and her reputation for making everyone in Hell Valley work so hard. Some of them meet the Earth People in the bush, smoke a little ganja, and exchange fish for ground provisions. Through them and other friends in the village who knew Mother Earth before she went naked, the Earth People are kept well informed of village activities and any gossip about them. The older Creole-speaking villagers regret the passing of traditional rural life and the depopulation of the coast. While valuing the benefits of piped water, state pensions, and a higher standard of living, they criticize the young men's expectations of an easy life: 'It come so all they want is fêting. They can't take hard work again.' They accord grudging respect to the return to the old life in the valley, all the more so as the Earth People themselves come from the town. Their own opinions about Trinidad's future parallel those of the Earth People: the oil is a natural part of the earth, the blood of the soil; and its removal is slowly turning the land into a 'cripsy', an unproductive arid desert; they too are suspicious of the newer farming techniques advocated by the government agricultural officers and, refusing pesticides and fertilizers, they continue to plant and harvest according to the phases of the moon; the oil wealth is transitory and will eventually cease, to leave Trinidadians starving in a once fertile land.

Their disagreement is less with Mother Earth's eschatological doctrines than with her practice of nudity, for no Trinidadian has gone naked since slavery. Trinidadians who have met her when 'putting out' regard her less as insane than as eccentric: 'She come half-way mad then.' She has, however, twice been taken by the police to the mental hospital in Port of Spain; there she was diagnosed as psychotic and given psychotropic drugs. Interviewing her myself with the Present State Examination (a formal mental health questionnaire) suggested that she had periodic episodes of hypomania after giving birth; she also has an overactive thyroid gland. In between episodes she is frequently despondent if not depressed. The explanation accepted by the group is that the Mother is only partially incarnated in her and withdraws at intervals (this withdrawal corresponds to depression, a different physical metaphor from Sabbatai's, mentioned in the previous lecture. The practical organization of the group at these times is left to her partner.

In the previous lecture, on insanity and religious creativity, I gave five possible conditions under which the statements of a mad person may be taken by his or her contemporaries as valid. We have here another instance of this. Mother Earth was not initially an important person (situation 1), but her episodes of madness, like those of Sabbatai Sevi, have been temporary (situation 2). The local concept of *folie* (madness) is more restricted (5) than the popular British one and emphasizes chronic mental deterioration, although it is also used in a consciously figurative sense. Sympathizers who are not members may accept that she is mentally ill while accepting the validity of her ideas (3), although her followers say 'If she mad, then we mad.' Trinidad can hardly be described as living in desperate times (4), but for the rural migrants to the towns and the remaining country people, the disappearance of an agricultural economy and its associated way of life has certainly been traumatic, particularly for the young male proletariat of the slums, unemployed and non-unionized.

Relations between Men and Women

The Earth People are generally celibate, but an idiom of sexuality pervades their ideas: the Son's act of 'interference' (rape) initiates post-colonial power as science, as well as the European appropriation of local women as slaves, domestics, midwives, and mistresses. Contemporary women, including Jeanette herself, have continued to experience something very like the original interference:

Every mother is The Mother . . . You got big house but you dead. You children yet to work and you got to pay for them to learn. You learn work hard and your necessaries . . . Half of children is born without love. They grow up with a frustration because their parents didn't come together with a love; so they have all sort of corruption. A man watch you and use you and laugh and he don't give you a dollar. And you get twelve big children . . . It is because of the Spirit [the Son] and the teachings that you have cause the men to be taking advantage on the mothers. Now the reason for that is the Spirit which is controlling that Flesh. He thinks he's the boss. So then he always use the mother as just a nothing. She's there to bring forth the children, clean the house, wash the clothes, do everything and because, look, he goes out and brings in a penny he thinks 'Well look I am controlling'. That's the Spirit of the Son, really. Well it shouldn't be like that. It should be a love and understanding between the both Flesh . . . Because, if I can humble myself to my husband and listen to him, he can humble himself too and listen to me. So then we will have a relationship with a free understanding between the both of us instead of one thinking 'I'm better, I am the boss'. Even when they get married it's worse because you marry a wife 'for better or for worse' they say but it doesn't be that. You don't really find it so often within families here. But then you have to say it's the Spirit still, because if the teachings was of the Mother it wouldn't have beating the woman neither. Because when you beat the mother—your wife in fact—you come just as if you hit your wife, you hit your mother, you hit your sister there, you hit your daughter there. So then it's the teachings that have us in this condition. We suppose to be living different, to have more love, but it haven't got that love; everybody is each for themselves.

Yet local women are not altogether blameless:

Even [among] the mothers you find the same thing. If she's doing a little job and her husband is doing a job sometimes she gets frustrated because, you know, she's working for her own money. Knowing that you working for your own money you feel too that you is boss too, so you do what you want. So the both of you all doing what you want. That isn't a living. Women thinks more materialise. And men are more natural. This is what I am seeing here in this country ... And that is really the Spirit [of the Son] because the Spirit try to hold the mothers more because, knowing that the mothers is the Spirit of the Earth, well then, he must have them more confused.[11] So then they make more spectacle of themselves than the men, too much of dressing, too much of material[12] ... Even now that the mothers reach to a stage that they don't want to be a mother any more. Most of them they don't want children; they use the contraceptive so that they can't have children. They don't really want that! They want a house, they want a car, you know they want all the material that they can get hold of instead of bringing forth their children. They find when they bring forth a child they can't go where they want, they can't do what they want: the children are confusing them. Contraceptive! We didn't plan to come here—the Spirit brought you—so how you plan now?

Childbirth, Motherhood, and Paternity

How can such an extreme individual experience as that of mental illness become translated into a shared cosmology? The first lecture touched rather generally on the idea of symbolic inversion, and this can now be teased out in more detail. Both in the centrality of the female and in her cosmogony Mother Earth deploys her life as a young mother. The idiom of childbirth is as fundamental to her account of creation as it is to her

[11] Mother Earth is explaining the usual local (and Caribbeanist) description of women as more 'respectable' than men (Littlewood 1993). As in other areas, she inverts the customary relationship, arguing that because women are essentially more 'natural', the Son has made particular efforts to change them to the opposite; and that this is through stealing their power of generation, once through cosmic and colonial rape, now through commerce and science.   [12] One of her characteristic puns eliding the physical (clothes) and the moral.

account of current relations between women and men: the physical development of each human child recapitulates the original cosmogony.[13]
While I was not offered a detailed account of Jeanette's earlier life,
motherhood had clearly been her most salient experience, as it was for the
women in the coastal villages and eastern Port of Spain slums who
recounted their lives to me. It is through her childbearing that Mother
Earth objectifies herself and her life to others as a universal principle, a
domestic mode raised to a cosmological order, a central experiential
metaphor by which she elaborates other ideas.

Jeanette's parents were not married in church. She was born in 1934 in
Port of Spain, the eldest of ten children. Her mother had come to
Trinidad from Grenada at the age of 13 to work as a domestic servant for
a White family, and Jeanette was born in her mother's thirties, to be
'raised with' the White children of her employer. She met her own father
'only once or twice' as she can recall; he died when she was about thirty:
'He call me then. I was not very interested but I go.' Her mother later
'friended with' a policeman, who was frequently critical of the established
church but was known for his ability to predict future events through
conjuration (bibliomancy).[14] From the age of 1, Jeanette saw her mother
infrequently and lived with various relatives, in particular her grandmother. She attended school sporadically, reads with difficulty, and cannot
write. At 16 she left her grandmother to live with a boyfriend. This relationship broke up and she returned with her child to her grandmother,
and then lived with one of her own mother's previous 'friends'[15] by whom
she herself had three children.

Well, it was a struggle, a very hard struggle for me, because I just been living.[16] I
never had to pay rent. I live with my first children's father for three years. He put
me out . . . I go by my mother. I remain there. I try to live with somebody else
again. It wasn't so easy. I leave, go back home, try again the third time. I leave
again, go back home and I decide to stay home. So then I been living and

---

[13] p. 30. There are close parallels with local women's accounts of a child's development as
a sedimentation out from chaos.

[14] Bibliomancy and 'high science' (to use the Trinidad term): popular European magic
found in farmers' almanacs and the 'De Lawrence books' published in Chicago; generally
concerned with theosophical and cabbalistic speculations on prediction, finding buried
treasure, and conjuring elementals (cf. Brooke 1994 for a similar complex developed as
Mormonism in 19th-century New York State). These 'science books' (which she would not
have read directly) may occasionally figure the world in human form (the Adamic body), or
explain the medieval European system of 'signatures' between plants, planets, animals,
colours, personalities, and so on, but generally they are used as recipe books for divination,
love magic, and sorcery.   [15] Lovers.

[16] Cohabiting and thus more economically vulnerable than if church married.

struggling, selling, doing whatever little I could do to make a penny for my children. When I get in with somebody we last until my belly is big—I'm pregnant again. They leave me. I have to fight again to mind my children but somehow or the other the spirit always sends somebody to help me . . . My spirit always be with me so that someone would help me, come and help me . . . But it usually end up I by myself, working again, selling again and feeding my children as much as I could.

As for most working-class Trinidadian women, emancipation from parents and accession into adulthood came from childbearing. She 'scuffled', borrowing, begging, getting by with help from relatives and boyfriends: 'a little job here, a next one there. I often plan to get marry but something happen. I ai' fuss.'

By the age of 37 Jeanette had borne ten children. Her views on sexuality and reproduction were then conventional: men and women are fundamentally different with characteristic personalities and interests, both contribute physically to the formation of the child, and a woman will bear her predetermined 'set of children'. For working-class Creole women, childbearing is the point of entry into autonomy in a way that secondary education, employment, chronological age, first menstruation or sexual intercourse, or marriage are not: 'You come a big woman now!' Bigger in belly, bigger in status. Childless women may be abused by others when arguments turn bitter ('mule' is the insult in Jamaica), while male preferences in female beauty still emphasize large buttocks and a 'grinding' pelvic gait which are explicitly emphasized as both sexual and maternal.

Through childbirth young women obtain publicly accepted obligations from the child's father,[17] for an unmarried father is supposed to assume some financial responsibility for his child's mother and for the child which only then may 'carry his title' (surname). To have children in marriage is less the expected option (and for some it is that) than the seal on mutual trust given the resources necessary for sustaining a marriage. Men may talk implausibly of women trapping them into giving money through falsely claiming they have fathered a child, but generally they accept this obligation willingly; and in everyday talk between themselves describe sexual relations in agricultural and culinary terms—women are land to be cultivated not only for planting but for realization of the

---

[17] As Handwerker (1989) notes, the economic advantages of women's fertility in Trinidad have now diminished as women have increasingly obtained employment away from household and family land.

produce.[18] A man's sexual reputation is determined by his fertility, not his virility. An 'illegitimate' child is not one without married parents but one who is not recognized by the father, with resulting shame for the woman whose child must then carry her own title, although this is frequently the occasion of much negotiation and retrospective changes. (Occasionally a de facto matrilineage of title may continue for a few generations.) Declaration of a child's father by a woman is frequently couched in ambiguous statements depending on the degree of intimacy with the listener, and later quarrels may lead to denials of earlier statements on paternity or even veiled accusations of 'badtalking' (a term that refers not only to gossip and lying but to sorcery and a variant of the evil eye). As Trinidadians put it, these matters are always 'according' (dependent on circumstances).

When in a relationship, whether church married or just 'living', the man might thus be simultaneously supporting his current partner and their children but also his earlier and 'outside' children. 'Paternity' is more than begetting: in Jamaica, but not as far as I could gather in Trinidad, his continuing financial support is regarded as a very physical feeding of the child, contributing after birth to its body.[19] For poor families the declaration of pregnancy by an unmarried daughter is generally the occasion for a formalized serious public row between her and her mother, in which (depending on the revealed identity of 'the man') the mother proclaims her own 'respectability' against her daughter's 'worthlessness': the daughter, less shamed than angry, may then leave to stay with other relatives and only return to her mother after some time. Observation of these episodes in the villages and in town suggests that they range from astonishment and indignation on the part of her mother if the daughter is still at school or entering valued employment, or if the father of the child is already married or 'living', to a fairly nominal but similar performance when the mother already knows about the affair but needs to declare her lack of responsibility publicly now that the girl has so evidently attained accountability. A promise to support the daughter made to her family by the man generally leads to a faster reconciliation, depending on their knowledge of his personality and prospects.

---

[18] Thus infidelity may be glossed as 'Man trespassing on my land' or 'There's more in the mortar beside the pestle.' Yet there is no West Indian recognition of male monogenesis or female pollution (except in Rastafari), for the 'earth' is not just an incubator but an essential and equal genetrix.　　　　　　　　　　　　　　　　　　　　　[19] Sobo (1993).

Interrupted Pregnancy and Birth

While infant mortality rates in Trinidad are not dissimilar to those of Western Europe, pregnancy is frequently said to be a period of particular vulnerability to sickness and envious sorcery by other women, particularly any having sexual relations with the father. In other islands attendance at a funeral by pregnant women is described as dangerous, as are attempted abortion, strong emotion or the sight of certain animals from the bush, accidents, or sickness, any of which may lead to difficult or even monstrous births.[20] Sexual intercourse is generally continued until late in pregnancy and is encouraged to keep the birth canal open. A common Caribbean image of health is an open and ripe ('fresh') body: frequent purging with infusions of local bushes and barks enable the body to be cleaned out periodically. And these are used particularly after the birth or for abortion. Induced abortion is less common than men suspect and, while attempted at some time by most adult women with whom I talked, is publicly regarded as murder. 'Freeness' refers simultaneously to personal autonomy, easy and flexible sexual relations, regular menstruation and childbirth, generosity and physical health; 'closed', like 'tied', is an idiom for virginity and infertility, prolonged labour, physical sickness and some types of madness, for marriage and respectability, for the reserved character of Whites as well as for village suspicions of sorcery, envy and self-centredness, and excessive worrying without ventilation. If sexual intercourse opens the body for a safe delivery, contraception is argued by village men and women of Jeanette's age to block the woman's body like sorcery, and is thus likely to cause aberrant growths elsewhere.

There are no longer any untrained village midwives, and women now give birth in hospital. For Jeanette:

My being pregnant and having to go to the doctor and hospital to make my baby I always see something in the hospital that I didn't like, and it is the young mothers. What I find that was wrong in those days that the young mothers should be taken care of more. Because they are young, in their first pregnancy, they don' know anything about it and they usually act inferior to which they should be acting (you know, they cry a lot, they bawl a lot), so by the time they are ready to bring forth the baby some of them are so weak. Nobody to sit down and talk to them. The nurses have no time, you know. I would usually go round the beds because most of my pregnancies, when I go in there, my water bag burst home and I think I am ready; when I reach there I am not ready; sometimes two weeks I am

---

[20] Kitzinger (1982); Sobo (1993). This was mentioned to me in Trinidad in malicious gossip about specific people but only rarely as generalization when discussing pregnancy.

still there, waiting on the pain to come, to deliver my baby. So then I would be helping the younger mothers by going and sit down with them, rub their hands, pass my hand on their face, talk to them, prepare them, tell them 'Don't cry—you know you are crying too much—you will get too weak—eat something—little thing to eat—they say you mus' eat something.' I did talk to them, pat them, show them. Sometime I get through with them, sometime they are very hard to get through with because they are studying the pain that they getting for days and they keep crying and crying. So I did talk to them. And these things use to make me feel good. It make me feel that I am doing something to help my people. I don't know . . . but I like it at the time. But yet I am in there for so long I still help myself by doing something, even self is to help share out some food sometime, until my pain come. Well my pain does be very short; if I start about ten o'clock in the morning, by the time twelve o'clock I am already deliver my baby.

But something happen to me in hospital once which I didn't like at all. Was with one of my babies. I don't really like the labour room because I find the bed is too high, it is too cold, the plastic they put on it is too cold. You have to lie down on this wet cold plastic and in my pain I like to be walking. Whenever a pain take me I jump off the bed, and I gone, up and down, up and down until it ease again, I go back and lie. But in the labour room you cannot do that: you have to bear that pain on the bed there. To me, I get more pain by being lying down there twist up. So I never like the labour room. So what I do is ease my pain on the outside, in the yard, and I remain there whenever it take me and walk, walk until it get very hot and I know when it is time to deliver, I jump up on the bed and my baby will come. When the baby come [this time] I call the nurse. The nurse did just pass and see me comfortable so, when she come back now, she say 'What happen?' I say 'the baby, the baby'. When she look she say 'Look what you making a mess, you making a mess in the place, look what you doing on the bed! You making a mess! Get up and go in the labour room! I bet you I push it back.' And she hold it, the baby, and push it! I fire a kick because I feel a pain. And when I fire the kick my foot pass near her face, when I start to cry one time. I say 'Sorry, I didn't really mean to do that but you push it and you hurt me.' You know and I cry and thing and I make it look [right]. That nurse, when she did that to me, I felt it.

In the next lecture I return to the question of her interrupted birth as a natural symbol for her religious experience and look at various Protestant sects—generally the less recognized—which have argued something similar.

3

Moments of Creation:
The Religious Embodiment of Women
Prophets and Divine Innovators

Explanations, Deep and Prosaic

To continue the story of Mother Earth: While, at the time, the temporary
return of the son back into his mother during an actual childbirth had
seemed just an unhappy fortuity, not uncharacteristic of what might be
expected from the *social* (snobbish, 'correct') midwives, it remained a
frightening experience on which Jeanette continually brooded. Not until
her visions a decade later did she begin to realize that this event had been
a prefiguring of a cosmic and universal truth: that the Mother's Son,
indeed all men, try to return into a woman's womb, to destroy her natural fertility and then emulate it as Science. And that it is respectable local
women such as nurses who are particularly enlisted in his endeavours.

This action of the Son—an 'embodied schema', as Mark Johnson
calls it,[1] in which Mother Earth uses her bodily experience figuratively
to interpret the world—recalls that of the culture hero or mediator in
those myths which celebrate a passing from matriarchy to patriarchy,
and from divine to human. Ethnographic, feminist, and psychological
explanations all emphasize the technology-bearing culture hero from the
perspective of men as an exemplary account which legitimizes their
power or resolves their sexual anxieties and jealousies. The hero frequently has a prolonged childhood or an abnormal or delayed birth as he
straddles the human and ultrahuman worlds.[2] Although Mother Earth's
ideas recall a pattern found in a number of cosmogonies elsewhere, we are

[1] Johnson (1987).
[2] Adelman (1992); Neumann (1963). Thus Jackson (1979), comparing two versions of a
Mande epic (in one of which the culture hero Sundiata is born extremely slowly while in
the other he returns after birth to his mother's womb) has argued that prolonged gestation
and prolonged infancy are cosmological equivalents. For psychodynamic explanations on
this, see the writings on 'the prophet as hero' by Otto Rank.

not concerned here with some shared myth arguably structured by a stable set of existing relationships, but rather with a novel schema, one certainly elaborated out of her available ideas and experiences but now proclaimed by the woman herself against the hero. It is difficult to see this simply as a shared legitimization of male power (though it does offer an explanation for current male dominance) or as the expression of men's personal dilemmas.

While I do not wish to speculate in detail on the putative 'deep moti- vation' (say, of a mother's 'incestuous' desire for her son being called to awareness as the nurse pushes the child back),[3] some consideration must be given to mother–son relationships in West Indian societies. Is there a local 'social vehicle', as Clifford Geertz calls it, which perhaps structures some existing sentiment of female descent? Or is it just that, as Edward Tylor once argued, the postulation of telluric (earth bound) mother deities is 'simple and obvious': Earth as the maternal womb, sky as semi- nal rain, or as chaos or whatever? (For 'paternity' and 'maternity' are hardly terms of the same order [4] and only recently has biotechnology dis- tinguished *mater* from *genetrix*: a new practice which of course enrages Mother Earth.) I heard no accounts of actual mother–son sexual relations in Trinidad: the suggestion was met with incredulous laughter rather than the disgust reserved for the rare vice of father–daughter incest. Nevertheless, the centrality of the mother–child relationship has been emphasized by Caribbeanists and by local novelists and politicians, as matrifocal, matricentral, or even matriarchal; most radically in the notion that the local family—always to be contrasted with its idealized European counterpart—is in some way usually 'denuded' of the father.[5] Women between themselves may lament the general irresponsibility of their men, joke that men are unnecessary except for sexual pleasure, and downplay (but hardly deny) the male contribution to procreation. Behind this matrifocal Caribbean family, argue some psychoanalysts, lurks the psy-

---

[3] It is difficult to question a divinity about the intimate details of her early life. Concern- ing actual physical incest with any of her sons I felt unable to enquire; for the reasons below I think this improbable. Her partner and her adult sons (including the one who was 'pushed back') found the possibility hilariously unlikely. Mother Earth died in 1984. In 1991 I asked her younger and more respectable sisters and her aunt: both derided the idea, but they said that she had been rather naive as a girl, easily 'led astray by men who took advantage on her'. I only met Mother Earth's own mother in 1991, three weeks before she herself died, when she was too ill to be asked about her daughter's experiences.   [4] Delaney (1986).
[5] R. T. Smith (1988) argues that the anthropologist should not interpret the Black family by comparison with the White ideal, but this is certainly what happens locally (e.g. Dann 1987: 14–22)

chological father—the White male—the historical rapist of the mother and the continuing representation of external power within the Creole family he has created.[6] Alexander has described the 'ancestral myth' of the West Indian middle class as one which traces descent back to a planter and his female slave,[7] and Trinidadian family stories may give names to the pair. The mother–child relationship is certainly the only kin tie which is expected to continue throughout adulthood, one which cannot be out-weighed by acquired relationships with others. Both sons and daughters may quarrel with their father as they get older or ignore him. But not their mother. 'Mother blood stronger than father blood', as the Jamaicans put it. She remains available as a mother for the whole of her child's life.

My psychoanalytic colleagues may perhaps argue here—and it is difficult to resist the intoxications of condensing down Jeanette's personal life, physical experiences, and cosmogony into a unitary psychosocial clo-sure, her visions as reflecting, or at least emblematic of, what Gananath Obeyesekere calls 'deep motivations'[8]—that the resolution of her Oedipal wishes for her biological father was thwarted by his absence; that these were then transferred to the doubly unobtainable White father (available in the psychic reality of imperial domination) to be temporarily resolved through bearing children to her 'stepfather'; in reaction against which nearly incestuous relationship she then chose a much younger man from a distant part of the island, and in joining the Shouter Baptists submitted herself, asexual, to God the (White) Father: a complex of unstable rela-tionships which were only resolved through her later identification with a Black female creatrix, thus apparently displacing the White and male principles onto a peripheral figure who interfered with her own pristine Nature, while at the same time she identifies herself with male as well as female, re-enacting but reversing the Son's return in her actions during the events she calls the Miracle.[9] In other words, the structuring key lies in a daughter–father rather than in a mother–son relationship, and the Son is only *a son* in that he provides an appropriate model of contingency, subordination, and rebellion.[10]

---

[6] For example, in the writing of Jacques André and Frantz Fanon.

[7] Alexander (1977).

[8] Obeyesekere (1981). To avoid the theoretical baggage of psychoanalytical terminology.

[9] Soon after her initial visions Jeanette found herself moving her arms down towards her womb, an event the group calls the Miracle, the moment when as incarnate Mother she recalled the veiling heat around the Sun–Son back into the Earth.

[10] The psychoanalytic perspective usually ignores Jocasta in favour of the tragic male hero. Olivier (1989), however, offers a feminist rereading which emphasizes the powerful desires she has for her son. Rather than look at Jocasta herself—like Oedipus, a somewhat

Psychoanalytic interpretations are not necessarily to be dismissed out of hand. But they remain more arbitrary than most: even if Mother Earth had told me more about her childhood experiences, we might generate a variety of somewhat different 'deep' narratives. Avoidance of sexual relations, however, may have a rather more prosaic rationale. Margery Kempe, an illiterate brewer in medieval Norfolk who had nearly died during her fourteenth delivery, interpreted a vision of devils as a call from God to abandon married life. Without claiming a general model of 'compensation' or 'resistance', it is hardly surprising that schemata associated with problematic childbearing are plausible for prophetic women such as Mistress Kempe, particularly those who elaborate a religious cosmogony which refigures childbirth. (She later identified herself with the Mother of Jesus.) Psychoanalytical speculation aside, an aversion to conjugal relations or the loss of children signal some personal departure from a conventionally ascribed identity. Male messianic leaders and prophets are frequently celibate or childless, as Max Weber noted, but this appears even more common among their female counterparts. While the death of young children or other family members may simply leave the woman with freedom to engage in new activities, the experience of losing her children may precipitate the potential prophet into action, perhaps in an attempt to restitute or make sense of her loss.

All four children of Ann Lee, an eighteenth-century Manchester factory worker who founded the Shakers, died in infancy, and one delivery by forceps was particularly prolonged, the child appearing reluctant to be born: 'She saw the deaths of her children as a series of divine judgements on her "concupiscence" . . . but once her health was restored, participation was infused with a sense of mission. What she had undergone as an individual she came to believe was really a universal struggle', her biographer tells us.[11] Only after her husband left her did Ann Lee assume her

---

unwitting protagonist in the original myth—we might consider the more motivated instance of Phaedra. She is enamoured of her stepson, Hippolytus: not her biological son admittedly, but Seneca's text is full of talk of incest—'Do you intend to be the common spouse of son and father? . . . Even the beasts abhor forbidden unions; instinct teaches proper respect for laws of generation'—and no psychoanalyst would baulk at 'stepson' for 'son'. Phaedra is the cousin of the Minotaur killed by her husband Theseus, who abducted Hippolytus' mother, an Amazon. If, with Jungian euhemerism (Lecture 4), we take the killing of the mother as the historical victory of patriarchy over matriarchy, then, as Phaedra carries out Venus' revenge for the heliocentric victory ('she hates all children of the Sun, and now through us she takes revenge for what was done to her'), incest—dubious paternity and thus 'mother-right,'—returns to undermine the novel 'father-right'.

[11] Andrews (1953: 8).

title of Mother; like Joanna Southcott and my Mother Earth, she was then accused of madness and sexual promiscuity, not unusual aspersions to be cast on the female religious innovator.[12] Sometimes these were deliberately provoked: when prosyletizing naked with the group, Mother Earth would open her legs towards a street audience, point, and call out, 'Here is where you all come from!' Christopher Hill records a seventeenth-century Puritan who disrupted a church service at Westminster by lifting her skirts up and inviting Christ to enter; as did some of the Camisards who inspired Ann Lee. Compare Gillray's 1814 cartoon of Joanna Southcott lifting her skirts up to the doctors' view and the street charivari of her giving birth to Shiloh.[13] Mother Ann was recognized as a divine Mother, and by contrast advocated celibacy after a vision showed her a 'full and clear view of the mystery of iniquity, of the root and foundation of human depravity', to cite her.[14] As among Roman Catholic clergy and religious orders, the extended 'weak' use of the terms Father or Mother with both prophets emphasizes their parenthood over other adults as members of a non-worldly family. Nurturing and power, but generally not generation.

The radical Christian tradition contains a number of men identifying themselves as embodiments of Jesus or God, or of such figures as Daniel, the Brother of the Almighty, or the Younger Brother of Jesus (discussed in the next lecture). And similarly prophetic women have argued affinities between themselves and biblical or quasi-biblical characters, both male and female. To take some modern English instances: Jemima Wilkinson, the Messiah; the Cornish Trumpeter (Revelation 8); Sarah Flaxmer, the Revealer of Satan (Revelation 12); Mother Joanna (Southcott), the Woman Clothed with the Sun, the Mother of Shiloh (Revelation 12; Genesis 49); Mary Evans, the Bride of Christ; Friend Mother (Luckie Buchan), the Holy Ghost. (I am not familiar with instances of men identifying themselves as female biblical figures.) If procreation for a woman involves two experiences with rather different agency, coitus and childbirth, then the less radical revisions still employ something like the former to mark the entry of divinity into her as a passive vehicle, whether as an envisioned identification or more concretely as destined motherhood of the incarnate divinity.

The extent to which the prophet may take herself as modelled on a mythical figure as exemplar, or as a chosen messenger, or as actually

---

[12] Ibid.; Hollywood (1995); Harrison (1979: 105).   [13] Harrison (1979).
[14] i.e. human sexuality (Mother Ann quoted in Holloway 1966: 57)

consubstantial with other-worldly power, seems to fluctuate with self-doubt and the acclamation of others. Joanna Southcott appears to have been pushed by her followers to a need to be 'proved'. Eventually she proclaimed in her sixties that she was about to give birth to a figure identified with the Second Coming of Christ. She had earlier identified herself as the Woman, then as Eve, then as the Bride of Christ.[15] Her self-ascription as Eve seems to have fitted with certain local ideas which took Eve as a potentially redeeming figure.[16] Mother Earth similarly draws on her past relations with men to use her emergent cosmology to explain their past behaviour to her. Unlike Joanna Southcott, she takes her pregnancy as the grounds for a grander revision which reduces God to her own jealous son.

Pregnant Embodiment

If we accept that new cosmogonies are often developed through immediate human preoccupations (as well as in more figurative idioms worked from an existing tradition), then we might wonder if their models of world creation will not be rather different for female than for male innovators; a woman's carrying a new being inside her for nine months is a fundamentally different type of procreation, as experience, memory, and project. She alone 'gives birth'. Whatever the local understandings of human generation, women are just more intimately involved through their body, and later through the child's post-natal nurture. Pregnancy may be less a customary trope than a real cognition and a real motivation. As Rabuzzi puts it, the pregnant woman recognizes herself as multiple: not just as her pre-existing self plus another, but in a new personal identity which distinguishes her from yet unites her to others in a 'near visionary' mode.[17] The woman ceases to recognize herself as a single entity, and the distinction between experiencing self and the world becomes diffused even as she retains a pre-pregnancy body schema which does not altogether disappear.[18] Her body's boundaries, its postures and actions, shift. She occupies a different space in relation to people and objects, with a different receptivity to not so external events. Relations between her parts change with a different weight, massiveness, and balance; she may find

---

[15] Southcott (1995: 2, 99).   [16] Ibid. 55, 59.   [17] Rabuzzi (1994).
[18] I am relying here on the accounts given by contemporary American women collated by I. M. Young (1984).

herself grounded in the earth as essential: 'In pregnancy I literally do not have a firm sense of where my body ends and the world begins.'[19] Agency alters as what were once automatic and unrecognized movements and gestures now have to be more evidently willed. Its inner movements are now those of another, but the sensations are the woman's sensations. Her location of self shifts to abdomen; her centre of awareness is now not only eyes but also trunk. A private internal world of life develops which is accessible only to the mother; at the same time she is aware that this aspect of her self will disembed, and that a moment is approaching when her subjective world will be differentiated, and part of her being will be objectified as an externalized other: yet an other which maintains an intrinsic relation to her. Some contemporary feminists have argued that pregnancy and lactation may be said to be non-Cartesian cognitions in that an absolute distinction between self and other becomes lost;[20] and certainly, in all of this, men and the earlier sexual act may become fairly redundant.

Pregnancy makes available a powerful body schema for wider cognizing of generation and multiplicity, emergent agency and connectedness, in other domains. While many bodily processes and actions may provide dual or multiple schemata,[21] none, I would argue, can be quite so resonant. The preceding paragraph drew on contemporary Western women's accounts, and while experience of pregnancy may be intrinsic, it is hardly invariant, dependent on a society's 'body techniques', as Marcel Mauss called them, and the woman's own understandings: pregnancy may be taken variously as the intrusion of an unwanted other or as a parasitic incubus, not least in male fantasy. Like childbirth, pregnancy may be cognized as willed or as 'other.' (Rarely, contemporary European women give birth without recognizing that they have been pregnant; and sometimes not even then.) While the pregnant woman may herself feel enhanced, for instance as more sensual, her associates may feel differently; a male is likely to claim joint or superior rights in the fruits of her body, and to maintain his own agency and meanings in the whole process; her physical comportment and costume may be constrained to enhance or conceal her pregnancy; other contingencies (material consequences, not being married, prostituting, affinal obligations, age, or previous miscarriages, children, and infertility) and the likely survival of the child constrain and

---

[19] Ibid.　　　　　[20] Ibid. And thus inherently more 'religious' (Jonte-Pace 1987).
[21] Eating, vomiting, excreting, digesting, menstruation, sexual relations, masturbation, dreaming, sickness, accidents.

determine her own cognitions, and thus their potential for wider meta-representations.

Contemporary feminists in Europe and North America have argued an opposition between 'birthing' and medical interventions. Hospital birth and its technologies are typically described as alienating the woman's subjectivity from her own agency in a process which is otherwise understood as 'willed' or which as 'inevitable' enhances an association between women and a natural world independent of human (here male) interventions. Mechanical intervention in labour is argued by the ecofeminists as a male rape of nature;[22] the woman's body is not only 'interfered with' (and Mother Earth uses an identical expression), but it is appropriated and objectified by men as a site of pathology, the pregnant body becoming vulnerable if not frankly dysfunctional. The use of instruments to evaluate the success of the process in the consensual world leaves her experience and knowledge as redundant, and childbirth becomes a procedure. Women are expected to remain passive; discouraged from walking about even in the early stages of labour, they deliver in a horizontal position orthogonal to gravity, often in stirrups, which reduce their ability to push, their legs held apart for speculum or forceps in a mimicry of copulation. Mother Earth's labour involved a similar perception of hospital delivery and of the officiating nurses. The thwarted birth she describes is not implausible in a context where the West Indian midwife has been said to describe women giving birth as 'animals' and tries 'to get [them] on the bed, where they were expected to lie still and be good patients'.[23] Midwives in Trinidad are precarious *ti-bourgs* ('respectable working-class', in British terms), themselves especially vulnerable to gossip about their own concealed sexuality, their relations with doctors, and their knowledge of abortion.

Gender and Variant Christianities

Motherhood provides a 'base model', as George Lakoff[24] calls it, an experiential metaphor for structuring birth, inheritance, nurture, marital relations, and kinship. But it is not of course one entirely independent of existing cultural context. Do West Indian understandings of motherhood already provide any explicit parallels for religious ideas? Very little.

[22] Kitzinger (1982); Caldecott and Leland (1983); Young (1984); Corea (1988); Haraway (1989). And, more critically, Calloway (1978).   [23] e.g. Kitzinger (1980: 93, 92).
[24] Lakoff (1987).

Maternity confers no especial religious significance. Sexual renunciation or concealment is associated with respectability, and thus churchgoing, yet nominal Catholics generally ridicule the idea of the Virgin Birth. Nor is Mary particularly revered. Waist-binding ('tie you belly') is still not uncommon among women in Trinidadian Baptist groups, in prayer and early pregnancy, sickness and later life, but is not locally elaborated, as among Orthodox Jews and Muslims elsewhere, as any separation of carnal and spiritual, but rather as both a spiritual and bodily support. Some anthropologists have made formal associations between the practice of 'labouring'[25] in religious revivalism (when women practise vigorous hyperventilation with synchronized foot and trunk movements while singing) to the mother's panting during the labour of delivery, but that is seldom locally noted. Jamaican women pressing down in childbirth have been described as 'calling down Jesus' into their bodies through their vagina,[26] but I found no evidence for that in Trinidad. Any equivalence would be regarded as decidedly obscene, although Jamaican Pentecostalists apparently state that the Holy Spirit enters them through their vagina, and expulsion of evil spirits follows the same route.[27] If sexuality has any association with Caribbean Christianity, it would seem to be—as elsewhere—as an opposition, yet Spiritual Baptist Mothers are certainly regarded as nurturing their congregation, on occasion healing or feeding them just as a mother does for her child;[28] and the Earth People's central rite of a communal meal was prefigured in Baptist and shango ceremonies of feeding the children of a local neighbourhood.

As general cultural innovations, women's cosmogonies of pregnancy and parturition have somehow to engage the interests of others, including men. We are not concerned with some momentary and empathic mimesis by Mother Earth's followers of an extraordinary experience [29] of thwarted birth, but with an active circulation of the images and transformations it offers, of engagement and reverberation with it at a variety of levels, appropriating it and socializing it, eventually codifying it. Generally young men, unemployed and functionally non-literate, her followers could share her concern with the situation of Black women, but they could hardly embody the meanings of her own parturition except in a reciprocal relationship: as her children, for they agreed that their historical paternity was, in a sense, through a European rape of African women.

---

[25] Known as 'trumping' among the Spiritual Baptists.   [26] Kitzinger (1982).
[27] Austin-Broos (1997).   [28] See Wedenoja (1989) for equivalents in Jamaica.
[29] In Abrahams's (1986) sense.

Space here does not allow me to examine their representation of Mother Earth's bodily experience as a new social formation. I will conclude with a brief comparison with other radical groups which have developed in Christianity: in particular those with similar cosmologies of bisexual or female divinity and which emphasize generation and nurturing, while simultaneously deprecating sexual relations. This last is hardly new given Christianity's residual apocalyptic expectations: to transcend sexuality, particularly incest, legendary Christian heroines had remained virgins or became men socially (Thecla and Margaret of Antioch) or even physically (St Uncumber grew a beard). [30]

While women have equal spiritual worth, maintained St Paul, in every-day life they are still subordinate to men.[31] St Jerome adds: 'As long as a woman is for birth and children, she is different from man as body is from soul. But when she wishes to serve Christ more than the world, then she will cease to be a woman and will be called a man.'[32] Though the Virgin herself stands for *motherhood* she is seldom an image of *fecundity*,[33] and the representations of sexuality, asexuality, and generation in Christianity (Incarnation and Virgin Birth, Immaculate Conception, the Church as the Bride of the Divine Bridegroom, the rapture of female saints by Christ), while to the critical observer they may derive their power from bodily prototypes, strive to maintain a purely figurative relationship to the sexual body. Margery Kempe, however, reports God as saying to her in a vision, 'Therefore I must be intimate with you, and lie in your bed with you. Daughter, you greatly desire to see me, and you may bodily, when you are in bed, take me to you as your wedded husband, as your dear dar-ling, and as your sweet son ... Therefore you can bodily take me in the arms of your soul and kiss my mouth, my head, and my feet as sweetly as you want.'[34] Similarly the thirteenth-century mystic Hadewijch spoke of Christ penetrating her: 'After that he came himself to me, took me entirely in his arms and pressed me to him and all my members felt his in full felicity.'[35] Speculation on exactly how God incarnated himself in Mary is generally avoided in theological speculation, or is highly figura-tive (such as Augustine's suggestion that it was through her 'ear' in the Annunciation), and a clear distinction is made between divine impregna-

---

[30] Warner (1983: 154).
[31] Gal. 3: 28; 1 Cor. 11: 3. (Paul or whoever wrote these letters.)
[32] Cited in Warner (1983: 154).   [33] Preston, introd. to Preston (1982).
[34] Kempe (1994: 126–7).
[35] Bynum (1991: 168). As Bynum's (1982) studies on 12th-century Cistercians argue, such images could go along with a perception of Jesus (or even God) as maternal.

tion and human birth ('conceived *by* the Holy Ghost, born *of* the Virgin Mary').

Although women in Western Christianity have provided the majority of devotees, they are rarely found in Christianity's higher echelons. As Mother Earth puts it: 'Outside they show a statue of the Mother, inside they is all Father . . . Rome is he, they have you under control, Church and State.'[36] Women are marginal in Christian practice, text, and fable, serving merely as intercessors or mediators between a Deity—represented on earth through a male priesthood—and his human subjects. By contrast, asserted the radical utopians, God is asexual or bisexual, on occasion female. Movements initiated by divine mothers like Mother Earth or Ann Lee have identified women's childbearing and nurturing with the natural world (as does the Church), but also with the original state of things before an interference. But rarely with human sexuality. Not surprisingly this identity of substance with spirit eschews a distanced male creator and either plumps for identity between Creatrix and Nature (Mother Earth) or an androgynous or paired Creator–Creatrix (Mother Ann of the Shakers was the second Christ Spirit born to the bisexual deity): immanent deities as containers of an unfolding creation rather than as conjurors of inanimate matter from nothing. Various radical revisions of Christianity have similarly countered the embodiment of the divine creation in the domestic father, while among the Shakers and Earth People any sexual activity has been avoided in imminent expectation of the End. Refusal of sex (and thus of repeated pregnancy and the death of children) has gone together with an enhanced status for women among many ecstatic utopians; as a sour cleric has observed, 'from the Montanist movement onwards, the history of [religious] enthusiasm is largely a history of female emancipation'.[37]

Many radicals argued sexual equality from the passage in the Apocrypha (1 Esdras 4), where Zorobabel lists the powers which by their nature women have over men. Like the earlier Cathars, Albigensians, and Old Believers, radical millennialists in the industrial era have oscillated between sexual abstinence and promiscuity, between 'rigorism' and 'scandal'.[38] Both practices repudiated procreation, with its association with property and the subjugation of women. Some of the American communalist projects of the eighteenth and nineteenth centuries attempted celibacy while others practised polygyny, polyandry, group sex, or free

---

[36] 'Rome' is frequently used as an equivalent to the Rasta 'Babylon' (worldly and oppressing state system)   [37] Knox (1950).   [38] Ibid.

love. As did Romantic poetry: Percy Shelley's *Queen Mab* similarly proposed a female cosmos, in which God and religion are simply man-made devices for legitimizing the tyranny of law and government; the Earth is now physically changing to initiate a period when time will cease and love will govern all. Shelley dreamed of anarchist utopias—'kingless continents sinless as Eden'—and such visions were integral to the American communalist experiments, religious and secular, which involved over a hundred groups and perhaps a hundred thousand people in the eighteenth and nineteenth centuries. Some emphasized rejection of the state, together with opposition to slavery and to conventional marriage, in favour of pacifism and economic self-sufficiency. Egalitarians, self-styled 'peculiar people', like Mother Earth they fulminated against racism, war, the criminal code, and the treatment of the insane. The Dukhobors of Canada still await the fall of temporal government when 'the complete unification of the nations would result'. Communitarians deprecated 'social' titles and given names, called each other Brother or Sister, and took themselves for a family. They adopted distinctive and sometimes deliberately paradoxical modes of dress and speech, the American Shakers transcribing spontaneous glossolalia into their everyday hymnals. Others experimented with all simultaneously: in the Spiritual Marriage advocated by Lucina Umphreville (the Public Universal Friend of New England) successive physical pairings with different partners continued until a couple found the perfect (celibate) match. On occasion Fabians and Theosophists too have attempted to 'transcend' sex.

Those institutions we generally account as 'religions' counterpose our imperfect world of human procreation to a transcendent world whose moral purposes offer us an understanding of our origin and end. Without passing comment on the not uncommon idea that in many particulars the religious is *necessarily* an inversion of the everyday (as argued variously by Edmund Leach and Simone de Beauvoir[39]), those movements we generally characterize as 'millennial' or 'apocalyptic' are concerned with a dramatic elision of the two worlds, through prophetic visions but more particularly in an end to their separation which will be experienced in this-worldly time (yet ending time as the now unified cosmos returns to

---

[39] Leach and de Beauvoir both argue that religion attempts to negate death and suffering: there are of course the usual problems of what counts as opposition or inversion, and at which level, and whether in local exegesis or scholarly analysis. Mother Earth may seem to stand Christianity on its head, but her revisions still rework many monotheistic themes in, for example, suffering as sin against the First Cause, a metaphysical dualism, a collective eschatology, and parallels to the Incarnation.

something like its original state or intention). Separations reconciled, sins purged, suffering dissolved, disease and death overcome, and so on. And through which sexuality and the pains of childbirth and the loss of children become redundant.

As the very differentiation between the sexes appears an inevitable fact of the temporal order of things and inherently tied to sexuality, apocalyptic interests may attempt to abolish sexual difference. Like some first-century Christians, the eighteenth-century American Rappites held that man was originally androgynous but that the biblical Fall had initiated our separation into two sexes who would once again be united through an androgynous Jesus: 'Just at this juncture the first fall of man took place, by which Adam violated his own inward sanctuary and his own female function by means of which he could have been (as Genesis I: 28 has it) fruitful and multiply without an external helpmate, after the order of a Hermaphrodite then, and after the order now, see Luke 20: 34–6.'[40] Curiously, like Jeanette's original mothers, these hermaphrodites had only one eye. Father Rapp was rumoured to have castrated his son and we might note a heterodox Christian tradition of mutilation as sexual renunciation (Origen); in an interesting paper Cristiano Grotanelli has recently likened this to peasant and anti-colonial resistance through self-mutilation. Orthodox speculation on frank androgyneity was, however, restricted to the human form after the Resurrection (Scotus). This is a close counterpart to Mother Earth's account of the Son's interference with the androgynous but parturient mothers, and indeed to the great 'Orphic myth' of contemporary ecofeminists.[41]

The Rappites too construed the human fall from its natural origins by the English word 'interference'.[42] The Shakers likewise taught that the original androgynous Adam, created by a paired male–female deity had been overthrown by the male Devil, the Christian's Father of all: redemption would be through the return of the deity in both male (Jesus) and female (Mother Ann) humanity: 'the Father's high eternal throne was

[40] Cited in Ardt (1965: 583).
[41] Adler (1986: 260–1); Corea (1988); Caldecott and Leland (1983). There are striking parallels between the cosmogony of the Earth People and those elaborated by the ecofeminists. Mother Earth could hardly have been directly influenced by ecofeminism (which may be formally dated to March 1980: Caldecott and Leland 1983), but she was certainly aware by the early 1970s of the American 'counter-culture' as represented in the cinema. If her ideas developed independently, I am not arguing for an inevitable 'women's cosmogony' but rather that the cognition of childbirth just makes this a very available schema (cf. Sered 1994).   [42] Ardt (1965).

never filled by one alone'.[43] Joanna Southcott at times seems to have argued that Christ would return to Earth as a woman and redeem us all in our original androgyneity.[44] Paired and androgynous deities are found in other revisions of Christianity such as Mormonism (Mother in Heaven), Christian Science (where God is sometimes called 'Mother-Father'), and Unitarianism.

Such revisions of the Christian progenitor are not limited to female initiators,[45] but I would suggest that for women they become more plausible. While one might be tempted to characterize monotheism's creation-at-a-distance as objectified 'uterus envy',[46] my argument here is not psychoanalytical, nor conventionally psychological, except inasmuch as we accept Marcel Mauss's idea of 'psychological facts not as causes, except in

[43] Andrews (1953: 158). Space prevents detailed consideration here of one 'Hermetic' or Gnostic tradition which proposes a malevolent male demiurge mistaken by humans for the First Cause. Similar ideas may derive from a continuing radical and popular 'counter-tradition' or simply as repeated reactions to the persisting Christian tradition (Littlewood 1993). If both Mother Earth and the ecofeminists revere maternity, the body as spirit, serpents, the moon, and sorcery as female power, for the ecofeminists these seem obviously derived from Bachofen via Jung; for Mother Earth they are oppositional possibilities realized anew. Any mythic corpus offers a variety of possible continuities, interpretations, and practices: the mystic meditating on the unity of all things; the pragmatic dedication to a saint; the fraternities dedicated to particular cults; the legalists and historians of religious authority; the ecstatic unity of worshipper and divinity. Each selects, revises, and contributes. In the medieval Gnostic, Hermetic, cabbalistic, and other 'mysteries', as these are available now in Trinidadian 'high science', we can certainly identify a progression from an undifferentiated first principle, usually female and spiritual, to sexually differentiated physical humans. High science, like ecofeminism, argues such a progression from an original matriarchy revering a supreme, parthenogenic but androgynous, moon goddess to solar patriarchy (Nelson 1979; Adler 1986; Albanese 1990; Weigle 1989; Sered 1994). For want of a better term, we may call this 'Hermetic euhemerism': an account of 'myth' in general which itself may be said to constitute a myth in that historical time is subordinated to some cosmological unfolding; its most developed variant is Jung's analytical psychology, which argues that the drama is recapitulated psychologically and physiologically in every individual, and that our shift to patriarchy has not been entirely beneficial: to fulfil ourselves men and women alike now have to return to a bisexual Great Mother inside us all (Neumann 1963). Similarly deriving from Bachofen, the other leading variant, euhemerism proper (in which history drives the myth rather than the reverse), as in Engels's Marxism and Freud's psychoanalysis, assumes that the shift has been irrevocable and, on the whole, is in our best interests. Ecofeminism has moved from such an evolutionary Freudian–Marxist euhemerism to the Jungian. The sources available in the tradition of high science are mythical schemata but also personalistic methodologies which I shall consider in my next lecture.

[44] Southcott (1995: 106–7).

[45] Christian Science (where God is sometimes called 'Mother-Father') was founded by Mary Baker Eddy; the Mormons ('Mother in Heaven') by two males; Unitarianism (an asexual or androgynous deity) has no identified founder except perhaps the Younger Socinus, and coalesced from a number of radical Protestant and then deist ideas. We might note the widespread attempt to feminize God by women in the major denominations since the 1970s (Weigle 1989; Sered 1994).   [46] The psychoanalyst Fromm called it 'pregnancy envy'.

moments of creation or reform'.[47] Pregnancy and childbearing provide a ground for complex social figurings of origin, agency, and theodicy, which for Earth Mother dramatically invert existing cosmologies (Christianity in Spiritual Baptism, Rastafari, and Catholicism; the shango cult[48]). Her schema not only structures a speculative cosmology, but in her own understandings allows some acceptance of this as a shared reality for others. As her children. For while her idioms of maternity—the earth as our Mother, herself as both Nature and the Mother of her group, creation as childbirth—may be idioms of parturition and nurturing, they are hardly those of active sexuality.

For the Earth People, the relevance of sexuality at the End remains vague. Sexual relations are not encouraged, but some members joined the valley together with their existing partners and they did, I think, continue to have sexual intercourse until the women left. Single members, generally young men, frequently complained to me about the relative absence of women, and Mother Earth placated them by explaining rather vaguely that all would eventually be resolved. Her more alarming proposal that men and women alike would soon return to a hermaphrodite form was possibly confided only to me.

If we take schemata of human procreation less as 'deep' motivations than as biologically cognized structurings of our own ontology,[49] inherent

---

[47] Mauss (1979*b*). Contrast Boas's rather Judaeo-Christian notion of cosmology as 'a projection into objective existence of a world that pre-existed in the mind of a creator'. If Anglo-French anthropology's disdain for psychology may be likened to a scientific control that endeavours to hold part of the data constant (here as the natural facts of psychology and physiology) so as to examine variation in the rest, it leaves Mauss's 'moments of creation or reform' somewhat mysterious. How 'large' is a social change to necessitate causes rather than cogs? And with the establishment of a new social formation are the causes to be understood as continuing as cogs? If psychoanalysis conflates the psychology of origin with the psychology of recruitment and persistence, Maussian anthropology generally remarks no association at all, relinquishing the study of radical social change to Weberian sociology (Jarvie 1964; Littlewood 1993).

[48] Shango in Trinidad no longer offers much beyond fragments of a Yoruba cosmogony, but we can trace a Son's incest with a primordial mother in some Brazilian and Yoruba sources on the orisha (power) Emanja (Littlewood 1993).

[49] Or more lucidly as: grounded but learnable, as cognitive categories, primary representations, conventional metaphors, focal metaphors, primordial image schemata, or intuitive notions of natural kinds (to take various suggestions from Boyer 1993). Compare Leach (1976) on his terms 'physiological basis' and 'biological foundations', where cognition appears simply in the shared culture which from outside the body employs the body as a metaphor: Durkheim's collective representation. (Similarly Douglas 1973.) In the case of pregnancy, we are not, however, dealing simply with the relationship between an available image and the collective acquisition of this knowledge, for pregnancy is also a cognition, motivation, and praxis, an inherent connection and interaction with others. (The last is

and immediate, which serve for such meta-representations as cosmological understandings, they can be deployed either figuratively or referentially, in representation or embodiment.[50] Continuing movement (and a variety of combinations) between representation and embodiment is mediated by context and reception as well as by personal intention and affect. Contra Durkheim, as a religious symbolization, pregnancy is inherently 'meaningful' in the sense used by Victor Turner and Gananath Obeyesekere. It is hardly arbitrary, for its deployment still evokes its intrinsic cognitions. As Mother Earth puts it, 'Your ancestor is you.'

argued in feminist jurisprudence.) Thus systemic and ethological rather than psychological evidence may be appropriate. We may argue a spectrum of instances from representations so grounded in intrinsic cognitions that they may be said to be psychological processes and most easily understood in neuropsychological terms, to embodiments of shared figurings such as Mauss's social 'techniques'. (And what we identify as the 'same schema' may pass from one to the other.)

[50] Compare 'shallow' or 'deep' symbolizations (Barrett and Lucas 1993), Victor Turner's 'ideological' or 'sensory' poles, Roman Jakobson's 'metonymic' or 'metaphorical' creativity.

4

In Defence of Euhemerus

Ultrahuman Individuals

The *lwas*, the Haitian gods who possess their initiates in vodu, comprise
a number of different families. The benign and nurturant *rada* spirits
came to Haiti from Dahomey with the slaves who served them; the *kongo*
spirits from further east, again during the slave trade. Many of the characteristics of these deities can still be identified in their African cognates—
in their personality, sentiments, and physical comportment, ritual
paraphernalia, and so on. One group of gods however, called *creole*, or
petro, appeared only during the period of Caribbean slavery: in this pantheon we find French mermaids and sea captains, bibulous peasants and
such historical figures as Jean-Jacques Dessalines, the first emperor of
independent Haiti, and more recently François (Papa Doc) Duvalier, the
physician who ruled Haiti from 1957 until his death in 1971.

These *petro* powers are hot, bitter, and vengeful. They overlap conceptually with the *gwedé* powers of death; indeed Papa Doc (who encouraged
schoolchildren to learn a new version of the Lord's Prayer: 'Our Doc who
art in Heaven') is said to have dressed like the most formidable of all
gwedé, Baron Samedi; now a god he, reciprocally, wears dark glasses and a
homburg, and talks through those he possesses in a nasal voice, his nostrils
plugged like those of the dead with cotton wool. The *petro* pantheon is
named from one Don Pedro, a Spanish-speaking slave in eighteenth-
century Hispaniola who is recalled as having preached violence against
the white slave-owners. About Don Pedro as a historical personage little
is known, but his vengeful personality remains to animate his cult.

In this lecture I propose to raise a question unfashionable in the social
sciences since Fustel de Coulanges and Herbert Spencer in the nineteenth century. May historical individuals like Mother Earth become recognized as ultrahuman personages whose sentiments, attributes, and
personality, however, recall those of the living human? Not the translation
of the dead into distant ancestral spirits, nor the well-studied phenomenon
of divine kingship, nor the near worship of dead heroes such as Mao

Zedong or James Dean, nor of the miracle-performing θεός ἀνήρ (god-man) of late antiquity,[1] nor even the apotheosis by which deceased Roman emperors (after Domitian when they were still alive) were regarded as 'divine', but the process by which during their lives individuals may become translated into personalized, unique, and novel divine beings who may then choose to intervene in our human affairs or else return embodied in living humans whom they inhabit with their person, and whose original sentiments and political context may preside over a whole category of local experience.

I am going to suggest that this process of divinization is particularly common among what Vittorio Lanternari has termed the 'religions of the oppressed'. I am not concerned with what we might term 'completed cultures'—if such there could be—but with the revelation of divine attribution, and in this with the currently discredited notions of incident and narrative. Nor am I suggesting this as a general model for religion. In a sense there is nothing so very extraordinary here: the phenomenon of spirit possession, as we shall see in the seventh lecture, presents an ethnohistory in which the spirits respond to and reinstate new events, objects, and personalities; the phenomenon of colonialism as spirit intrusion is well represented in the classic accounts of *sar* (or *zar*) possession in East Africa (by Lewis, Constantinides, and Boddy[2]), and colonial memoirs of Africa once frequently recounted the reappearance of the deceased district commissioner as a (generally benign) spirit. (Among the Wataita of Kenya, Harris[3] reported in the 1950s, *saka* possession in women could be occasioned by the appearance of bicycles or motor vehicles, and I recall from my fieldwork in Trinidad a whole family possessed by a new sewing-machine they had allegedly stolen.) Religious experience is always represented through events and contemporary history even if it cannot easily be equated with them.

While local genealogies may record the apical ancestors as somehow closer to the world of spirits than one's recently deceased relatives, in this the human personality of the long-dead person is generally unremarked in their later descendants. Their human uniqueness, as it were, fades away. I propose here some fairly modest speculations on a more personified process of divinization—what the Victorians knew as euhemerism, and what more recently we may be inclined to regard as an extreme instance of the biographical fallacy. Less the transmission of event into structure than the transmission of person into structure: if you like, a severe case

---

[1] Brown (1982).   [2] I. M. Lewis (1969); Boddy (1989).   [3] G. Harris (1957).

of the routinization of charisma. I would suggest that a nineteenth-century explanation for religion which we now deride as conjectural intellectualism may nevertheless be of interest in certain contemporary instances, particularly anti-establishment movements.

Euhemerus of Messene was the Hellenistic author, around 300 BC, of a fantasy travel novel, *Hiera Anagraphē* ('Sacred Scripture'), which now survives only in fragments. In this, Euhemerus tells of an imaginary voyage in the Indian Ocean to the island of Panchaia in the Indian Ocean which recalls perhaps Sri Lanka. Here he finds documentary evidence that the Hellenic gods were simply great heroes who had been deified after death by their grateful people; this argument we now term 'euhemerism' in its more extended form—that myths are surviving local accounts of real incidents in human history. The Greek myths themselves already contained accounts of human or semi-human heroes being translated at their death into full divinity, or into stars or whatever; Plutarch describes how Egyptian priests showed interested tourists the actual grave of Osiris; humans are granted immortality in the Vedas, as they are in Greek and Egyptian myths. Euhemerus simply reads this as a uniform process of civilization. Euhemerism became particularly appealing in a period when Alexander's successors required worship from their citizens on what they supposed were Asian principles, the Ptolemies having their secular power personalized under their more transcendent title of *soter*: protector, guard, saviour. The early Roman poet Ennius wrote a euhemerist piece in Latin to question the divinity of Jupiter; this too has not survived, but was later cited by Christian apologists such as Lactantius to decry the independent reality of the Greek gods. Like Herbert Spencer,[4] anthropologists too have sometimes credited mythical 'heroes' (but seldom, as with Spencer, actual gods) with some previous existence as humans.[5] Fustel de Coulanges offers less a 'strong' euhemerism (in which only the high eternal gods are derived from specific 'superior persons'—as the anthropologist Evans-Pritchard[6] termed them) than a domestic origin for religion in which 'hearth-fire demons, heroes, lares, all are confounded';[7] in Coulanges's schema all ancestors are translated into something like minor gods of one degree or another because no death can be conceived as final, for the living are still emotionally attached to their deceased relatives who have to be fed and placated.[8] He calls this 'the worship of the dead';[9] let us call it 'weak' euhemerism.

---

[4] Spencer (1876). [5] Lang (1884: 199). [6] Evans-Pritchard (1977).
[7] Fustel De Coulanges (1864: 32). [8] Ibid. 19. [9] Ibid. 21.

As a general explanation of godhood, euhemerism is now regarded by anthropologists as implausible. Divinity is primarily a social not a historical or psychological phenomenon. One of the last professional anthropological pieces on the 'historicity of myth' was perhaps Meyer Fortes's astringent review[10] of William Perry's *The Primordial Ocean* in 1937, the latter a characteristic piece of University College London's solar diffusionism splendidly subtitled *An Introductory Contribution to Social Psychology*. The idea, however, persists in what we might term popular 'Hermetic antiquarianism', a set of ideas to which I shall return.

At a fairly banal level, however, deities are surely always modelled on human persons: omniscient and eternal they may be, yet they are liable to become angry or jealous, to be forgiving or otherwise (what Samuel Johnson's dictionary termed 'anthropomorphism'). But this is hardly euhemerism—strong or weak—in which historical individuals have remained among us as gods. It is of course Christianity that its critics have argued as the most striking instance of euhemerism: the doctrine of the Incarnation proposes, not that the man Jesus was deified by over-zealous followers (as Muslims and other unitarians argue), but that the pre-existent Deity appeared in the guise of—or as—a man. (For, to prove successful, any ontological promotion must surely sell itself in some such reversal: for how could one deify a man who was *already* God in human form?) Christian theology has been much preoccupied with the exact relation between God and Jesus. The 'Judaizers'—as they were once called—emphasized the humanity of Jesus as the Messiah: for the Jewish Messiah has never been properly divine. The extent to which Jesus recognized himself as 'divine' is lost in subsequent hagiography, but we know there were disputes between those followers emphasizing his humanity and those—the 'Hellenizers', like St Paul and St John—who downplayed the human Jesus in favour of the Christ, the divinity made flesh. So, as appears with Zoroaster or Buddha, but probably even more so, we have two opposed directions, the downward embodiment of the other-worldly (incarnation, as stated in doctrine) and the upward divinization of the natural (apotheosis, as seen by observers and critics). Deification during life leads to certain intellectual problems at the death of the historical individual. The Christian argument here is perhaps best left to its apologists, but we might note that the argument over the two natures of Christ has continued: Nazarenes and Ebionites were opposed to the Gnostics and Docetics, the extreme universalizers who argued that the

---

[10] Fortes (1937).

Jesus who died was no longer divine but simply a man, God—who cannot die—having departed his physical body before the Crucifixion, an idea here curiously allied to those of the Monophysite churches such as the Copts which have proposed the incorruptibility of Christ's body from the first moment of the Incarnation.

With complete identity between deity and prophet, the divinizing principle has of course to downplay the immediate *social* attributes of the deified human; and in St Paul's letter to the Galatians we find a rejection of much of the Jewish context of Jesus's beliefs and practices—the context which an ethnographer of early Christianity would require to understand the incarnate deity's human actions.[11] It is doubtful—given that all our sources are relatively late and Christian—if we can seek to uncover a non-Christianized (and hence non-divine) historical personage Jesus; I want to turn today to some more contemporary instances where one can place empirical knowledge of the historical individual against subsequent deification. We might note that such deification of the prophet may be resisted (Islam in general) or reversed (eighteenth-century French deism and Unitarianism in North America).

So far I have been rather vague about what we might properly refer to as a divinity. To demonstrate the occurrence of something like 'strong' euhemerism (as opposed to the 'weak' forms of 'ancestor worship' or 'divine kingship'), I propose that we require:

1. A situation in which one already makes a clear distinction between the world of everyday experience and an other-worldly ultrahuman order (Paradise, Olympus, the Transcendent, or whatever).
2. But in which humans at death do not generally pass to authority in the other world; certain high beings in the ultrahuman world, one or more, have a pre-eminence and power which generates, and in part controls, our sublunary world. Let us call them 'gods'.
3. Some humans, during their life or afterwards, may claim or are awarded identity and authority with these gods as one of their limited number, or indeed as the single eternal and omnipotent deity; as Andrew Lang, not incidentally a euhemerist, put it: 'ancestral spirits raised to a higher power'.[12] What may be described as ontological promotion.[13]

[11] One can note similar issues arising in the *volkisch* turn in German 19th-century Protestant theology: Jesus as a Jewish rabbi (David Strauss); or as a Roman (Ernest Haeckel); as not being a historical figure at all (Arther Drews), but an image of God (Albert Schweitzer) or Wotan (C. G. Jung).   [12] Lang (1884: 199).

[13] I am grateful to Dr Nick Allen, who suggested this appropriate term.

If this sounds a rather Western and monotheistic schema, I am indeed going to look primarily at instances within monotheism or drastically revising it. Can it ever occur? Given that the Christian Incarnation was a more or less once and for ever event, the latter is more common: the process we can characterize as euhemerism has now to be one of imitation, scandalous heresy. (I shall leave aside Asian religious systems, in which we find a complex cross-cutting of divine heroes, avatars, deified religious leaders, minor divinities, incarnations, and godlings.)

The Incarnate Earth Mother

You will recall from my second lecture Jeanette Baptiste, the 39-year-old woman who left Port of Spain to live on the coast of Trinidad together with six children and her partner. Jeanette experiences a series of revelations which become the foundation of her subsequent group, the Earth People. She comes to understand that Christian teaching is false. Rather, our world is the work of a primordial Mother whom Jeanette identifies with Nature, with the Earth, and with her own body. Nature gave birth to a race of Black people, but her rebellious Son (the Christian God) re-entered his Mother's womb to steal her power of generation and succeeded by producing (or forcing her to create) White people. The Whites, the Race of the Son, then enslaved the Blacks and have continued to exploit them.

Jeanette herself takes the name Mother Earth as the primordial Mother Nature in bodily form, but the Mother will only fully become her at the End. 'They say the Christ is returning in the twentieth century, but I am the Christ.' She was also identified previously in human history as Eve in opposition to both Adam and his Creator, as the Devil against God, and (for the human Jeanette was once a habituée of 'sword and sandal' cinema epics) as Polyphemus against Odysseus, as Dracula against Frankenstein, as Cleopatra against the Romans, as Rider Haggard's She, and as the reggae singer Jimmy Cliff's Queen of Africa. (A living divinity must presumably employ this sort of euhemerism herself to cut down her mythic rivals by arguing that they are only misreadings of her own physical actuality.)

Here we have an instance of a prophetic woman identifying with a divine being: not one already known but a novel one which nevertheless translocates certain aspects of existing deities and heroes—particularly the Christians' God and their Devil—and whose overall schema certainly recalls the model of divine power and human disobedience offered by popular Christianity, say in the tales of the medieval Golden Legend. Mother Earth cannot offer us an instance of 'natural religion' like those proposed by eighteenth-century theologians such as William Paley: her actions take place within and against an already existing religious system. (And we must be similarly wary of using the development and organization of a religious community as a convincing model for civil society.) One radically new development is her notion of creation: which recapitulates Jeanette's own personality and her earlier experiences of physical motherhood, and with which her group have continued to resonate after her death not only in doctrine but in comportment, sentiment, and affect. In this, they are, as they say, Her Children: gentle but resolute and implacable. Jeanette's personality has been translated both into an organization of her group as a family and into its individual replication in each member.

Divinization in the Protestant Tradition

The radical Protestant tradition, particularly in the countries colonized by Europeans, contains a number of men identifying themselves as Jesus or God, or such figures as the prophet Daniel, or the Younger Brother of Jesus. And, similarly, prophetic women have argued affinities between themselves and biblical or quasi-biblical characters, both male and female. How does individual human action and experience become translated into that of a divine exemplar? While an emphasis on psychological aspects here appears more germane than for 'theories of religion' in general, my earlier ascription of insanity is perhaps less an explanation than a denigration (though grandiosity is not an infrequent symptom in psychopathology). While it is true that my instances of divinization occur in small and generally transient groups (and thus lack the characteristics which Evans-Pritchard argued make the explanation of religion primarily sociological—its shared cultural context, its uniformity, its obligatory nature), it is the acceptance by others of divinization as legitimate that differentiate it from our normal ascription of madness. It has to resonate with the experience of others. (Which is not to say that divinization is to be considered as especially psychological: custom and habit are as much psychology as resonance with novelty.) The most useful interpretation here is perhaps that proposed by the psychoanalyst Erik Erikson[14] for charismatic leadership: in periods of locally recognized change or contestation, the new leader's personality and experiences exemplify for others

---

[14] Erikson (1958).

their own uncertain situation—and its solution. As the anthropologist Godfrey Lienhardt put it, 'the "vision" of one man then becomes accepted by his followers as a source of their own distinctive collective experiences'.[15] We might wonder if those groups in the Christianized world which particularly divinize—women, the colonized, the poor—are so marginal that resistance which is successful (for only this comes to our attention) must necessarily take a more dramatic form, and that to align their aspirations with divine or natural processes is to provide an objectivized charter for radical action, enabling them to challenge the dominant order in which, as an apparently seamless and thus unquestionable whole, its immediate practice as well as ultimate justification have consigned them to marginality. In this sense, 'divinization' is the possibility of subdominant protest framed in a cosmological idiom.

Why women? Figuring the relationship between cosmos and human in terms of sexuality or parturition appears virtually ubiquitous in human understanding, whether as implicit trope, as conventionalized analogy—or as some expressly concrete generation, what Robertson Smith once called 'sexual analogies of a crass and physical kind'.[16] Indeed it is difficult, as I argued previously, to conceive of any formal set of cosmological ideas (including male religious expression and counter-intuitive Western science) which do not in some way eventually evoke our everyday sensory modes. Revisions of Christianity by women prophets in the English tradition have frequently favoured such a repeated unfolding—or disembedding—of an immanent creation rather than divine generation at a distance: the prophet herself may be a fairly passive vehicle as bride or womb for a male divinity (Margery Kempe and Joanna Southcott), but may sometimes appear as the female aspect of a bisexual godhead (Ann Lee, the Manchester factory worker who founded the American Shakers), or most radically as our ultimate divine source now embodied in human form (Mother Earth).

It is difficult to assess a personal and consistent identification with divinity from the refutations written by clerical persecutors, but there appear a variety of personal elisions between woman and divinity: from a heightening of conventional analogy in which a mystic like Julian of Norwich or Margery Kempe is spiritually penetrated, to a closer identification with divine or divine beings (many English Ranters and the Canadian Dukhobors have argued they were in a way divine, particularly their leaders, and Quakers and some Beguines such as Marguerite Porete have

---

[15] Lienhardt (1964: 134–5).   [16] Cited by Stocking (1996: 69).

come close), to a novel and total incarnation as embodied Protestant divinity (Joanna Southcott, Jemima Wilkinson, Ann Lee, my Mother Earth).

Assumptions of 'divine identity' in religious visionaries are not infrequent, if less common than that of the merely human prophet who claims a divine origin for their message. Divinity may be offered to religious leaders in their lifetime and refused: on his visit to Jamaica the Rastafari informed a bemused Haile Selassie that he was God, but he declined the honour; nor did Jiddu Krishnamurti accept Godhood when the English socialist Annie Besant proposed it. The seventeenth-century Jewish messiah Sabbatai Sevi (the first lecture) alternated between deprecating the near-divination suggested for him by some of his Christian followers and sending out letters signed 'God', and both Cromwell and Napoleon were acclaimed as the Messiah by groups of grateful Jews. There has recently been a near-scandal among the Christian Scientists, whose deity is virtually bisexual; they were offered a very generous donation in exchange for nudging Mary Baker Eddy, their founder, to a more divine position. They declined.

'Divinity' appears to cover a variety of rather different understandings. In the case of Mother Earth she certainly seems to take a transcendent identity rather different from that of her followers, and one which appears modelled on the incarnate Christ. She represents in her physical being a First Cause, eternal and pre-existent. Jehovah is subordinated to a role as her Son, and other monotheistic divinities—Allah, Jah—are identified as partial understandings of either Mother or Son. Yet the Spirit of the Mother is immanent in everything where it contends with the Spirit of her Son. The Mother literally embodies physical Nature, consubstantial with the whole of creation, with the very ground of being, less some familiar sort of deity than a concentration, a leading cusp of a Spinozan unfolding. Her biblical idiom passes over into pantheism or even hylozoism; the Son (her understanding of the Christian God), it is true, will be exiled to his planet and thus perhaps remain distinct as a principle, but the rest of Nature will, in a very real sense, return to her, to be reconciled in its original form. Whether she will then maintain some separate identity is none too clear; for these questions are of no great interest to her nor to her followers. Although she would disdain a title of Deity, Jeanette does certainly recognize herself as the pre-existent and omnipotent power. Yet we can present her as a materialist in her emphasis on our return to the Earth; a certain Christian two-memberedness persists, represented in the embodied Earth and in her Spirit. I find it helpful to read these as immanent and transcendent aspects of the same Mother: in cabbalistic terms the 'lower' and 'upper roots'.

What actually constitutes the claim to 'divinity' is not then as obvious as it might seem. While Jewish messiahship comes close and certainly needs to be considered as a marginal case, we might restrict the argument to those cases in which full identification is made with a *single* omnipotent deity. All the Dukhobor leaders have claimed to be either God or Jesus, a claim which has, naturally enough, antagonized other Canadians, yet the Dukhobors also say, 'Let us bow down to the God in one another.'[17] Similarly, the Black Muslims of the United States have argued that all Black people are divine, although their founder appears to have initiated the idea when claiming that he (alone) was divine.[18] Attributions of divinity may be assumed by outsiders who conclude from a personal interview with the leader that he alone is regarded as divine when he is merely rather provocatively asserting the divine nature of all men. This may have been the case with the Dukhobors. How are we to interpret the encounter in the 1780s between Robert Hindmarsh, a Swedenborgian, and a man in Shoreditch who told him that 'there was no God in the universe but man and that he himself was God'?[19] Pantheism, the divinity of mankind, or a more personal assumption of divinity? Or perhaps just a statement that no death is 'natural', as with the Jamaican Rastas? Another problem is the self-protective dissimulation of many sectarians: ultra-Orthodox Jewish Hasidim may privately accept their particular *rebbe* as the Messiah even if he would deny this, and Sun Myung Moon appears to encourage the Unification Church to promote him to Godhood while never publicly admitting it.

There appear to be various related positions, all of which may be held simultaneously by different members of a group, or at different times: the leader alone may be recognized as divine and has appropriate absolute authority; or the whole community (or all people or creation) are divine; or else the community or mankind just have some sort of 'divine spark', the presence of the Holy Spirit or another emanation of divinity, within them; or else an essentially materialist message is necessarily couched in a prevalent biblical idiom. A situation in which it seems that only the leader is divine, but which then turns out to be one where all followers are divine (the Dukhobors, Black Muslims, perhaps Rastafari), might actually mean in practice that the leader has less authority than in a movement

---

[17] Woodcock and Avakumanic (1968: 92). [18] Lincoln (1961: 73).
[19] J. E. C. Harrison (1979: 40).

where he alone claims the status of a prophet or of some not-quite-divine figure such as the numerous Spouses of Christ, Brothers of the Almighty, or Women Clothed with the Sun whom we find among radical Protestants. As with the Quakers and Shakers, the group may move from one position to another, usually but not always from divine leader to the divinity of all (compare Father Divine, below). As with the Earth People, what appears to the outsider as an extraordinary claim may not be of any great importance to the group themselves in the course of everyday life; Mother Earth's followers are cheerfully abusive to her—as a 'doctrinal' obligation—except when she sets herself to offer them formal declarations of faith delivered from her position as their mother.

The radical Puritans in seventeenth-century Britain furnish numerous instances of ontological promotion. Some clearly distinguished themselves as personally divine or semi-divine, but others, like George Fox, were perhaps merely demonstrating the radical idea that a chosen generation were enacting the Last Days, or else were part of the general Ranter and Quaker 'spreading out of divinity' through provocative antinomian acts and statements. As such we may take the respected Independent minister William Franklin, who decided he was God and became a Ranter, or the Hackney bricklayer who said he was as much God as Jesus Christ had been, both described in Christopher Hill's marvellous book on the interregnum sects *The World Turned Upside Down*.[20] Pantheism or blasphemous atheism? The distinction is difficult to draw given the prevailing biblical idiom: beards and long hair were common in imitation of Christ when John Donne's son observed that everybody in Massachusetts seemed to be 'Christ the Messiahs'.[21] Nor can we assume that individuals or groups were consistent; or in the case of the Ranters altogether serious . . .

Living divinities have appeared transiently in Afro-American societies, as with Mother Earth: particularly in those groups we currently term 'Afrocentric'. An early Rasta, Leonard Howell, seems to have lost his following when he claimed personal divinity. Alexander Bedward, a Native Baptist pastor, identified himself as Christ and in 1921 publically attempted, unsuccessfully, to ascend into Heaven. In Trinidad one of the members of Michael X's Black Power commune, Hakim Jamal, claimed to be God, and the White founder of the Jonestown community in Guyana was said by some followers to be divine. From the 1930s until the 1950s the most notable instance, Father Divine, headed a large and

---

[20] Hill (1975).   [21] Lovejoy (1985: 89).

influential Black church in the United States incorporating a network of factories, stores, and housing projects known as 'heavens'.[22] As with Mother Earth and Mother Ann Lee, Father Divine provided banquets of free food during a period of economic depression—for up to 5,000 people per day; like other divine leaders, he promised eternal life to his 'angels' who took new names, Honey Bee Love, Snow White, Happy Heart, and so on. (Mother Earth's followers are named after local plant foods, Banana, Orange, Cane, Coconut, Cassava, Breadfruit: the deified leader frequently extends a parental role as the source of food.) Recourse to professional medicine was prohibited, for Father Divine was credited with miraculous healing powers; and at a meeting in 1936 his church, the International Righteous Government Convention of the Divine Peace Mission, unanimously passed the motion that 'Father Divine is God'. The idea was not altogether original to him; Father Divine had started off as the follower of another God who assigned him a junior divine status (God in the Sonship Degree); disgruntled early followers who felt that everybody was God had then left the movement in disgust. As they put it, 'God in you, God in me, Everybody be God.'[23]

What we may call the 'diffusion of divinity' to all members appears characteristic of groups which have outlasted the awkward death of their divine or near-divine founders, the Black Muslims, Shakers, and Muggletonians. From the very beginning the Quakers discredited aspirants to individual divinity such as James Nayler, who triumphantly entered Bristol on a donkey strewn with palms to cries of 'Hosannah',[24] and their notion of the actual divinity of all members dwindled rapidly into one of a 'divine spark'. Among the Dukhobors pantheism and messianic leadership appear to have coexisted quite comfortably for over a hundred years, but for a larger and proselytizing group, the death of the divine founder is difficult to negotiate, and the group collapses; early Christianity may appear the exception, one requiring, as psychologists would put it, cognitive dissonance in its followers at Pentecost. Jesus's divinity we may presume was conferred posthumously.

How do Individuals Choose Divinity?

Mother Earth told me she had started off, like any good prophet, with regarding herself as the privileged vehicle of divinity, and then it seems through a transfer of agency and the acclamation of others gradually

---

[22] S. Harris (1955).   [23] Ibid.   [24] Fox (1694); Hill (1975).

allowed this indwelling to displace other aspects of her personality. As like Mother Ann Lee of the Shakers, 'What she had undergone as an individual she came to believe was really a universal struggle.'[25] The extent to which, in a given situation, the prophet takes herself as simply imitating a divine figure as exemplar, or as being a chosen and unique messenger, or as actually consubstantial with other-worldly power, fluctuates with self-doubt, unexpected contingencies, and the acclamation of others. Joanna Southcott, a well-documented West Country instance to whom I referred in my last lecture, appears to have been pushed by expectations in 1813 from her Methodist and Anglican followers (who were coping with a sudden decline in their number) to a public attempt to be 'proved'.[26] She eventually proclaimed that at the age of 65 she was about to give birth to Shiloh, a figure she somewhat uncertainly identified with the Second Coming of Christ. Earlier, after a number of problematic love affairs, she had identified herself as the Woman, then as Eve, then as the Bride of Christ; in all cases fighting the Devil, who had seduced woman in Eden: 'For as the dispute began with the Devil and the Woman, it must end with the Devil and the Woman,' now to redeem humankind, as she puts it in one of her pamphlets.[27] Declared pregnant by nineteen of the panel of twenty-four doctors who examined her, she died some months after the expected date of delivery. Her self-ascription as Eve seems to have fitted with certain Hermetic speculations among local Protestants who took Eve as the redeeming figure who, as Genesis has it, would finally bruise Satan's head. Yet Joanna comes close to pantheism in one of her debates with Satan when she affirms 'we shall be as gods' (presumably after Genesis 3: 5). Nor was her refusal of Satan's offer of marriage altogether idiosyncratic, given that much of her cosmology memorializes her Dissenting farming background: thus Satan had tried to 'ruin' her just as other men had tried, unlettered people like her followers can read the Bible more truly than the learned, and so on. In her pamphlets there is a fluctuating identity between her own objectification as 'the woman' of her personal experiences which she narrates to others and 'the Woman' who will crush Satan. Similarly, we are never quite sure when we should assume she is talking of 'the man' as a particular individual who has previously let her down, or as Satan, man as Adam, or even man as all humankind.

Mother Earth offers us a consistent and considerably more radical revision of Christianity, now depreciating. Unlike Joanna Southcott but in a similar way to Mother Ann Lee, Jeanette takes her pregnancy as the

---

[25] Andrews (1953: 8).   [26] Hopkins (1982).   [27] Southcott (1995: 2, 99).

grounds for a grander assumption of divinity, one that does not tack and turn as did the unfortunate Joanna's, but which irrevocably reduces God to a representation of her own jealous son. If Jeanette's personality still animates her movement, I fear Joanna's story ends in farce. At her death she left a sealed box with directions that it should be opened at a time of national crisis in the presence of the assembled bishops of the Church of England. The box was opened in 1927, at the request of the National Laboratory of Psychical Research, one suffragan bishop actually being present, and was found to contain some coins, a broken horse pistol, and a copy of a rather doubtful novel, *The Surprises of Love*, by John Cleland.

Was the postulation of strong euhemerism by earlier anthropologists necessarily 'debunking' of religious belief? I would venture to suggest that euhemerism remains a popular idea for the materialist-in-the-street as much now as in the eighteenth century: Q. (adherent): 'Well who then *are* the gods?'; A. (sceptic): 'They are simply your deluded projections of your leaders' (or something like that). Take, however, the contemporary instance of antiquarian supernaturalism—not only of the Glastonbury, Templars, Stonehenge, menhirs, pyramids, and leylines sort of popular anthropology, but the related ecofeminism of the mystical wing of the women's movement. Here euhemerism becomes doctrinally central. Like Mother Earth and Robertson Smith, the ecofeminists argue the Queen of Sheba as evidence of a primitive matriarchy, and the usual schema which owes much to Bachofen and Engels is less that of the divinization of historical personages than of the divinization of their actions: starting from a 'shamanic' Neolithic culture in which femininity is prized and which worshipped its leaders as the Goddess under various names—Isis, Hathor, Danu, Ishtar, Nana, Astarte—along with matrilineal descent and property-owning by women. From about 3000 BC in this history, the Goddess was gradually ousted by Indo-European invaders with their horses, masculine battleaxe cults, and gods of fire and storm: an Ur-kultur of phallocentrism represented in the cosmologies of the ancient Middle East and Aegean: Indra defeats Danu, Baal defeats Lota, and so on. The Goddess comes to be represented as a defeated serpent or dragon, paternity is now recognized, and female chastity and virginity prized in a patrilineal if not patriarchal system. Like related Afrocentric ideas, ecofeminist antiquarianism seems to have been strongly influenced by University College London heliolithic diffusionism; as late as the 1930s Elliot Smith at UCL was teaching that the Egyptian gods were deified kings.[28]

---

[28] G. E. Smith (1932: 83).

We are All Gods

The most polished variant of this popular euhemerist anthropology is perhaps to be found in C. G. Jung's analytical psychology, which proposes in phylogenetic mode that the historical fall divinized as myth is now recapitulated physically and psychologically in every individual's personal development. The historical shift to patriarchy has not been in our best interests; to fulfil ourselves, men and women alike now have to return to the irrational Great Mother inside us all, on the route to full self-deification. In a recent revision, in what we can term the 'science fiction cults' (Scientology, Solar Temple, Heaven's Gate), Christian deities are regarded as imperfect understandings of real, albeit galactic, events. Popular euhemerist explanations, it seems true, were conceived of primarily as a materialist debunking. But they have themselves become religions or potential therapies, anti-ritualist and transformative, self-examinations aimed at 'knowing yourself', as the expression of both psychotherapists and the Gnostics has it.[29] They seem capable of articulating a variety of pragmatic resistances, frequently in association with the revaluing of women's social position; for, to reverse the ancient revolt of the solar hero against his mother, we elide both history 'out there' and its residues in our contemporary make-up; through recapitulation every individual continues within them the conflict between Mother and Son, female and male, life and science, moon and sun. The psychological, the geographical, the historical, and the mythical collapse into each other. We are all gods.

I have emphasized the example of divine women rather than men because I think they show more distinctive and radical claims to divinity in Christianized societies. The extent to which we choose to regard these claims as fitting into an existing religious schema, the extent to which they presume a new one, is arbitrary. In the passage from human to divine the historical personage casts its shade over the institutions over which divinity presides: the angry and vengeful Haitian deities of Papa Doc and the Emperor Dessalines, the nurturing humanitarianism of Mother Earth and Mother Ann, the sheer glorious incompetence of Joanna Southcott. It is not only in the case of standardized spirit possession in Haiti—or in the devotee's Imitation of Christ, or in my instances of strong euhemerism—that the follower engages in an accessible mimesis of the divine deceased. We might propose that all new religious dogmas and institutions involve us in some way in identification with their innovators' unique personal characteristics.

[29] Pagels (1982).

5

Therapeutics of the Divine:
Healing as a Hasidic Religious Idiom

Religion and Healing

While Western monotheisms radically distinguish the sensible world
from its ultrahuman reality, an explicit image of 'healing' has been common to the restoration of the body to health and safety, to the deliverance
of a 'wounded spirit', and to indeed the preservation or redemption of a
whole community (compare Greek *soteria*, Latin *salvus*). Prophets and the
founders of new religious dispensations commonly engage in, or are
recorded by later hagiographers as having employed, miracles of healing.
They assert a double cosmological register—physical and spiritual—usually enhancing the very separation, yet at the same time they show that it
may be mediated by certain individuals; indeed their very authority
appears to be justified through their tapping higher realities to heal sickness and insanity, as well as to predict or avert other misfortunes, evil
forces, or disasters to the community. The expectations on a prophet to
reconcile the two worlds through healing—and his occasional resistance
to these—are well demonstrated for Jesus in the Christian Gospels
(Mathew 4: 23, 8: 16, 9: 32, 12: 22; Mark 5: 25), together with his use of
the idiom of healing for an increased turning of the troubled spirit to the
spiritual, through confession and absolution, with conversion of the sick
soul to a fundamentally new perspective.

Do prophets actually derive their claim to authority from their ability
to heal bodily ills, which then serves as a conscious analogy for salvation
or spiritual healing? Or are the two idioms locally inseparable, as anthropologists conventionally argue for small-scale communities? Or indeed
does physical healing itself derive explicitly from an altogether ultrahuman idiom? Without close knowledge of the local etymologies of the
available terms, or of the sequence of actions of the prophet given later
interpretation, appropriation, and hagiography, it is difficult to give historical or conceptual precedence to either. While small-scale non-

monotheistic communities may provide an active physical healing role which is closely allied to knowledge of, and action in, a more transcendental world, as well as to pragmatic leadership and the countering of sorcery (the circumpolar and Amerindian shaman is a well-studied instance, and one popular through its contemporary image of the wounded healer transcending physical suffering through spiritual struggle), it is conjectural in the extreme to assume, as did an earlier generation of anthropologists,[1] that the everyday psychology of Western monotheism emerged from a less differentiated complex. Whether early Christianity itself can be said to have refined a novel Jewish dichotomization of 'physical' and the 'spiritual', or whether it exemplified a Hellenistic reaction, a more totalizing and unitary discourse, is debatable. The Jewish scriptures certainly seem to offer many accounts of physical healing through divine intervention, but close textual reading merely exemplifies the complex interparticipation of the sacred and the profane, whether glossed best by our own notions of 'sickness' or something closer to 'ritual pollution'.[2] It might be argued that physical suffering has an immediacy, a compelling urgency, which is prior to interpretation (whether in our cultural history or in the immediate experience of sickness) and which is then available to serve as a 'natural symbol'[3] for the imposition of social meanings. To do so is perhaps unwise, given that our knowledge can only be about episodes of sickness recognized within a social context. All we can say is that local ideas recalling our distinctions between 'physical healing', 'social healing', and 'spiritual healing' may have a close, or not so close, relationship within a particular community, depending on what I call here the 'tightness' of a double register and its possible cross-associations.

It has been argued that the seventeenth-century Jewish Sabbatian movement, and thence the subsequent development of Hasidism, appropriated certain more 'monistic' and participatory ideas and images from Christianity.[4] Certainly, Christianity, while always maintaining an absolute distinction between the bodily and the spiritual, has offered clear passages between them which are not typical of rabbinical Judaism: the Incarnation and the Assumption; Roman Catholic healing pilgrimages (now usually justified as purely spiritual ventures—what Csordas[5] terms a 'consolation prize'); the validation by Vatican doctors of the miracles which continue to justify sainthood; religious nursing orders, and the

---

[1] Stocking (1996). [2] G. Lewis (1987); Eilberg-Schwartz (1992).
[3] Douglas (1973). [4] Scholem (1973). [5] Csordas (1983).

involvement of most major denominations in hospital-building and health care; the ambiguity between 'missions' as medical or conversionist enterprises; the elision of conversion and 'spiritual healing' of physical illness in contemporary evangelical crusades; the religious origins of the hospice movement. Certain groups (the Salvation Army and the Seventh-Day Adventists) virtually define their mission in terms of healing physical sickness, and counter accusations of opportunism by arguing the ultimate unity of the physical and the spiritual in any healing. All Western cosmological systems, Christian or otherwise, argue for sickness being contingent on disharmony within the ultimate order, closely allied to their notions of evil.[6] Certainly, beyond the pragmatics of immediate sickness lies some ultimate theodicy which, as its etymology implies, we can posit as 'religious'.

Some psychotherapists have argued for a distinct lineage in which their own practice derives from Western religious healing.[7] Ellenberger [8] suggests that Jung's elision of the spiritual and the psychological emerges directly from the Protestant *Seelsorge* (pastoral Cure of Souls) of the nineteenth century, with its secularization of the 'guilty conscience' into the 'pathogenic secret'. It has been argued that Freud drew on Hasidic themes,[9] but he argued for a justification of his practice through immediate empirical evidence rather than in a cultural tradition. As a science, biomedicine too argues for this non-relativist emphasis on the immediate and the pragmatic rather than on the ultimate sources of suffering—on the anthropologist Evans-Pritchard's 'how' rather than 'why'; but for the practising Christian or Jewish physician, healing occurs under a transcendent and unknowable order—exemplified by Ambroise Paré's well-known 'I bound his wounds and God healed him.'

A detailed exposition of any heuristic distinction between 'religious' and 'physical' healing in Western societies is beyond the scope of this lecture. Suffice to say that the distinction, as derived in everyday English, may be variable; may place a particular priority of origin or understanding on the one or the other; and that the coalescences, distinctions, and contradictions between the two have been so varied and numerous as to make any simple relationship debatable and of uncertain value. Nevertheless, in individual experience the ultimate elision of sin and sickness, and their removal through some 'higher' power, are particularly powerful, whether in the experience of salvation or in subsequent dilemmas and illness.

---

[6] Parkin (1985).   [7] Janet (1925).   [8] Ellenberger (1970).   [9] Bakan (1958).

The term 'dualism' is used variously to refer to this distinction (*a*) between immanent and transcendent; (*b*) between corporal and spiritual (and thus temporal and religious authority); or (*c*) between what we may term good and evil; in Pauline Christianity, as in the Jewish cabbalah, these three 'slid together'.[10] In this lecture I am using the term primarily in the first usage, one which is closely allied to the second while not altogether independent of the third. In the second and third senses, Judaism is arguably less dualist than Christianity: 'I form the light and create darkness: I make peace and create evil: I the Lord do all these things' (Isaiah 45: 7).

We are not concerned here with whether the conversion of individuals to the new religious perspective can be usefully termed 'therapeutic'—a current interest—so much as with the public apologies for physical illness offered by its members. Such testimonials, and those offered by their leader, are, however, referred back to the moment of awakening to the moment's ideals, an experience which is frequently couched in a therapeutic idiom.

The Lubavitch Hasidim of Stamford Hill in London are members of a worldwide Jewish movement, whose leader, the seventh Lubavitch *rebbe*, lives in New York. (He actually died five years ago: I am taking the liberty again of using the ethographic present.) Every year he receives hundreds of *kvitlekh* (petitions) about episodes of sickness and misfortune. He responds to many with reassurance and advice, sometimes suggesting that the household's religious objects are impure and should be checked. A 60-year-old rabbi living in the community recalls how he became dangerously ill following a heart attack: after discharge from hospital he continued to experience chest pains, so his concerned wife wrote to the *rebbe* in Brooklyn asking why this had happened and what could be done. The *rebbe* replied simply that 'one should check one's *mezuzot*'. (The *mezuzot* are parchment scrolls inscribed with the *shema*, the affirmation of faith in God, enclosed in a metal or wooden case and placed upon the door frames of an observant Jewish home.) After a thorough examination of the family's *mezuzot* by a scribe, it was found that in one, in the ordinance 'Thou shalt love thy God with all thy heart' (Deuteronomy 6: 5), the word for 'heart' was wrongly spelt. A new, kosher, mezuzah was obtained and subsequently the man experienced no more chest pains.

---

[10] Brown (1989: 48). For a more extended consideration of how the various scriptural and post-scriptural texts did, or did not, distinguish between *nephesh* ('soul', 'spirit') and *basar* ('body'), and for possible Hellenistic influences, see Preuss (1978), Bottomley (1980), Rubin (1988), Gilman (1992), Eilberg-Schwartz (1992).

Both husband and wife maintain that the error in transcription was the ultimate cause of the illness, and its correction was essential to his recovery. The *rebbe*'s knowledge was, in their words, 'truly miraculous'.

The incident certainly recalls the conventional understanding of a 'miracle'. Cause and effect are recognized in the material world through our everyday sensory experience, but also on occasion through direct knowledge of (or actual intercession by) a transcendent other-worldly register which ultimately justifies suffering, one which is generally opaque to full human awareness but which we can supplicate if not sometimes actually constrain.

The so-called 'interpretive turn' in the anthropology of medicine in the 1980s, like its phenomenological successors, claims a greater closeness to individual agency and intention than that achieved through an objective criterion of efficacy derived from biophysical medicine: for biomedicine is now recognized by social scientists as a map, not a mirror. While I have criticized elsewhere anthropology's complete abandonment of the objectified naturalistic body as one valid commentary on human experience, my concern here is rather different. Does the emphasis on 'meaning' do justice to the explicit concerns of those involved situationally as sick individuals? Medical anthropologists still imply some greater validity to their own 'holistic' methodologies, in, typically, suggesting that the flux of experiencing should not be reified into entities, and that a dualist epistemology is in some way misconceived. The generality of bodily afflictions are, however, experienced as real, as immediate and arbitrary; neither 'symbolic' nor demanding rhetorical transformation, they have a compelling physical urgency which demands instrumental redress in the same register. While we may sometimes, particularly with chronic afflictions, be driven to a search for significance and justification, we are generally concerned with immediate practical amelioration: with countering the 'first spear' as best we can before worrying about the second, to use Evans-Pritchard's African idioms.

To argue for the primacy of an interpretive or semantic approach is problematic given that 'meaning' itself refers to a multitude of types of understanding, and 'interpretation' is a residual anthropological category. If biomedicine is relegated as merely one local interpretation of the physical world, then 'experience-near' anthropology remains an academic interpretation of a (local) interpretation, and one that still offers an intellectualist meta-narrative in proposing that humans are essentially driven by their quest for meaning. (The interpretive genre paradoxically enhances dualism through displacing the truth claims of scientific medicine onto that discipline itself.) I do not argue here for a particular sense of 'meaning' or 'symbol', let alone a psychological or linguistic explanation of human signification and representation, except to say that I favour the observations of many of the authors in the volume *Symbol and Sense* edited by Foster and Brandes [11] that one can locate the same 'symbolizations' on a spectrum between the expressly referential and the figurative, the shallow and the deep, and that movement between the two modes seems mediated by intention, context, or affect. As I will argue, movement in the referential direction may be such that lexical representations become objectified as entities in themselves, less meanings to be unravelled than themselves directly gaining ontological status in the cognized world. [12]

[11] Foster and Brandes (1980).

[12] Sperber (1985); Parkin (1982); Barrett and Lucas (1993); McGuire (1983); Wagner (1986); Lakoff (1987); Tambiah (1990): cf. Foucault (1970): ontological status whether in everyday life (Berger and Luckman 1966) or in anthropological theory (Boyer 1986). Are 'cultural transactions' for anthropologists just shared agreement, in which case the process is perhaps of more interest to social psychologists and rhetoricians than physiologists? Moerman (1979) had cited research on 'psychosomatic illness', on biofeedback and immunology, as well as links between the body's neutral, endocrine, and autonomic nervous systems, to argue (like Mauss 1979*b*), for specific 'pathways' linking the physical and cognitive registers. For Dow, too, the relationship between somatic and symbolic (what he terms 'emotion') can be characterized as analogous to that of a 'thermostat' such that processes in the individual's unconscious-somatic systems are altered through the manipulation of symbolic parameters at the social level. Csordas (1988) takes the now conventional phenomenological 'single register' view to argue that Dow's analogy is too 'mechanistic' in still accepting the naturalistically understood body as a distinct element in the system. This internal communication, he argues, is predicated on our common-sense and medical tendency to distinguish and reify the social, the self, and the somatic, such that we must then specify mechanisms of bridging and causally transacting between them. These of course are akin to the distinctions often made by the participants themselves through the same common-sense 'Cartesian' assumptions, leaving a vagueness as to how for them the symbolic may ever relate to (or even refer to) somatic processes as naturalistically understood—the domain of miracles. And Csordas's assumption that the naturalistic body and the social body are totally incommensurate domains is radically more 'dualistic': unless the naturalistic body is assumed to have no real existence at all, an idealist position which recent medical anthropologists have sometimes seemed to approach. Kirmayer (1993) keeps the two in play by suggesting transient cultural and individual constructions linking them (which he terms 'metaphors', analogous to Dow's 'emotions').

Nevertheless, at the level of ethnography, I would agree with Csordas (1988: 139), Schieffelin (1985), and Kapferer (1993) that 'an approach grounded in participants' own experience and perceptions of change may arrive at a more pragmatic conceptualization of healing as a cultural process [and that] what is needed . . . is specification of how therapeutic processes effect transformation in existential states' through the ways that symbols are deployed in actual situations (Kapferer 1993). And this phenomenology may be considered quite independently of the sort of successful therapy which tends to be favoured in ethnographic accounts. For 'therapy' may be said to occur independently of the presence of a healer, and indeed is frequently incomplete or even mysterious from the position of either healer or patient.

The earlier structuralist schema had required what the anthropologist Edwin Ardener termed 'P-structures': in other words, paradigms or blueprints which had some primary instrumental or formal relationship to the secondary registrar, whether as base and superstructure, myth and experience, or simply template and artefact.[13] Structuralist models of healing such as that of Claude Lévi-Strauss seemed to correspond closely with local

With the medical anthropologist's shift of interest from causal mechanism to contextual meaning and intention, from signifieds to signifiers, the Western practice which itself approximates most closely to the new readings of 'traditional' and 'alternative' therapies remains that of psychotherapy, now itself concerned less with the alleviation of symptoms than with promoting self-knowledge. The goal of removing any specific symptoms with which the patient presents for therapy has been replaced by that of facilitating a new shared interpretation, currently glossed under idioms such as 'personal growth' or 'self-actualization', 'awareness' or 'raised consciousness'. This sense of 'things locally hanging together' recalls current critiques of biomedicine by Western complementary practitioners which argue for an integrated and meaningful process of healing, to be contrasted with professional medicine in which, while any disease may (or may not) be cured, the patient certainly feels worse. There is considerable ambivalence among Western complementary practitioners as to whether they need to be evaluated by physiological criteria, or whether their efficacy lies in some other set of understandings which are impervious to the biological assumptions of scientific medicine, understandings which indeed may be obscured through a 'false objectivity'. For the physician these doubts are of course disingenuous, at best seeking to mask 'real' failure through self-serving protestations of holism, at worst frank irrationality and charlatanism: a perception of the fringe which has been simultaneous with the modern professionalization of medicine.

If the quest for meaning and interconnectedness by medical anthropology has relinquished the naturalistic body to the physician, it has become difficult to distinguish 'healing' from other social patterns except by analogy with Western medicine; and thus the very subject-matter of medical anthropology becomes uncertain. In a perceptual regress from the immediate object, 'sickness' becomes reframed into 'affliction', 'healing' into 'performance' and 'transaction' (e.g. Kapferer 1993). This reading of the naturalistic perspective through the history of ideas, as primarily a social interpretation (in Sperber's 1985 terminology) of bodily processes rather than as reflecting any arbitrary reality 'out there', leaves the anthropologist generally removed from the immediacy of biomedical sciences while commenting generally upon their social practice. Yet, like the complementary medical practitioner and the psychotherapist, the anthropologist is professionally relegated to the residuum of problems 'medicine cannot yet treat'; in either case irrelevant to biomedicine's criterion of practical efficacy, and, while nominally 'holistic', practically Cartesian in agreeing with the physician that like cures like, what was once called the 'psychogenic', even if this is no longer the favoured idiom. Symbols of healing now engage not the naturalistic body but the symbolic body. By contrast, complementary medicine on occasion still tries to maintain that what is recognized as non-physical can causally and 'really' alter the physical. And there remains a continuing medical interest in how shared social meanings may determine physiological change, particularly in subdominant groups 'close to nature'—as in the occurrence of synchronized menstruation among related groups of women or in the mechanisms of 'psychogenic death'. For, in the words of one pioneer of the 'placebo effect', 'the mechanisms of the human body are capable of reacting . . . to symbolic stimuli, words and events which have somehow acquired special meaning for the individual' (S. Wolf, cited by Easthope 1986: 63).

[13] E. Ardener (1980).

exegesis in societies where the body and its sickness were indeed already highly 'mythologized': where upper and lower register, mythic reality and bodily experience (and, as in this lecture, social group), were understood as already reflecting and re-creating each other in a ubiquitous and closed narrative, where psychology was a cosmology, mythic reality being experienced by individuals as in accordance with events and actions which were not seen as situationally specific, nor generally justified as personal agency—not altogether surprisingly, given anthropology's earlier organicist analogies of social structure. This is not to say that individual agency could not be recognized in such tightly ordered schemata, but that some implicit sense of the overdetermined complex was always assumed to be borne in mind by—or rather to constitute—individuals; and any innovation by them took place through various combinations of identification and negation.

I would argue that the demise of such tight structuralist isomorphisms is not only an attribute of changing intellectual fashion or the demise of colonial objectification, but that everyday life in the apparently 'timeless small-scale societies' with which anthropologists have been generally concerned *has* generally become more pluralistic and subjectively instrumental: certain religious groups excepted. In even less 'tight' societies, such as the pluralistic postmodern Western world where biomedicine, while arguably evoking core notions of self and agency, has considerably less representational coherence and certainly no obvious formal homology with some ultimate reality, we may expect the notion of 'mythic healing' to become more extraordinary for both observer and participants. Taking 'myth' in its restricted sense as a narrative about personages in a sacred world and time akin to some ultimate reality (compare Kirmayer[14]), it may be argued that Western biomedicine offers no such *narratives* but simply *paradigms* of sickness reality which only implicitly recall the ultimate justification of our world.[15] The greater the gap between divinity and experience, the more miracles are indeed 'miracles'.

The Origins of Hasidism

Hasidism developed as a popular movement in eastern Europe in the eighteenth century.[16] Its immediate founder was the Master of the Good

---

[14] Kirmayer (1993).　　　　　　　　　　　　　[15] Lock and Gordon (1988).

[16] For accounts, see Buber (1948); Dresner (1974); Katz (1961); Mintz (1968); Sharot (1982). The attribute Hasid ('pious one') had previously referred to the Jewish rebels against Antiochus Epiphanes (2nd century BC) and to the German followers of Rabbi Yehuda he-Hassid (13th century CE).

Name, the Baal Shem Tov, popularly known by the acronym Besht. Two events have been identified as instrumental in its emergence: the Cossack insurrections of 1648–9, which killed tens of thousands of Jews in Poland and Ukraine; and the subsequent Sabbatian crisis. Buber and Sharot [17] both emphasize the increasing gap between the urban rabbinate and the rural Jewish population after the death of Sabbatai Sevi (whom I described in the first lecture) whose messianic claims and antinomian acts had swept the Jewish Diaspora with promises of immediate redemption and speedy release from all their trials. When Sabbatai converted suddenly to Islam, some followers returned to rabbinical Judaism or converted to Islam or Christianity. Others maintained Sabbatian ideas under the guise of orthodoxy, citing the cabbala to explain how Sabbatai had committed the ultimate transgression of apostasy: for the Messiah had to descend to the lower levels to redeem the divine sparks exiled there since the beginning of time.

The relationship of Hasidism to the Sabbatian movement remains controversial and some scholars deny any direct continuity. [18] The Besht, a clay-digger and itinerant healer of humble origin, taught that every present moment contained the possibility of redemption for each individual and for the community. Every person, whatever his status, wealth, or learning, could participate in this cosmic process. Between the scholarly elitism of the rabbis and the apocalyptic messianism of the Sabbatians, the Besht's followers put forward an egalitarian interpretation of the cabbalistic teachings which I consider here. They taught that God was to be known immediately in all aspects of life, since the physical world existed with him and within him, and he could be reached through everyday activities. People were encouraged to 'cleave to God' and experience him through ecstatic song, prayer, and dance, and even, initially, by the use of tobacco and alcohol. Any act—eating, work, sexual relations—was a religious act if the intention was to attach oneself to God.

The Besht was apparently well known in his hometown as a healer, 'a master of practical Kabbalah, a magician'. [19] It has been suggested that he

[17] Buber (1948): Sharot (1982).

[18] Scholem (1954) argues that the Sabbatian attack on the literal law through an antinomian enactment of cabbala both reflected and amplified the development of secular Judaism, opening up the ghetto to more universalized and psychologized ideas as the medieval Jewish accommodation with feudal power collapsed through the growth of local nationalisms (Katz 1961). Like Sharot (1982), Scholem (1954) sees Hasidism as a 'neutralisation of messianic elements into mainstream Judaism', while Bakan (1958) goes so far as to talk of a 'dialectical synthesis' of the two. For a review of the debate, see Sharot 1982.

[19] Scholem (1954).

employed the existing practices of the miracle worker to persuade people of his ethical teachings. 'There can be little doubt', argues Sharot,[20] 'that the Besht's reputation for miracle making was accepted as an important proof of his charisma and of his teachings.' While he generally employed recognized physical methods such as herbal remedies or bleeding with lancet and leeches, like other *baalei shem* (local healers and magicians), he would sometimes use a prayer or the secret names of angels to exorcise a *dybbuk* (earthbound spirit) from the body of a sick person or out of a house.[21] *Baalei shem* protected the individual against sickness, and against such misfortunes as infertility, miscarriages, fire, theft, and the evil eye. They reframed non-Jewish folk therapies in a Jewish idiom, and employed the sacred writings of the rabbinical tradition for practical magic, together with the names of God and the angels and prophets, sometimes as anagrams, acronyms, acrostics, and inversions derived from them. The *mezuzot* had perhaps originally been amulets of this sort, and they retained their thaumaturgical function despite rabbinical attempts to transform them into simple emblems. When a child was ill or a woman in obstructed labour, the Torah scroll was laid on top of them. Psalm 20 was read over the mother to alleviate the pains of childbirth, for its nine verses corresponded to the nine months of pregnancy, and its seventy words to the seventy pangs of labour. The Besht himself was famous for his blessed coins and psalms or other formulas written on parchment enclosed in a small metal case which contained the names of angels and imprecations against malevolent powers.[22] Fifty years after his death the *Shivhei ha-Besht*, a book compiled by a follower, relates many stories of his ability to heal:

I heard from the Rabbi of our community that Rabbi Leibush of the holy community of Meserich visited the Besht for the Days of Awe. Before Rosh Hashanah [the New Year] he became sick. The Besht was busy curing him on the eve of Rosh Hashanah and the entire night as well. When he went to the beth hamidrash [study hall] at the time for prayer, Rabbi Leibush became faint and felt very weak. They tried to tell the Besht, but they were afraid to shout and he did not hear them. When Rabbi Isaac of the holy community of Meserich saw that the Besht did not respond, he shouted to him in a loud voice. The Besht answered 'Why didn't you tell me?' He hurried home and found the Angel of Death standing at the head of the bed. The Besht scolded the Angel of Death severely and he ran away. The Besht then held Rabbi Leibush by the hand and he recovered immediately'.[23]

---

[20] Sharot (1982).   [21] Trachtenberg (1977).   [22] Ben-Amos and Mintz (1970).
[23] Ibid. 116.

The Besht's teaching was systematized by this biographer, Dov Ber of Meserich (1719–72), known as the Maggid (Preacher), who took the existing term 'zaddik' (righteous man) for the local leader of a Hasidic group. The founder of Lubavitch, Rabbi Schneur Zalman of Lyady (1745–1812), who studied under Dov Ber, later commented, 'we drew up the holy spirit by the bucketfull, and miracles lay around under the benches, only no one had time to pick them up'.[24] According to some, Hasidism would not have spread with such rapidity nor attained such dimensions but for the 'extraordinary galaxy of saintly mystics' it produced during its first fifty years. Hasidism holds that only the zaddik can attain the highest form of *devekut* (attachment to God at all times with one's thoughts always on him). Other Jews have to attach themselves to a zaddik, through whom in turn they can become attached to God. (The term *rebbe* is now used virtually synonymously with zaddik.) The zaddik develops the spirituality of his adherents while at the same time, through his mediation with God, he can secure favours for them in both mundane and divine matters.

After Dov Ber's death groups following various zaddikim developed in Ukraine and Poland, each known by the name of their centre of activity. Their leaders are now recalled through a particular quality or activity: some were distinguished for their fervent devotions, others for their ecstatic visions, spiritual insight, or miraculous healing. Their surviving texts are characterized by an accessible popular style rooted in folklore: anecdotes, homilies, marvellous tales, puns, jokes, and semantic paradoxes. Despite accusations of antinomianism and even pantheism, Hasidism spread rapidly in Poland and was introduced to Lithuania by Schneur Zalman, who developed the variant called Habad, which reintroduced the more intellectual elements of cabbala—but now into more general accessibility—through his *Tanya* ('Book of Teaching'), the major text of Lubavitch.

Both Orthodox Jews and secular Zionists have maintained an ambivalent relationship to Hasidim, at times critical of their overt emotionalism and dependence on miraculous *rebbes*; on other occasions taking them as the authentic voice of Jewish spirituality and identity. Hasidic folk tales have now become widely accessible through the popularizations of Martin Buber.[25] By the nineteenth century, Lubavitch was accepted as a 'rationalist' form of Hasidism which could appeal to the educated. It fought to secure economic and political benefits for all Jews in eastern Europe, and de-

---

[24] Wiener (1969).   [25] Buber (1948).

veloped a number of charitable and educational projects. Discouraged from migrating to America because of the dangers of secularism, the majority of Hasidim were to die in the Holocaust, but the sixth Lubavitch *rebbe* organized communities outside eastern Europe from which in 1948 most of the survivors settled in New York (Brooklyn), London (Stamford Hill), Israel (Jerusalem and Kefar Habad), Canada (Montreal), and Belgium (Antwerp). It has been generously estimated that by the 1980s there were perhaps 250,000 adherents and close sympathizers worldwide.[26]

The Lubavitchers of Stamford Hill

Stamford Hill is an inner-city area in north-east London, with a population of around 27,000 people in an area of three square miles. There are now nearly a 1,000 Hasidic families living here, about 200 of them Lubavitch. Although today 'Stamford Hill' is virtually synonymous with Jewish ultra-Orthodoxy, this was not always the case. Before the Second World War many local congregations were United Synagogue or Sephardic, who later moved out to the more affluent suburbs. Today, less than half of the population of Stamford Hill are Jews, mainly lower-middle-class tradesmen, religious teachers, and small businessmen.

The number of Lubavitch families increases every year, not only through the encouragement of large families but through conversion.[27] The majority of the adult Stamford Hill community are British converts from non-Orthodox Judaism who are more likely to speak English than Yiddish. According to my colleague Simon Dein, some informants have even been adherents of Western-based Buddhist and Hindu sects although they were born Jews. Many had already been familiar with popularized accounts of the cabbala or with that continuing counter-culture interest in matters Jungian and Hermetic. Rarely a Christian may convert to Orthodox Judaism to then join Lubavitch. The community conduct mass campaigns to reclaim 'stray' Jews: public meetings where rabbis preach, *mezuzot* campaigns (checking that local Jews have kosher *mezuzot* on their doors) and, perhaps the most striking of all, the 'mitzvah tank', a truck going round the streets inviting male Jews to enter and lay *tefillin*. For Orthodox Jews, relations between the mundane and the

[26] Sharot (1991). On Lubavitch in New York, see Mintz 1968; in Montreal, Shaffir (1974); in London, Kupferman (1976), Wallach (1977); on ultra-Orthodoxy in Jerusalem, Bilu *et al.* (1990).

[27] The idiom of 'conversion' is somewhat inappropriate: rather Lubavitch 'reclaim' Jews to Orthodoxy.

ultrahuman are mediated through a number of objects. At one level the whole household may be said to be 'sacred' in opposition to the Gentile world but additionally there are three more specific 'ritual' (transactional) objects to which this lecture and the next refers. *Tefillin* are phylacteries, worn during prayer on the head and on the arm near the heart, which contain scriptural texts written on parchment exhorting the Jew to love God and to subject to him everyday life, thoughts, feelings, and actions (Exodus 3: 1–10, 11–16; Deuteronomy 6: 11, 13–21). Identical texts, affixed in a case to the door frame of the main entrance as well as of every living room of the house as the *mezuzah*, summon the Jew to consecrate his home, making it an abode worthy to be blessed by the presence of God. The *tallit*, a prayer shawl donned by adult males during morning and additional prayers, has eight fringes at each of its four corners.

Besides encouraging every Jew to be more observant, Lubavitchers attempt to attract into their group educated young single adults, and campaigns are sometimes held on university campuses. 'Conversion' is less a sudden accession of faith than a gradual process in which the individual 'returns', employing more and more Jewish rituals in his or her daily life. Joining may cause conflict with the families of the converts, especially when a student gives up university studies or career.[28] Daily activity within a Hasidic group is determined in principle by Halakha (the Way), largely derived from the Talmud, the rabbinical compilation of legal, ethical, and historical writings. Minimum standards of observance for all the community include strict *kashrut* (food must be ritually pure; milk must neither be cooked nor eaten with meat), together with Sabbath and festival observance. For men there is regular attendance in the prayer house and daily study of the sacred texts, with conservative clothing, beard, and covered head. For women, an enthusiastic attitude to child-bearing is expected, with modest dress including covered hair (married women cut their hair short and cover their head with a *sheitl*, or wig), and in most groups regular prayer (not always in the synagogue) and some religious learning. Marriage and parenthood are sacred acts, and couples are expected to adhere to the laws governing family purity. Marriage of members is arranged by a *shiddukh* maker and agreed by their fathers, and at least nominally by the *rebbe*; choice of spouse depends on their family's

---

[28] Joining involves a gradual detachment from significant others outside the group with increasing interaction with established members, approximating to the general model of conversion proposed by Lofland and Stark (1965). This is not the place to argue why, in a generation after Auschwitz, certain Westerners should seek to 're-enchant' their secular world.

yihus (wealth, lineage, and learned background). Children are educated in single-sex Jewish schools, with secular education valued less than Jewish learning; in their late teens some are sent to residential seminaries. Rarely university education may be considered appropriate. As for other Orthodox Jews, the Lubavitch injunction to study affirms it as a religious experience which brings the scholar ever nearer to God.

Hasidim do not have careers; they earn a living. Favoured occupations include small businesses, especially those serving the wider Orthodox community such as food stores, or teaching and other religiously linked occupations, (slaughterer) *shohet*, (beadle) *shammes*, or (circumciser) *mohel*, and the rabbinate. Families tend to be large: one couple has sixteen children living in two adjoining houses. The average number of children per family is seven; parents are expected to trust in God to help them provide, educate, and care for large families. During fieldwork it was found that people usually adhered strictly to the Orthodox public norms. Occasionally a degree of flexibility is agreed in the interpretation of religious law; one woman from the community went to live in the north of England far from the nearest synagogue, to which the *rebbe* allowed her to travel by vehicle on the sabbath.

Although there is some association with other local Hasidic groups and occasional intermarriage, there are frequent tensions: the Satmar, who retain the kaftans and hanging sidelocks of the east European *shtetl* (the traditional village or small town community), argue the Lubavitchers' adaptation to 'modernity' has been too enthusiastic, while some Orthodox Jews accuse the current *rebbe* of messianic ambitions. To an extent, one may take these other Hasidic groups as continuations of small *shtetl* communities linked by descent and endogamy, now concerned with preserving the group's traditions and boundaries in the modern world, while Lubavitch's use of new communication technologies, its public profile, and emphasis on conversion argue for many similarities with contemporary 'new religious movements'.

In a study of another Hasidic group, derived like the Lubavitch from the pre-war world of the *shtetl*, I noted that the mundane and the religious remained 'tied together' through the mediating symbolisms of everyday actions.[29] The term 'kosher' was applied simultaneously to food, clothes, non-menstruating women, books, and ideas. The geography of community prayer house, home, room, clothes, and body were carefully ordered, each commenting on and reflecting the others. Prayerbooks were divided

---

[29] Littlewood (1983).

into sections which corresponded with the rooms of a house and the parts of the body. The Halakha gives contemporary Hasidim explicit norms for all daily activities but also, through a complex numerology employing the numerical value of words and letters, cardinal numbers (the number of good or bad observances, gifts, objects, alms) and ordinal numbers (sequence of a text or family birth order), it inscribes the social and physical worlds in a tight network. There is no act or event, good or bad, which is arbitrary or neutral. Indeed it can be said that contemporary Hasidim aspire to have no 'secular' life in that all everyday events and actions are aligned to a divine reality which is always to be held in mind. Members of the community isolate themselves where possible from the non-Jewish world. They argue a practical advantage in their distinctive attire which makes them less likely to go into sinful places. Mixing with goyim (non-Jews) is minimal except for business purposes, for they are said by some to be impure and polluting: a not uncommon idea is that their souls are somehow inferior. Mary Douglas,[30] following Durkheim, has argued that the Orthodox Jewish concern with the boundaries of the physical body—with its entrances and exits, with food, purification after excretion and menstruation, and masturbation (whence semen provides embodiment for evil powers)—follows a concern with the boundaries of the body politic faced with the ever present threats of assimilation and intermarriage. Certainly, for Lubavitch, return to Orthodoxy is primarily through ritual actions which inscribe a gradually increasing sanctity onto the individual body marking it off from the world of the goyim.

The *akeres habayis*, the Hasidic wife, is the mainstay of her family, whose domestic role is praised, particularly in guaranteeing the purity of food and household, and thus her family's health. These tasks are not recognized as 'symbolic' in the vernacular sense—that is not instrumental—for failure to perform, for example, the prescribed clearing of the house of bread before Passover allows sickness to intrude. While Lubavitch women argue that household tasks are sacred, many consider themselves more independent than other Hasidic women and to have a higher level of education, and some claim a responsibility equal to that of the men in doing the *rebbe*'s work. Several women are involved in 'reclaiming' other Jewish women to religious Orthodoxy and, compared with women of other Hasidic groups, they are less discouraged from attending the synagogue.

---

[30] Douglas (1970).

The Rebbe

Every room in a Lubavitch house has several pictures of the last *rebbe* on the walls, as a young man and as a nonagenarian. I should note that the current account is based on fieldwork (carried out by Simon Dein and myself) prior to his death in 1994. Families take great pride in showing pictures of their visits to him, especially at Dollars, when he distributes a dollar (signifying charity) to every one of the hundreds who visit him in Brooklyn on Sunday mornings.

Menachem Mendel Schneersohn has led the group since the 1950s. Lubavitchers describe him as 'the most phenomenal Jewish personality of our time', and it is through his direction that Lubavitch has developed its distinctive outward orientation. Born in Russia in 1902, he became a 'Torah prodigy', is said to be fluent in ten languages, and—unusually for Hasidim of his generation—received a secular higher education, a degree in engineering from the Sorbonne. Many miraculous stories are told about him during the fourth meal by which Hasidim seek to prolong the sabbath: he sleeps for just one hour a day, and fasts for three days in the week; he 'gives Torah' for several hours without needing a break; he meditates weekly at the grave of the sixth *rebbe* with whose soul he communicates; he predicted the end of communism in eastern Europe a year before it occurred. Although he has never visited Israel, nor indeed left Brooklyn for the past forty years, the *rebbe* is widely credited with single-handedly halting at least one set of Middle East peace talks, and with directly influencing the 1988 Israeli elections.

Many of these 'miracle tales' have personal resonances. Mrs Levy visited the *rebbe* for Dollars some ten years ago and asked for a blessing for a *shiddukh*. She was carrying several books, which she dropped accidentally in front of him. On her second visit last year he looked carefully at her and said 'Be careful with your books!' Another informant approached the *rebbe* about his son, who was physically handicapped and for whom he was unable to arrange a *shiddukh*. The *rebbe* gave him two dollars, one for himself and one to take to Israel; not understanding the reason behind this he went nevertheless to Israel taking the second dollar with him. In Jerusalem he happened to speak to a Hasid on a bus sitting opposite him and recounted the problem of his son. The other was astounded, for he himself had a disabled daughter and had written to Rebbe Schneersohn to find her a partner: the *rebbe* had given him the identical advice. Subsequent friendship led to the marriage of their two children. Those tales told about earlier zaddikim recall European fairytales—stories of lost children, secret parentage, tribulation and reward, buried treasure, ghosts and dybbuks, miraculous escapes from Cossacks and Nazis (such as the stories of Bashevis Singer). A common theme is the fundamental distinction between Jew and goy, and the near impossibility of passing from one to the other.

Succession to a *rebbe* is usually dynastic. Menachem Schneersohn is the son-in-law of the previous *rebbe*, and in his father's line the descendant of the *alter rebbe* (Schneur Zalman). Under his leadership Lubavitch institutions and activities have been established throughout the world to cater for the educational needs of the alienated Jew and 'late beginners' who would otherwise be unable to attend either a *yeshiva* (rabbinical college) or girls' school.

The process of joining Lubavitch is characterized, not only by the appropriate use of ritual objects, but by an increasing *hitkashrut* (attachment) to his person and to his work. Among the most important gatherings of the community are those that commemorate the deaths and key events in the lives of past zaddikim. Lubavitch are expected to be familiar with their lives, works, and teachings (*hasides*), and the movement's sense of itself is a moral history understood principally through their written works and stories about them. In its shallow chronology Hasidic *rebbes* are recognized as the incarnations of previous *rebbes* or of biblical prophets, and scriptural events have a contemporary action or significance; biological evolution is denied. Children are taught to revere the zaddik, and in everyday conversation Lubavitchers frequently discuss his objectives and his teachings, particularly his extraordinary personal powers and wisdom. Couples engaged in marital intercourse on the sabbath are enjoined to fix their minds on him. Through him mundane happenstance takes on new, deeper meanings: what might otherwise be seen as 'coincidences' are to be understood as brought about by the *rebbe*'s intervention. He is the guide on matters of spiritual and physical health, education, marriage, and business:

Miriam Hirsch had always intended to visit the Rebbe in America for Dollars, but had never had the necessary money. One Sunday, her American sister in Brooklyn went to see him. Mrs. Hirsch was unaware of this but admitted that on that particular day she had thought a lot about the Rebbe. Her sister didn't mention Miriam to the Rebbe but was unexpectedly given two dollars. She sent one to London. Mrs. Hirsch understood that the Rebbe was aware of the thoughts of every Jew; he knew how she was worrying and therefore gave her sister two dollars: 'Truly a miraculous man.'

Lubavitch are prepared for the arrival of the Messiah. They envisage a time very soon when the world will change fundamentally, for sickness, envy, greed, and hatred will disappear. Several rabbis argue that many existing institutions will probably remain, a commonly mentioned instance being capitalism. The appearance of Moshiach is now imminent: conventionally, 'If he does not come today he will come tomorrow.' When asked why he has not yet come, the following explanation is often offered: in each generation there are thirty-six righteous (but hidden) men, one of whom is a potential Messiah, but not enough merit by Jews has been acquired for him to emerge. Many Lubavitchers suggest that perhaps now there is enough merit, and admit that they thought Rebbe Schneersohn might be the Messiah, an idea which he, like other *rebbes*, has done little to contradict.[31] They point out that he is the seventh *rebbe*, and that Moses was of the seventh generation after Abraham.

The next lecture will engage more closely with how the 'miracles' are generated by holy texts which themselves refer to bodily experiences.

[31] Beeston (1992).

6

Therapeutics of the Divine: Healing and Redemption as Mutual Transformation in Hasidism

In the last lecture I discussed an ultra-Orthodox Jewish group the Lubavitch Hasidim, emphasizing the 'tight' construction of their symbolic and physical world. In this lecture I am less concerned with the physical projections of the individual into a cosmos than with a later development: how the already projected cosmos is now referred back again to the experiential body in practical healing; and how embodiment and representation can be regarded as two contrary processes.

Cabbala

Through daily readings, Lubavitch makes accessible to the Hasidim the once esoteric knowledge expounded in the texts known as cabbala. The term *kabbalah* ('tradition', 'that which has been received') had been used since the eleventh century of the Christian era for that diffuse tradition of Jewish mystical thought said to be hidden in the religious Law and which was received from the remote past, from Ezekiel, or even, in some accounts, through Adam from the angels before the Fall. Gershom Scholem, the pre-eminent historian of Jewish mysticism, has argued for a continuity with Jewish Gnosticism, which had sought to reconnect the immediate and divine worlds which rabbinical Judaism had so austerely divided: 'the Kabbalah was a mythical reaction in realms which monotheistic thinking had with utmost difficulty wrested from myth'; an 'eruption of subterranean forces [which attempted] to construct and describe a mythical world by means of thinking that excluded myth';[1] a return back across the 'abyss' which had developed between the registers of the physical and the spiritual.[2] Scholem suggests that the rabbinical tradition of

[1] Scholem (1965; 98, 99).   [2] Scholem (1954).

established institutions and canonical texts had provided no help in dealing with disaster and sickness, or indeed with the spiritual vacuum left by the Sabbatian apostasy. Cabbalists, however, have never seen themselves in opposition to rabbinical Orthodoxy but rather as its commentators and developers.

Cabbala is said to have first been communicated as secret teaching only to a privileged few, but by the early modern period it had become a more open pursuit, a trend particularly evident in Hasidism. It speaks of the ultimate ultrahuman order as now manifest in man, and as one which can be directly known through study or ecstatic experience, and upon which we can call and obtain practical power in this world. We may argue, as does Scholem, affinities with South Asian religious systems, Christian and Islamic mysticism, and particularly with the sort of Western theosophico-astrological tradition currently recognized under the rubric of New Age thinking. The material world of our experience is to be understood as an imperfect reflection of hidden, 'deeper' (or 'higher') underlying principles, knowledge of which serves as a practical key to confer insight and sometimes power over everyday events. Instead of the rigorously dualistic cosmogony in which the inscrutable and austere Hebrew Deity suddenly creates the material world out of nothing, and across which gap occasionally pass angels or the souls of the dead, we have here a mythic narrative gradually unfolding in cosmic time through which the progress of individual souls can be mapped, with infinite gradations of being between God and man. This metaphysical reality is often figured in anthropomorphic, if sometimes explicitly allegorical, terms; as gendered and embodied, emanating in physical space, with impulses and motivations not entirely dissimilar from those of humankind.

The most important of the more than 3,000 extant cabbalistic texts is the Zohar, the bulk of which was probably written in Spain by Moses de León (died 1305); its themes were elaborated by Isaac Luria (1514–72) in Palestine among the Iberian Jews exiled in 1492, in what is generally known to scholars as the Lurianic cabbala. The Zohar, a lengthy collection of tales, anecdotes, homilectics, and commentaries, is in late literary Aramaic with occasional Hebrew, Arabic, and Spanish expressions, the whole interwoven with paraphrases, neologisms, allegories, oxymorons, verbal paradoxes, and invented quotations. There are frequent digressions retelling *aggadah* (one or other popular tale) and on medical and demonological questions.[3] Its recurrent themes are the nature of the

---

[3] Preis (1928); Trachtenberg (1977).

Deity and the way he made himself manifest in the universe; the mysteries of the divine names; the soul of man, its source and destiny; the nature
of evil and suffering; the importance of the written and oral Torah; and
the promised Messiah and our future redemption.

According to the Zohar, the Infinite En-sof, who has in himself neither
qualities nor attributes, made his existence perceptible by projecting ten
successive channels of light which served as media for his manifestations
in the finite. These ten channels are the Sefiroth (numbers, elements,
spheres), which in the Zohar are understood as the names, indeed the
actual qualities and agencies, of God: the intelligible divine attributes
which make up all existence. The Sefiroth are figured in different patterns, but may be divided into three triads or dimensions. The first triad
represents the immanent intellectual power of the universe, the second
triad the moral world, and the third the physical universe. The tenth Sefi-
rah is the female aspect of divinity, the Shekhinah, now manifest in the
physical world, and which Adam, the first man, mistook for the whole of
divinity. The human individual is to be understood as a microcosm of the
whole universe by which each person reproduces what is above in the
celestial worlds. The Sefirotic structure of man simultaneously reflects
and is reflected onto that of the universe, and the Sefiroth may be represented as concentric circles, as the Tree of Being, or as the Cosmic Man
(the lower parts being the outer circles of the first representation).[4] They
may be identified with certain numbers, letters, and colours, and they are
gendered: in the first triad, Wisdom—masculine, the father, the giving
element—is counterposed to Understanding—feminine, the mother, the
receiver; the offspring of their conjunction is Knowledge.

Later cabbalists describe four distinct realms corresponding to different
orders of Sefiroth: in descending order of divinity, Aziluth (Emanation),
Briah (Creation), Yetzirah (Formation), Asiyah (Making, the divine
archetype of the material world). The four are both simultaneous and
successive,[5] structured by the Sefiroth in a similar pattern and subject
to common influences. Anything which involves one level cannot fail to
involve all others, for 'from an activity below there is stimulated a corresponding activity on high'.[6] There is an intrinsic relationship between

---

[4] A common representation, allied to that of the circles, is that of a nut: sensible experience is the shell which has to be broken to reach the 'real' essence. This is a common figuring in any system in which, as in biomedicine, a distinction is made between 'reality' and
'appearance'; in biomedicine the physical is the kernel, in Hasidic medicine it is the husk.
Other systems of cabbala offer either a more personified Deity or one more ethereal, who,
as in Christian Gnosticism, is counterposed to the demiurge mistakenly represented in Genesis as the Creator.   [5] Scholem (1965).   [6] Zohar (1934).

what we may gloss as the 'material' and 'spiritual' worlds, each not only influencing but continuously participating in the other as prefigurings and memories.[7] And these relationships may be understood through a complex but variable numerology in which the twenty-two letters of the alphabet are exchanged (*temurah*) or substituted for their numerical value (*gematria*). The absence of numerals, vowels, or punctuation in the written Torah (the first five books of the scriptures) leaves it open to a bewildering number of interpretations. Some have argued that there are actually 600,000 possible interpretations of the Torah, corresponding to the 600,000 holy souls each of whom has a letter in the Torah.[8] The scriptures begin with the second letter, *beth*, to show that God's manifestation is on both levels, for the Hebrew alphabet is itself the direct manifestation of the divine, as are the shape of the letters and even the spaces between, each possible pair of consonants forming a gate for the passage of divine energy. The Torah (and the alphabet) is represented variously in cabbalistic writings as the individual physical body, the body of the Jews as a whole, or even that of God: some maintained it existed before the creation of the physical world.

A rigid distinction between 'material' and 'spiritual' (the worlds I have called 'embodiment' and 'representation') is hardly perceptible given the everyday as an immanent unfolding of the divine language. As Scholem remarks, 'The Torah is to [Jewish mystics] a living organism animated by a secret life which steams and pulsates below the crust of literal meaning; every one of the innumerable strata of the hidden region corresponds to a new and profound meaning of the Torah.'[9] Cabbalistic texts embody a variety of complex, sometimes playful, shifts and cross-cuttings between 'depths' of interpreting the Torah, from the referential to the figurative: *peshat* (literal reference), *remez* (conscious allegory), *derasha* (talmudic commentary), and *sod* (mystical). These four levels are known by the acronym *pardes* (orchard).

No unfettered speculation, even *sod* remains closely constrained by adherence to the literal interpretation of the Law and the authority of the *rebbe*, and its sources lie within the religious texts and practices of all Jews. There have been no radical innovations in Jewish mysticism since the seventeenth century, but, in Martin Buber's words, Hasidism transformed the once esoteric cabbala into a 'folk ethos'. Unlike most other

---

[7] Bloom (1984).

[8] This requires further complexities as there are only 340,000 physical letters in the Torah.   [9] Scholem (1954: 14).

Orthodox Jews, our Stamford Hill community have immediate knowledge of cabbala, for, as part of their education, every Lubavitch child studies *Tanya*, which is based on Lurianic concepts. *Tanya* (*Likutei Amarim*) was compiled by Rabbi Zalman, the founder of Lubavitch, and is regarded as 'the written law of Habad'. Other Orthodox groups adhere to the old talmudic ruling that only married men over 40 with a good knowledge of the Talmud may proceed to cabbala. (Much of the Zohar employs erotic imagery in figuring the exile and eventual reconciliation of divine and mundane: the human conjunction of husband and wife on the sabbath night is a realization of the union between God and his exiled Shekhinah.)

Another current name for Lubavitch is *Habad*: an acronym from the Hebrew words Hokhmah, Binah, and Da'at (the first–intellectual– triad[10]) They refer simultaneously to personal experiences and to the Sefirotic realm where these are reflected. Anything occurring in the mind mirrors that occurring in the universe as a whole. Indeed, like other religious systems which approach pantheism,[11] the Sefiroth are as much a psychology of the human mind as a cosmology. Hokhmah (Wisdom) is the intuitive flash by which an idea emerges into the mind. Once it has come into being, the thought becomes actualized through deep reflection as Binah (Understanding). When the idea becomes an actual part of the person engaged in contemplation, the third stage of Da'at (Knowledge) is attained. The psychological and spiritual body of man 'participates in', rather than 'represents', the same principles and structural counterparts as his physical body. 'If we want to know something about the ultimate reality of the world we live in, and how God the creator manifests himself through this reality, we must begin with a study of the human being.'[12] In Jewish mysticism our phenomenological world is far from illusory (as it is in Buddhism) but one end, as it were, of ultimate reality.

Thus Lubavitch speak of the Sefiroth, not just as being symbols or allegories or even resonances, but as immanent in bodily experience. 'We were formed after the supernal pattern, each limb corresponding to something in the scheme of wisdom' (Zohar: ii., 212; cf. Genesis 1: 27). One young rabbi describes how the Torah is figured thus in the Zohar as the 'blueprint' (his words) with which God provided himself for the physical creation: the Torah contains 248 positive and 365 negative *Tanchuma ha-Kadum* (Injunctions) and these 'upper roots' have their respective manifestations in the 248 'limbs' and 365 'sinews' (or blood

---

[10] p. 92.   [11] e.g. Horton (1983); Tambiah (1990).   [12] Mindel (1974).

vessels) of the male body. Each limb of the body embodies one of the commandments, and each sinew and each day of the year embodies self-restriction. (The *Tanya* argues that the spiritual aspects of these 613 parts comprise the individual soul.) In this way every observance (or breach) of the commandments of the Torah directly causes, through its counterparts in the human body, a reaction in the corresponding portion of the world of Sefiroth: in Zoharic terms, each is the 'clothing' of the other. In his *Tanya*, Schneur Zalman associated specific parts of the body with other psychological and moral attributes: 'the evil spirit is in the left ventricle of the heart, and the love of God flames in the right ventricle'. While there are intrinsic homologies between the two realms, the correspondence is realized practically not only through mystical computation but through such transactional objects as the *tallit*.

Healing and Restitution

Sickness has its place in the divine schema. Luria's development of Zoharic cosmology postulates an initial voluntary contraction (Zimzum, self-limitation) of the Infinite to make room for the finite world of phenomena. Into the vacuum thus formed the Infinite projected his light, providing it at the same time with the 'vessels' which were to serve as the media for its manifestations in creation. Some of the vessels, unable to endure the inrush of light, gave way and broke. The breaking of the vessels caused a deterioration in the worlds above, together with chaos and confusion in the worlds below. Instead of uniform distribution throughout the universe, the light emitted by the Infinite was broken up into sparks illuminating only certain parts of the material world; other parts were left in darkness, their sparks trapped in matter. This confusion was aggravated by the failure of Adam to restore the fragments, and thus human history is born in exile. The universe remains in a state of disharmony, and the mission of every Jew, say Lubavitchers, is to restore (*tikkun*) the scattered divine sparks back to the Godhead through performing *mizvot* (divine commandments and thus ritual and charitable deeds): 'the perfection of the upper worlds waits on the perfection of the lower worlds'.[13] The distinction between the more divine and the more

---

[13] Scholem (1954) suggests that the scattering of the sparks may be read directly as the historical exile of the Jews, restitution as redemption. Sharot (1982) points out that while Luria himself did not expressly relate his schema to the recently past Iberian expulsion of 1492, we, as observers, can note a Weberian (or euhemerist) affinity between historical event and subsequent myth. Certainly there is occasional explicit reference to this by others,

human elements in the cosmic unfolding may be understood as one of dimension, distance, time, quality, procedure, potential, or indeed sometimes identity. Sickness and evil thus refer not to some malevolent power external to the created world of experience, evil in a strong sense,[14] but to a lesser state of being of this world which can be redeemed in this life or in another incarnation. 'How, Reb Zusya, do you explain evil?' [his] students asked. 'What evil?' said the rabbi with wide wondering eyes. These students pointed out that Reb Zusya was himself suffering from illness, pain and poverty. 'Oh that,' replied the rabbi, 'surely that is what my soul needs'.[15]

The Lurianic cosmogony—the 'great myth of exile' as Scholem[16] calls it—informs the Lubavitchers' explicit concepts of 'health' as knowledge and order obtained through following talmudic teachings. It refers simultaneously to physiological and psychological dysfunction, to failure to perform ritual correctly, to disharmony and conflict within the family, and to the historical exile of the Jews—all as a separation from the divine. The original 600,000 souls have become fragmented and now seek to be restored.[17] To recover one's health is, in some small measure, to restore our alienated world. Stamford Hill Lubavitch commonly argue that the 'universe itself is now in need of healing', for which they quote the Lurianic cosmogony. Since the shattering of the vessels God himself is in exile. If there is a single image, a core symbol [18] which incorporates and subsumes others, and which captures the manifold connotations of sickness and misfortune, what the anthropologist Victor Turner termed a 'root paradigm', it is that of exile and restitution.[19] 'The very nature of man . . . makes him an admirable intermediary between the material and the spiritual. By means of these religious acts, not only are the material things spiritualised, but the infinite light is, at the same time, diffused in the physical world.'[20] While not answerable to the Mosaic Law, the goyim—

together with a shared idiom. In prayer Hasidic men tie a cord around their waist to separate the spiritual upper part of their body from the mundane lower half, for *aliyah* is physical height as well as ascent to the divine, and more recently the term for secular migration to Israel (Jacobs 1973). In the arguably manic-depressive illness of Sabbatai Sevi, *aliyah* described his periods of elated mood, and thus his messiahship (Lecture 1).

[14] Parkin (1985).   [15] Wiener (1969).   [16] Scholem (1954).
[17] Mintz (1968); Ben Shimon Halevi (1974).   [18] As Ornter (1973) calls it.
[19] Sullivan (1987) proposes that the 'most important figure or symbol in any given religious tradition is the source of healing'. Our identification of an overarching representation is of course likely to reflect immediate concerns: in which case his observation is tautologous. Yet the heavy semantic load embedded in 'core symbols' ('enabling symbols'; Lawson and McCauley 1993) is perhaps fully accessed only in particular situations.
[20] Mindel (1974).

non-Jews—are subject to the covenant God made with Noah, and thus have some small role in *tikkun*. It is the *rebbe*—the dynastic leader—who is to do most, for he alone can safely descend into our material world among the shattered vessels to redeem the exiled divinity, to mediate evil into good, ignorance into knowledge, sickness into health.

Healing through the Rebbe

This is the theoretical map through which healing operates. What of its actual practice? The conventional understanding of a 'myth' is that it is some narrative about ultimate reality to which we have particular recourse when everyday cause-and-effect explanations are inadequate (when 'overloading the rational device triggers a symbolic processing': Dan Sperber[21] following Malinowski); and which to the observer exemplifies our society's fundamental values. Social anthropology continues to debate the relationship of normative myth to everyday praxis, the representational to the instrumental. Laughlin and Stephens, like Sperber, argue in Malinowskian terms that myth is 'the quintessential form of a symbol system, operating to organise experience around a society's core symbols. A society's core symbols are invariably orientated upon the zone of uncertainty—that is, the set of events giving rise to significant effects for which there exist no readily perceivable causes for a large number of society's members.'[22] Certainly, the Jewish myth of exile and restitution has served as a 'template' to articulate the destruction of the Temple and the subsequent Diaspora, antisemitic pogroms, the Holocaust, and the establishment of Israel. Yet, as a written text it has a continuing existence through time which provides an 'archive', as Foucault calls it,[23] from which individuals take elements to figure their collective history and their personal dilemmas—and as the non-arbitrary and referential exemplified by instrumental (magical and healing) cabbala.

In spite of his earlier radical sympathies, the historian Scholem takes Jewish mysticism as a major determinant of modern rationalism. Defending it against accusations of superstition, he argues that practical cabbala and magic (and indeed Hasidism) are degenerate forms: shifts, as we might say, from the figurative to the concrete and the instrumental. Indeed, Hasidism emerges not only from cabbalistic texts but through the everyday medical practice of early modern *shtetl* communities. Zoharic

---

[21] Sperber (1980: 39).   [22] Laughlin and Stevens (1980).
[23] Foucault (1970). Or 'template' (E. Ardener 1980).

passages were used before Hasidism to cure sickness or to serve as pro-
tective amulets against the evil eye of envious neighbours and against
dybbuks.[24] They can be read in multifarious ways: not only as a divine
unfolding—a type of contemplative field theory—but as a pluripotent
map of direction by which the dualism of everyday life, the material and
the divine, can be practically transcended.[25]

In listening to public accounts given by Lubavitch of their healing, they
retain a normative 'top–down' textual quality: individuals suffer apparently arbitrary affliction here below, and then, through some recourse to
the transcendent world, are healed. It was initially difficult in fieldwork to
look through these narratives to see how individual experiences and social
relations might simultaneously embed the mythic structure.[26] The multitude of possible (and conflicting) correspondences between the physical
and spiritual worlds which the Zohar theory offers are hardly accessible
to every contemporary Hasid; as with other apparently closed nosologies
based on correspondences,[27] quite variant explanations are volunteered
for a particular crisis, from a fairly abstract theodicy to the concrete and
immediate efficacy of transactional objects. Among Lubavitch it is
through the person of the *rebbe* that Zoharic cosmology is usually opera-
tionalized in immediate situations to be used as an exemplary account.
Compared with the other Hasidic groups in London, individuals seem
less likely to employ practical (magical) cabbala; informants are reluctant
to talk of possession by dybbuks (a powerful consequence of failed con-
jurations) but this explanation is occasionally volunteered in cases of consistently deviant personal actions. One local rabbi was prepared to say he
had witnessed it but was reluctant to give details. Another rabbi has elaborated his own treatment of jaundice using a white dove based on Zoharic
complementarities.

---

[24] Trachtenberg (1977).

[25] While I have emphasized here a linear image of exile, this can be figured also as a three-
dimensional containment and catharsis, well represented in public and household ritual.

[26] Anthropological fieldwork with conversionist groups is distinctive in that they continue
to offer presentationalist justifications of normative actions (Littlewood 1993). Unlike other
illness narratives (Good 1994), these have a fixed and formal (Lawson and McCauley 1993;
cf. Early 1982) tripartite pattern—appeal to *rebbe* about a problem, *rebbe*'s response, resolution of the problem—which recalls the exemplary legends Hasidim recount of past zaddikim. They may be taken as standardized and edifying testimonials, emblematic
self-presentations for other Hasidim and for the anthropologist as a potential convert: to use
Crapanzano's (1992) term they have become 'meta-pragmatic'. Thus the story (Lecture 5)
of the misspelt *mezuzah* has already been recorded among Brooklyn Lubavitch in very similar terms, but there about a set of *tefillin* (Mintz 1968: 334).

[27] Foucault (1970); Littlewood (1983).

How then do the Lubavitch of Stamford Hill act when they become ill? Their first thoughts, they say, are always about immediate pain and disability, then they consult their family or friends for a practical remedy to alleviate it, and later perhaps a Jewish physician sympathetic to the community: one of the two Orthodox, but non-Hasidic, general practitioners who live locally. According to one of these doctors, their medical treatment is generally accepted, but a common practice is to write later to the *rebbe* asking why one became ill. Not every illness episode results in a *kvitl* (petition to the *rebbe*) being written. This is done, say some, when the illness is judged to be life-threatening by patient or doctor, or when the patient does not like the treatment given by the doctor: Mrs Goldstein explained that she wrote to the *rebbe* only because her doctor's advice had been 'too simplistic'. The *rebbe* is consulted particularly when the patient does not get better despite receiving physical treatment.

The *rebbe* does not respond to every letter, although it is said that he reads them all. Even when he does not reply, Lubavitchers maintain that he still sends out a *bracha* (blessing) to the person writing to him. Not infrequently he advises against surgical interventions, for 'they make their living by cutting, I make my living by not cutting' (Rebbe Scheersohn, cited by Wiener).[28]

Samuel Drazin is a 35-year-old married man who was interviewed on several occasions in Lubavitch House. He had just written to the *rebbe* about a persistent toothache which he had experienced for some months. He had visited two dentists but no obvious physical cause had been found. The first dentist told him that he could not see anything immediately wrong with his teeth—'in fact, for someone of your age, your teeth are in very good condition'. He could certainly not account for the pain. The second dentist asked if Mr Drazin was under a lot of stress, and he left with the impression that the dentist thought it was in his mind. 'I've never had much faith in dentists,' he says, 'they cannot do a lot for you.'

The pain became so bad that he could not sleep. It affected his concentration at work. He tried several types of proprietary painkiller without much effect. His wife suggested that he should visit a homoeopath which he thought was a good idea, although he knew very little about them. Homoeopathic remedies did not alleviate the pain, although he felt more relaxed.

[28] Wiener (1969).

Born in East London in 1957, Mr Drazin had grown up in Stoke Newington, on the borders of Stamford Hill. His father, who died five years ago, had worked as a baker for most of his life, a calm gentle man, in contrast to his mother, who was 'very anxious' and fussed over his childhood ailments (she died suddenly four years ago). An only child he recalls his childhood as generally happy; after leaving school with few qualifications, he completed a two-year catering course. Although he had a non-Orthodox Jewish upbringing (indeed he rejected religious ritual and only fitfully observed the sabbath), he had met several Lubavitchers as an adolescent, but had not paid much attention to them. After leaving college at the age of 20, he was unemployed for two years—'there was not much work about and I wasn't very interested in doing catering jobs'. Having a lot of free time and 'lacking in direction', he started to visit the Lubavitch centre in Stamford Hill 'in order to learn more about my religion'. Over several months his participation in Jewish ritual increased. Starting with daily laying of *tefillin*,[29] he soon began to attend thrice-daily religious services.

He bought several *mezuzot* and put them up on the doors of his flat. His nights were now spent at *shiurim* (study sessions), where he learnt *Tanya*. After a year Samuel Drazin moved in with a Lubavitch family, who introduced him to his future wife, Rachel, who also came from a non-Orthodox background. They now have eight children aged from 6 months to 10 years. Mr Drazin now works as an administrator in Lubavitch House, the administrative centre of the community. A friendly and charming man, always immaculately dressed in a white shirt and tie and wearing a Homburg, with a long flowing grey beard, he speaks openly about his health, emphasizing that he is certainly not one to be preoccupied with minor aches and pains, but that this toothache was very bad. He had never been 'really ill' before. Mr Drazin had written to the *rebbe* on several occasions in the past, for in his early days as a Lubavitcher he had some doubts about becoming Orthodox. The *rebbe* had reassured him that this was the right thing to do, and encouraged him to perform further *mitzvot* (prescribes ordinances). He met the *rebbe* last year for Dollars and recounts how his 'heart was filled with joy'. Now, quite despondent, he sent a *kvitl* to the *rebbe* asking about his toothache. The *rebbe* responded by offering a blessing and emphasizing that one

---

[29] Lecture 5, p. 84.

should check one's *tallit*. Mr Drazin examined his prayer shawl to find that one of the strands was distinctly worn. Here indeed was the explanation of his toothache, for the thirty-two strands on the *tallit* correspond to the thirty-two teeth. A worn strand may cause pain in a tooth. He triumphantly emphasized again how the physical and spiritual worlds reflected each other, for after replacing his tallit his toothache had disappeared in a few days. For him the episode of illness and the *rebbe*'s response recalled his original 'spiritual healing' on joining the group.

My second instance, like that of the misspelt *mezuzah* in the last lecture, provides a formal homology between the words of a text and the physical body. Sometimes the *rebbe*'s explanation is not validated so immediately:

Rabbi Nifield is now 60 years old. He recently had a small stroke, which left him paralysed in his left arm (although it did not impair his walking or speech). He has suffered from hypertension for some years, but admitted that he had not taken it as seriously as he should have, although he had been in hospital on several occasions with angina. Following the stroke he spent a week in his local hospital, where he was given physiotherapy, which only slowly helped his weakness. Being a rather impatient man, as he put it, he wrote to the *rebbe*.

Born in Poland, Jacob Nifield came to Britain in 1936 at the age of 4, the third of ten children, his parents a rabbi, 'a very learned man who spent all his time studying', and an 'ideal Jewish mother, a very quiet woman'. Both parents died several years ago. Jacob grew up in an ultra-Orthodox environment and carried out the prescribed rituals from a very young age. He spent a year in a Jewish seminary in northern England and became a rabbi at the age of 26, and has been teaching since in Lubavitch schools. He is married with ten children ranging from 11 to 32 years old. His wife is reputedly a distant relative of the *rebbe*, whom they have visited in America on a number of occasions.

He is a rather austere 60-year-old man, dressed like many older Lubavitch in a long black coat and broad-rimmed Homburg. He has a particularly long beard, and is serious in manner and always rather impatient. 'When do you think that I will get better?', he asked repeatedly. Rabbi Nifield has written to the *rebbe* in the past about the education of his children, especially as to whether his sons should proceed to rabbinical training. He was impressed by the *rebbe*'s wisdom in this matter, and several of his friends had been helped after writing about health and financial problems. He proudly recalled that he had visited the *rebbe* on three occasions for Dollars: 'Every day you hear more stories about his miraculous power.'

The *rebbe* now responded to Rabbi Nifield's letter by offering a blessing and suggesting that he check his *mezuzot*. His wife took the *mezuzot* to a scribe, who thoroughly checked the scrolls and casing, only to find they were ritually pure. He could not understand this. Could the *rebbe* be wrong? 'No, the *rebbe* is never wrong; if he says the *mezuzot* are not kosher, they really are not kosher.' He sent a second letter to the *rebbe* telling him of the first scribe, but the *rebbe* responded by suggesting the *mezuzot* were checked again. A second scribe was found, but he too found them to be kosher. A third letter to the *rebbe* brought the same reply. The third scribe spent a long day examining the *mezuzot*, working until the early hours of the following morning. It was only then [30] that, holding up one scroll, he found the problem: a small beam of light shone through a hole in one of the letters. The hole rendered the *mezuzah* unkosher. Rabbi Nifield had the scroll replaced and immediately regained some movement of his left side. Three months after his stroke he had only some slight weakness in his left arm.

Several people were asked by my colleague Simon Dein about this healing. How did the *rebbe* know that there was a problem with the *mezuzah*? Rabbi Nifield himself responded immediately: 'the *rebbe*'s soul represents the soul of the whole Jewish nation. He is aware of the life of every Jew. Every Jew's actions are known to him.' When we asked if it could possibly be a 'coincidence', he objected, 'Of course coincidences occur, but I have heard too many accounts of the *rebbe*'s healing for my healing to be a coincidence.' He likened the *mezuzah* to 'a suit of armour in the spiritual realm. It protects a person from influences which can cause illness. An unkosher *mezuzah* simply makes a person more vulnerable.' Again Rabbi Nifield took the opportunity to emphasize that the physical and spiritual realms were interrelated: the woman who fails to take *mikveh* (the prescribed monthly bath) after her menstruation may bear a defective child.

---

[30] The early dawn is the best time to study cabbala and kindred matters: the Hebrew words for 'mystery' and 'light' are equivalent in gematria.

The *rebbe* is consulted on a number of health-related issues apart from immediate sickness. A serious concern is infertility, which is considered disastrous for Lubavitchers with their emphasis on large families.[31] While the *rebbe* himself is childless, he is considered to have particular foresight about infertility:

Rabbi Lehrman was very concerned about his wife, who had still not become pregnant after five years of marriage. Repeated hospital tests had not demonstrated any physiological abnormality either in himself or in his wife, so he wrote to the *rebbe*. About a week later, when (rather unexpectedly on a business trip) he was able to visit the *rebbe* in person, the *rebbe* told him, 'Your fears are irrelevant.' He was surprised by this and asked what the *rebbe* meant, to be told 'your wife is already pregnant.' He telephoned home to learn that his wife was indeed pregnant.

The *rebbe*'s replies may indicate that he has talked with the petitioner's deceased parent's soul, and they frequently cite well-known texts and aphorisms, employing puns and rhymes in Hebrew or English (such as health–wealth) and logical paradoxes, as well as explicit instructions. Do the *rebbe*'s words themselves have power, or does he just have a better knowledge of divine matters? When questioned by sympathetic observers, the Lubavitch *rebbe* has agreed he has personal power to help others unite the seen and unseen realms,[32] for he argues, 'there is a continuous relationship between the creator and the creation'. He can cure by physical touch, or through a *mezuzah* he has blessed.[33] The imagery

---

[31] Magolin and Witztum (1989), in their discussion of Sephardic interpretations of infertility and impotence, suggest that a common explanation is having been 'tied' by jealous sorcery.

[32] In the accounts cited here the petitioners argue that they expect, through the *rebbe*, to effect some definite change in the natural world: in Ahern's (1979) terminology, following Austin, their petitions were, like spells (Tambiah 1990), performative, 'strong illocutionary acts'. Although offered retrospectively as efficacious, it is likely that at the time many were 'weak', simply performed as immediately appropriate or 'felicitous' (Lloyd 1990) or little more than wishes, Wittgenstein's 'actions of instinct' (Tambiah 1990: 56); and they of course have a perlocutionary context which I do not detail in this lecture.

[33] Although the narratives emphasize the *rebbe*'s knowledge, collections of exemplary stories published by Lubavitch emphasize something more like instrumental power over the physical world. The term 'miracle' is commonly used. An 18-year-old boy, Rafi, is seriously ill with leukaemia (Lubavitch Publications 1992). The hospital doctor advises an immediate operation, but Rafi's tearful brother tells his teacher, who contacts the *rebbe* only to be advised that the operation must be delayed until he has prayed on the sabbath. The doctor, an atheist who is furious at this interference, decides to proceed. He arrives late at the

employed by Rabbi Nahman, the founder of the Bratislav Hasidim, was that of a 'banker' who could receive the bad qualities of the supplicant and exchange them for good. Woocher prefers the analogy of a 'mirror', while one Lubavitch rabbi who has studied psychology likens the *rebbe* to a mediating archetype who lowers himself to the petitioner's level of spirituality; *rebbe* and Hasid 'invest' in each other, spiritually as well as financially.[34] Strikingly, he argues that for the *rebbe* to teach someone who does not absorb the knowledge is like masturbation—indeed the *rebbe* may actually experience a nocturnal emission as a consequence. The Lubavitch *rebbe* physically takes on and redeems the transgressions of the Hasid.[35]

hospital after being held up with a burst tyre; the nurses report that the instruments have gone missing, and he has to postpone the operation. The boy's condition suddenly improves and the operation is no longer necessary. Many Lubavitchers offered us the word 'charisma' for their *rebbe*'s power, the term suggested by Weber (1947*b*) to designate situations where an individual who embodies a group's concerns through 'extra-social qualities' leads them independently of tradition, physical coercion, or role-bound status. Sociologically, charisma is less an explanation of social action than a description, one defining element in a typology; what is significant is not the 'personality' of the leader, but their social function as symbol, catalyst, and message-bearer (Littlewood 1993). He or she may be relatively unimpressive as a practical leader, serving like Sabbatai Sevi (Lecture 1) as the locus on which current pre-occupations are placed. In the popular sense, however, 'charisma' refers to something like 'strength of personality' or even 'ultrahuman power'. The *rebbe* approximates better to Weber's 'traditional authority' or even the 'divine king' of Oxford Africanists. In Hasidic stories he recalls another anthropological figure: the trickster of folk tales, outwitting the powerful official or greedy peasant, on occasion ironically defeated through his own stratagems.

[34] Schachter (1979). Which recalls the presentations of food and money offered by the *shtetl* Hasid to his *rebbe* which the latter then redistributed (Zborowski and Herzog 1962)

[35] (Like Christ.) One rabbi reading an earlier draft of this lecture written by Dr Dein and myself argued that the emission was impossible. See also Hoffman (1981). A more appropriate image may be that of a 'condensor' or 'container' (Parkin 1992; Lutzky 1989), an idiom which becomes a little clearer when we consider the converse of a miracle: the 'scandal' of medieval Christian terminology. In Feb. 1992 the *rebbe*, then aged 90, had a stroke. The medical details were unclear, although local newspapers such as the *Jewish Chronicle* reported that it was minor and he was making a good recovery. Lubavitch House requested that all Jews recite psalms once a day. Although apparently not seriously ill, the *rebbe* was unable to give out Dollars, or to respond to petitions. Members of the community were asked why he himself had become sick, and what they thought this sickness meant. Among the explanations given was this one from a young rabbi: 'The soul of the Rebbe represents the group soul of the Jewish people. His suffering represents the suffering of every Jew. It is like a body and head, the Rebbe being the head of the Jewish body. The two cannot exist independently. If the body is sick it can give rise to a headache. If the brain does not work, how can the body function? If every Jew does not perform good deeds the Jewish body will become sick and in turn the Rebbe. If more Jews perform these deeds the Rebbe will recover.' In order to heal their leader a new Torah was written in New York, and every Jew asked to donate £1 towards a letter in it. Another rabbi explained: 'All Jewish souls are tied to the Rebbe's soul. In the Torah there are 600,000 words (328,000 complete words and

Representation and Reality

The secret world of the Godhead is a world of language, a world of divine names that unfold in accordance with a law of their own . . . Letters and names are not only conventional means of communication. They are far more. Each one of them represents a concentration of energy and expresses a wealth of meaning which cannot be translated, or not fully at least, into human language.[36]

If the 'efficacy' of the *kvitl* and its response may be regarded as an illo-cutionary manipulation of transactional symbols which stand for events in the material world, then it is difficult to find a formal system of heal-ing in which the two can at times be so closely tied together. Informants say that even our transcriptions of the healing miracles printed in this book have some power to heal. We have here an elision of the material and its divine representation so profound that it is not easy to imagine any Hasidic observance which is not a type of physical healing.

Scholem[37] argues that 'those who carry out the *mitsvah* always do two things. They *represent* in a concrete symbol its transcendent essence, through which it is rooted in, and partakes of, the ineffable. But at the same time they transmit to this transcendent essence (which the later Kabbalists called the "upper root" of ritual action) an influx of energy.' If psychiatrists and anthropologists have postulated correspondences between, or actual causal effects across, a 'double register' of body and representation in 'symbolic healing', the Zohar and hence the *Tanya* are perhaps unique in the extent of mutual influence. Man has two souls, argues the *Tanya*, the animal and the divine, each dialectically constitut-ing the other; the divine spiritualizes the material as the material spiritu-alizes the divine. Language is not an obstruction, nor even the path, to ultimate reality, but rather its actual nature. The letters of the Torah are not just God's Law, but the very name of God; indeed they *are* God, the

272,000 incomplete words). In the world there are 600,000 general souls which each divide up into many more souls. These general souls are linked to the Rebbe's soul. By writing a perfect Torah the Rebbe's soul becomes perfect again and this will affect his body.' He described how the *rebbe* must first undergo a descent into the shattered vessels before he can ascend to a higher level, taking with him some of the hidden sparks. This descent is associ-ated with a decay in the physical body. The rabbi intimated that perhaps this was a prelude to the messianic arrival. He admitted that it was quite possible that the current *Rebbe* was indeed the Messiah. 'Every descent of the Zaddik means an elevation of divine light' (cited by Scholem 1954). (Before the *rebbe*'s death in June 1994 Lubavitch initiated a public 'Moshiach campaign' implying he was the Messiah, and expectations of some sort of 'res-urrection' have surfaced since his burial.)

[36] Scholem (1965: 124).   [37] Mindel (1974); Kehot Publication Society (1981: 778).

upper roots of our physical world. The ten Sefirot together form that great unutterable Name of God which is the act and goal of creation; and hence of human history. Representation (upper root) and embodiment in the sensible world (lower root) necessarily participate in complementary causalities.

All 'mystical' ideas developing within Western monotheism are, like miracles, concerned with reconciliation of the two registers. Rather than just representing matters as two qualitatively distinct registers, the divine and the physical, with certain rare passages between them (miracles), the concentric spheres of the Zohar allow participation in either the divine or the physical directions—a stereomorphic cosmos but one in which any event or entity is located simultaneously at the centre and the periphery.[38] A 'miracle' in the sense of a radical but temporary resonance across the two registers, a local drama of the structural anthropologist's or psychotherapist's transaction of the bodily through the symbolic, is thus hardly novel—for, in a sense, here everything and nothing is miraculous. In Zoharic theory physical healing and spiritual healing are the same event, even if the contemporary Hasid visiting his family doctor hardly has the latter foremost in mind. If the Zohar, as a theory of representation, anticipates the interpretive turn in the anthropology of medicine in its concern with directions and procedures rather than with entities (albeit with what Bloom [39] terms its 'wandering meaning'), in reconciling structural order with moral agency, it goes further in retaining the physical as valid as the representation. Representation itself is an aspect of the natural world.[40] Where all is symbolic in that everything both represents

---

[38] The Cosmic Man is made up of all men (Ben Shimon Halevi 1974), 'members and parts of various ranks all acting upon each other so as to form one organism' (Zohar). If we need a figuring, the notion of a fractal (in which each part replicates the whole; Mandelbrot 1977) is more apposite than of a single spiritual–physical dyad: perhaps Pribram's hologram or Wagner's (1986) holograph, the linguistic trope of synecdoche or the participatory symbols of Lévy-Bruhl's primitive mentality.

[39] Bloom (1984).

[40] In Bolinger's (1980) words, 'the culture inserts a sign and gets back a symbol', as the increasingly referential word itself becomes materialized as an independent entity, Tambiah's (1990) 'objectified charisma'. (See n. 33.) While a similar potential exists in Christianity—'the word made flesh'—we might argue that it is more esoteric theology than instrumental practice although there are analogues in the sacraments and in popular healing (Cramer 1993; McGuire 1983), and of course in Islamic medicine (Parkin 1992). Bloom (1984) proposes that the deity of the cabbala may be (mis)read as language; for Scholem (1954) he exists as a theory of representation. Foucault (1970) takes the late medieval 'signatures' (in which natural object and name were intrinsically linked, as in Hermetic and cabbalistic typologies) as not properly a theory of representation at all but rather one of resemblance through sympathy, mimesis, repetition, and transformation: representation proper requiring the Renaissance distinction between an object and its name, which itself is

and embodies everything else, there are, in a sense, no 'symbols': everything is concrete reality, everything 'works'.

In everyday practice things are rather different. Scholem,[41] here surprisingly akin to countless guardians of religious orthodoxy, warns us against too deep a cabbalistic immersion in the Infinite, in which everyday actions become translated as the ineffable and back again. Explaining why he had not written down his ideas, Luria is supposed to have said, 'It is impossible, because all things are interrelated. I can hardly open my mouth to speak without feeling that the sea burst forth its dams and overflows.'[42] The *rebbes*, ever aware of the eruptions of cabbala embodied in the antinomian madness of Sabbatai Sevi (first lecture), set firm rules for the incorporation of Zoharic speculation into the practice of everyday life, always subordinate to the prudent rabbinical ordinances. To attempt to coerce rather than supplicate the upper register (theurgy) was of course sorcery, and if Hasidim still sought access to the strong dangers of ultimate power, it was to be only through the circumscribed intercession of the *rebbe*. While scholarly Lubavitch may endlessly argue about the minutiae of cabbala, their founder disdained such miraculous interventions, yet it is through the person of their current *rebbe* that ultimate redress is mediated. Hasidim refer to him as a 'channel' between the physical and the spiritual registers.[43] In his mediations the *rebbe* reorders

not of the natural order but arbitrary (and hence the natural world cannot be replicated or coerced through such devices as numerology or alphabetic order). He notes the primacy given in the European systems of signatures to Hebrew, the universal language spoken by Adam which retained something of the material creation. The recovery of this or some other language which directly embodied (or later, represented) reality was a recurring Renaissance preoccupation (Eco 1993). The more figurative numerology of religious texts by cabbalists proceeded from already existing referential practices: Hebrew lacks numerals, so numbers have always been represented by a letter of the alphabet (on which, see Crump 1990), and there had long been a popular tradition that misspelling the paraphrases of the divine name in a Torah was likely to visit serious sickness and misfortune on the community (Trachtenberg 1977). Even a misspelt Torah was too powerful to be safely destroyed and was buried in a vault.

[41] Scholem (1954).   [42] Scholem (1971).

[43] Sharot (1982). Or the 'channels' of structuralism (Laughlin and Stephens 1980). Any dualist epistemology, whether religious or scientific, has difficulties in justifying the nature of the links between the two registers. Again we have to be wary of assuming a uniform local understanding: for the less scholarly or recently 'reclaimed' Hasid, the *rebbe* is often not so much a channel as a thaumaturge. (Contrariwise, most people regularly check their *mezuzot* anyway.) If mediation between the two registers occurs typically through a particular individual, it is difficult not to locate in them some personal 'magical' power (Tambiah 1990; cf. McGuire 1983): what Scholem and Bastide, following Andrew Lang, term a 'degeneration' of religion as a cosmological figuring. Frazerians would argue the converse—for the figurative as the degeneration of the instrumental: as does Robertson-Smith (1927) in his account of the origins of Jewish religion.

the everyday experiental dualism which cabbala always threatens to banish: in the terminology of these lectures, a double register now re-emerges in a distinction between material experience and its ultimate meaning, between the physical world and some determining transcendent reality.

If we are justified in talking of cabbala as a 'folk model', then it is one with a close reflexive engagement with wider Western knowledge, including now biomedicine. Contemporary Lubavitch do not live in an eighteenth-century enclave, and their emphasis on conversion constantly invokes the individual remaking of secular and sacred worlds. Their exemplary illness narratives do not simply articulate Zoharic cosmology and personal suffering, but justify the normative rules of a small community, one always preoccupied with its own continuity and boundaries, and with its vulnerability in the wider political world. But for which rules individuals may argue quite various religious justifications; for no single interpretation of sacred texts can ever be taken as completely valid. Judaism is characteristically praxis, not *doxa*.

In conclusion, I would suggest a reading of healing and restitution through the Zohar.[44] Western monotheism's double register of immanent and transcendent has, I have argued, formal and historical continuities with that of material and representational, naturalistic and personalistic, in contemporary science. Both cabbala and contemporary anthropology essay an epistemological turn away from such a dichotomized universe in which the meaning of one world was simply to be read as the reality of the other. The complex correspondences and isomorphisms between lower and upper roots in the Zohar certainly allows for Hasidic recourse to an ultimate reality by which immediate suffering occurs and is resolved but only imperfectly as a distinct realm we may recognize as otherworldly. If this healing is itself amenable to the conventional procedures of sociological inquiry, as I have attempted here, the mythic corpus to which it refers is nevertheless one which articulates problems of reconciling embodiment and representation identical with those of anthropology: yet an interpretive turn so radical that it is still able to encompass our material reality as reality, albeit a reality dialectically constituted through its own representation.

---

[44] In Bloom's (1984) terms, a misprision or creative misreading, analogous to Freud's physiological reading of Brentano, or Lévi-Strauss's sociological reading of Jakobson. Arguably this is less of a 'misreading', for both cabbala and contemporary anthropology offer not dissimilar epistemologies of signification, and Ellen (1977) proposes that 'analytical classifications' such as the Zohar are particularly amenable to the procedures favoured by structural anthropologists.

In my next lecture I shall continue with the theme of material versus representational in a quite different and apparently secular context—that of the new moral epidemic of multiple personality disorder, and then in my last lecture sum up these two types of understanding.

7

Satan and the Computer:
The Euro-American Revival of
Spirit Possession

In this lecture, I shall consider how a near-supernatural cosmology is generated out of radical personal experience in something many commentators have compared to the witch-finding hunts of early modern Europe, and, in its personal manifestation, to the anthropologists' spirit mediumship. And in this I would suggest we have something approaching a 'natural model' for the phenomena I have been considering.

Multiple Personality

In the late 1970s, following revelations about the widespread sexual exploitation of female children, cases of multiple personality suddenly began to emerge in the United States, particularly after the well-publicized account of 'Sybil'.[1] Questions of authenticity and medical suggestion were immediately raised. Corbett Thigpen, the psychiatrist who had treated Christine Sizeman—well known through the earlier film based on his 1957 book *The Three Faces of Eve* [2]—argued that spontaneous multiple personality like Eve's was rare. After the film made him famous he was besieged by *multiples*, as individuals with multiple personality disorder (MPD) were now called. Thigpen comments that of the thousands of patients he saw in the following thirty years only one was genuine, that is spontaneous and prior to medical intervention.[3] At least one new case emerged immediately after the individual saw the film.[4]

Besides the presumed aetiology of early sexual trauma, multiple personality differed from the previously described nineteenth-century double

---

[1] *Sybil* (Schreiber 1973) was followed by other popular accounts: *The Five of Me* (1977), *Tell Me Who I am Before I Die* (1977), *The Flock* (1991), and a male case, *The Minds of Billy Milligan* (1981). The first published case of satanic abuse was *Michelle Remembers* (1980).
[2] Thigpen and Cleckley (1957).   [3] Burne (1993).   [4] Spanos (1989); Ross 1994.

consciousness in the sheer number of personalities, frequently young children, who now appeared. Sybil, the first well-publicized case attributed to repressed memories of sexual abuse, developed sixteen personalities. Eve, who had retired from public view presumed cured, returned with twenty-two personalities, and then recalled having been abused, to chair the recently formed International Society for the Study of Multiple Personality and Dissociation. An increasingly active group of patients, Speaking for Our Selves, publicly attacked sceptical doctors,[5] while those professionals who were sympathetic provided expert legitimization in 1988 with a generally supportive journal called *Dissociation,* and devised a number of rating scales to measure dissociation and to determine MPD. Significantly, following the example of Sybil's psychiatrist, therapists now often ascribed to each personality proper names by which they were directly addressed in treatment. The spontaneity of the syndrome has continued to be argued in the medical press, particularly whether 'repressed memories' can be truly recalled to awareness decades later.[6] Some doctors maintain that, if properly sought, MPD is found in 10 per cent of psychiatric patients, while popular 'recovery manuals' presume half the female American population have been sexually abused and are thus 'latent multiples'. The question of induction through mass publicity or through the particular procedures used (hypnosis, guided imagery, trance work, body massage) is countered with the argument that genuine MPD is the response to a hidden trauma, indeed a type of autohypnotic self-healing in which the pain is so intense that 'the self leaves': the public recognition of 'latent' or 'secret MPD' simply enables multiples to come out and seek the professional support they need or to recognize the condition in themselves—less medical suggestion than appropriate diagnosis. Patients maintain that television reports and films about MPD enable them to give expression to something already there since their childhood rape.

Over 100 different secondary personalities (now known as alters) associated with one physical body have been identified. A single body's alters may have consistent differences in handedness, facial expression, cerebral bloodflow, and EEG recordings; up to sixty points' difference in IQ scores, with their own characteristic visual abilities, handwriting, vocabulary,

[5] Kenny (1981).

[6] MPD (called dissociative identity disorder, apparently to reduce the consequences of giving the emergent states proper names (Hacking 1995)) is now recognized as a disease by the American Psychiatric Association (DSM-IV) and, less certainly, by the World Health Organization (ICD-10).

speech patterns, and immunological responses; they have diverse memories and personal and family histories, and different ages, gender, ethnicity, and sexual orientation. They are often suicidal, self-mutilating, self-hating, and sometimes violent. The personality immediately presenting to the doctor is troubled but bland, while the secondary personalities often admit to being 'playful' or 'wicked'. Not only do larger numbers of discrete personalities emerge, but these seem generally aware of each, coming and going relatively freely outside clinical sessions, conversing together as they scheme, quarrel, choose appropriate wardrobes, obtain spectacle prescriptions consistent with their various ages, or arrange their own personal television and book contracts; if the multiple is European rather than American-born, one or other alter may speak only the language of origin.

Medical treatment of the new epidemic initially recalled that of the neurologists of the previous century: hypnosis and persuasion to discharge the pathogenic secret and then reintegrate the secondary personalities with the original self, or else exhortations to just 'go back', as the nineteenth-century physician Morton Prince had then put it. As before, the secondary personalities often objected to being killed off. But now, with the appearance of the multiple activists (and their alters) on television, the support of feminist therapists emphasizing the politics of rape, and through well-publicized court defences that the personality in the dock was not the same one who had committed the crime (unsuccessful, but sometimes only after defence lawyers have persuaded the court that the defendant when giving evidence should be sworn in separately under all their different personalities [7]), the alters have gained a public voice and demand their legal right to an independent life. Frequently young children, these alters are now accommodated rather than integrated or exorcised, for their very existence as secret memories has become a public testimony to the reality of the abuse of young women. Indeed, killing them off is regarded by the multiple movement as murder, as the concealment of one crime by another—'revictimization'—as the male physician simply re-enacts the original abuse. The preferred therapeutic option is now to keep all the personalities in play, establishing explicit therapeutic contracts with each to encourage 'mutual awareness and communication' between them in what has increasingly come to

---

[7] Kenny (1986); Merskey (1992). A current court case involves a woman accusing a man of inducing one of her alters, a naive young girl, to emerge so he could rape their body more easily.

resemble family therapy,[8] the goal being termed 'co-consciousness' (although some therapists still postulate an Inner Self Helper as the convener of the group). Hypnotherapists encourage the *survivor* to meet and comfort their abused earlier self, or instruct the alters to 'come out and play' only in dreamtime. Drama therapists instruct each individual in their therapy group to take on and role-play one of the alters elicited from one individual, the whole group then enacting that body's mental state.

Satanists and Extra-Terrestials

What of this to those interested in religion? In the 1890s some American doctors sympathetic to Spiritualism had accepted secondary personalities as benign visiting spirits and were less inclined to kill them off.[9] This interpretation too has returned, but now in a demonic variant: sexual abuse of working-class children in both Britain and America has been linked (on implausible evidence [10]) with male witchcraft, cannibalism, and child sacrifice.[11] Satanic explanations have been encouraged among teachers and social workers by evangelical Christian networks which practise exorcism and generally favour a diabolical interpretation of human malevolence and misfortune.[12] A British psychiatrist with a clinical

[8] Or indeed, judging from Ross's accounts, a popular television soap opera. Like the spirits of vodu, an individual's alters may constitute a society: one patient manifested two 'communities' plus cadet subcommunities, each of the two larger groups itself containing three sets of 'families', and within each family three sets of paired alters known as 'sisters' (Ross 1994: 143). Other recent variants are that the person who had raped the physical patient was only an alter of her father, or that a continued incestuous relationship with the father involved only one of the patient's alters (ibid. 170, 173). Less personified alters can be recognized by the patient as simply consolidations of her free-floating attitudes or emotions such as self-hatred and depression, which can thus be 'exorcised' out of her through specific psychological therapies or pharmaceutical drugs: 'the Stranger Within was very scared of clomipramine' (ibid. 282).   [9] Kenny (1981: 343).

[10] Victor (1993); La Fontaine (1994).   [11] Jaroff (1993); Sinason (1994).

[12] Csordas (1992); Victor (1993); e.g. Koch (1972). Such as the Institute for Pregnancy Loss and Child Abuse Research and Recovery (*The Times*, 4 Mar. 1994, 17). Why teaching and social work? Both are low-status, poorly paid professions, with a high proportion of women, and a good deal of publicly defined responsibility and personal commitment to young children, yet with little independent authority, no consistently accepted intellectual rationale or body of accepted practice, and vulnerable to sudden swings of public policy and professional justification. Their practitioners are constantly faced with balancing their client's wishes and capabilities against (in the earlier socialist social work, malevolent) state institutions. La Fontaine (1994: 31) argues that they 'are reluctant to accept that parents, even those classified as social failures, will harm their children . . . Demonising the marginal poor and linking them to unknown satanists turns intractable cases into manifestations of evil.' MPD itself has been identified as especially common among social workers and nurses (e.g. O'Dwyer and Friedman 1993), who are also identified with the not unrelated pattern of

interest in child sexual abuse has recently stated that 10 per cent of our adult population are practising Satanists.

A British textbook for treating survivors of satanic abuse written by clinicians at London University[13] does not follow some American psychiatrists in recognizing alters as alien demons, but suggests rather that the Satanists themselves use hypnotherapy to induce secondary personalities. It proposes that therapists have not taken seriously their patients' accounts of

a war-time atrocity in peace-time England. Men and women . . . worship Satan as their god in private houses or in churchyards and forests. In so doing they literally turn upside down any moral concept that comes from Christianity. They practise every sexual perversion that exists with animals, children and both sexes. They drink blood and urine and eat faeces and insects. They are involved in pornographic films and drug-dealing as a way of raising money. They are highly organised, successful in their secrecy and have a belief that through their pain and abuse they are getting closer to their god.[14]

The contributors admit that their own therapeutic role must preclude any ascertaining of the 'truth' of memories of satanic abuse but also that those apparently seeking to discredit their work publicly, generally doctors and jurists, are ritual abusers themselves.[15] (MPD therapists frequently present themselves as beleaguered or oppressed pioneers facing 'the pervasive hostile counter-transference' [16] of their colleagues.) The book proposes that survivors should be treated in extended sessions in special sanctuaries to be set up in the near future.[17] A professor of psychology at the University of Utah has argued that this (satanic ritual abuse) conspiracy, involving Satanists, the CIA, and Jewish cabbalists, has produced 'cultified multiples' who are currently under surveillance by the Utah Police Department of Public Safety.[18]

Munchausen's syndrome by proxy, the induction of symptoms in their children by isolated mothers in establishing a parenting relationship together with a male hospital doctor (Littlewood 1991*b*). (Here again issues of verification have dominated the issue.) And we can note a similarity with other illnesses commonly reported among nurses, particularly eating disorders and deliberate self-harm (ibid.); the extent to which these too involve some new dissociated identity is currently argued by therapists, while parallels between self-denial in eating disorders and in women's religious experience have frequently been argued (Littlewood 1995*a*). (Compare *trumba* spirits in Mayotte who may either barely eat or else eat excessively and then purge their host's body (Lambek 1981).)

[13] Sinason (1994).   [14] Ibid. 8, 3.   [15] Ibid. 63, 204, 280.
[16] Ross (1994: 109).   [17] Sinason (1994: 278).

[18] Transcript of Fourth Annual Eastern Regional Conference on Abuse and Multiple Personality, Virginia, 1997.

American psychiatrists have proposed that the sexual abuse which results in MPD is carried out not only by the child's family and by Satanists but by extraterrestrial 'effectors' who abduct, abuse, and then return the victim; one Harvard University clinic has now treated more than seventy of these 'experiencers'. Nineteenth-century Spiritualists had described visits to alien flying machines, and Schnabel [19] gives a detailed account of the recent development of the various experiencer (or 'abductee') networks involving observers of unidentified flying objects, science fiction writers, psychologists, and psychiatrists: coteries who met on the New York cocktail circuit, exchanged clients, franchised new techniques, sponsored conferences, and appeared on rival television chat shows. In the late 1940s, with the start of the cold war, a number of sightings of flying saucers were initially taken seriously by the US Air Force but then discredited by a number of government commissions. (Enthusiasts have continued to argue a collaboration with the aliens from outer space by the US government and the United Nations.) Originally green in colour, by the start of the civil rights movement the aliens were observed to have become somewhat darker or at least grey. Accounts of physical abductions of humans first appeared in the early 1950s, initially benevolent in intent but by the 1960s involving 'medical examinations', usually of a gynaecological type with the women's legs spread in stirrups.[20] These accounts progressed in a few years to uncovered memories of rape as the abductees began to discover bruises and other marks on their bodies which to critical observers recalled medieval stigmata. Starting in the 1970s, hypnotic therapy was used to 'regress missing time cases' whose memories of the events had been erased by the abductors: by the 1980s more than a 1,000 women in therapy had successfully recalled being abducted, inseminated, and returned to earth, only to be reabducted for the harvesting of their hybrid offspring. (Fewer men were abducted, generally to be sexually aroused and have their semen piped off.)

Extrapolating from a questionnaire study of the public in 1991 suggests that over 15 million Americans have now been abducted. By the late 1980s the small number of abductee scholars who still favoured benevolent alien intrusion had gravitated to New Age and near-death experience (NDE) groups in order to contact these higher powers; those arguing for malevolent agencies aligned themselves with the existing sexual abuse theorists including many in the Christian Right and feminist mental health networks. Under ever 'deeper' hypnosis, some survivors were now

[19] Schnabel (1994).   [20] Bryan (1995).

able to recall sexual abuse in an earlier life form, as Eve did by 1989.[21] (Multiple personality aside, 28 per cent of American psychotherapists accept that hypnosis facilitates recall of memories from previous lives.[22]) Schnabel describes the disputes between the different abductee therapists, their conflicts with rival experts for lucrative television time, film and book contracts, the attempt to monopolize the more important abductees and to discredit those of competing cliques, and the unsuccessful proposal by the psychiatrists involved to exclude amateur therapists from conducting hypnotic regression (backed by their consensus DSM-III diagnosis of adjustment disorder with mixed emotional features, i.e. anxiety and depression caused by the alien abduction[23]). Objections that the abductees could be shown by psychological tests to be 'fantasy-prone individuals' were countered with the argument that this personality trait was a response to the abduction.

That most abductees reported being removed from and returned to their beds at night has been suggested by sceptics to recall common temporal lobe and hypnogogic phenomena such as sleep paralysis and out-of-body experiences which may be locally understood as incubi such as the Old Hag phenomenon among Newfoundland fishermen.[24] Indeed, on mapping cerebral localizations of the body's sensory input, the vagina is represented on the orbital frontal lobes, adjacent to temporal lobe seizures which are not infrequently experienced by women as sexual penetration; while dream-time erection and nocturnal emission are of course common experiences for men.

The multiple selves are variously identified as the possessing aliens themselves, as their hybrid offspring, as the psychological representation or psychic reincarnation of the human perpetrator, as living or deceased family members, as 'transcendent spirit helpers', as new attempts at self-healing, or as the lost person of an abused childhood. Christian psychiatrists and clergy who offer 'deliverance ministry' describe them as invasive incubi, or as congealed ancestral vices and the vengeful spirits of aborted foetuses passing down the 'generation line', an idiom recalling the psychologist Ribot's rather less dramatic description of the traumatic memory as a 'mental parasite'.[25] These variant identifications are not

---

[21] Hacking (1995).   [22] Crews (1994).   [23] Schnabel (1994).
[24] Simons and Hughes (1985).
[25] Horn (1993); A. Young (1995). Or indeed as induced by witches trained in hypnotherapy who 'lay down' (Hacking 1995) 'cultified multiples' (Mulhern 1994) programmed both to interfere with any future therapy and to relay information about the therapists back to the cult.

restricted each to a therapeutic school; university professors of medicine teach their students how to distinguish anthropomorphic alters who are merely split-off psychological functions from those who are to be firmly diagnosed as extraterrestrials or demonic spirits.[26]

The reality of multiple personality has not gone unquestioned. The spontaneous 'recovery' of memories of sexual abuse in MPD has recently been challenged. Therapeutically encouraged legal suits by adults against their parents for having sexually abused them as children, and against their earlier doctors for having failed to diagnose their MPD, have been met by counter-claims against the individual's therapists of inducing a 'false memory syndrome' in distressed individuals who are persuaded to recall non-existent sexual abuse (akin to false confessions to the police), encouraged by the expanding 'survivors' movement' with its television confessions of MPD.[27] Damages against the parent for sexual abuse have been of the order of up to $5 million plus lawyers' and doctors' fees; and the Roman Catholic Church in the United States has reportedly paid $500 million secretly to have claims of child molestation against its priests dropped. By 1993, 7,000 people had joined the anti-MPD False Memory Syndrome Foundation, whose therapists specialize in counter-techniques and who liken the whole issue to the Salem witch trials. Indeed, there have been recent instances in rural American communities of self-accusations of satanic cannibalism volunteered by newly 'born-again' Christians.

Some Context

Whether at this point we read multiple personality as an idiom of distress, as a psychological defence against sexual abuse, or as a genuine cosmology, whether we grant it some existence as a distinct psychophysiological entity, socially induced or requiring public acceptance to bring it into the open, its local context and meanings are significant. Can the wave of multiplicity be related to a coherent group of professional interests, or to some more diffuse sensibility of the times, or to recent changes in

[26] e.g. Mack (1994); Ross (1994: 125). Professor Ross, who proposes coercive exorcism, notes that 'The reductionist, atheistic bias of modern psychiatry which dismisses the reality of demons is just that, reductionism. It is not science.'

[27] Horn (1993); Loftus and Ketcham (1994); Wright (1993). (Compare self-accusations of witchcraft in Ghana: Field 1960.) In one case resulting in a twenty-year prison sentence, the self-accusation issue generated a multitude of books in 1993–4 (Crews 1994); the abuse therapist Ross (1994: ix) argues that the study of dissociation alone is far too extensive for anyone to have read the literature.

women's social experience? In terms of immediate context, we can recognize in it a committed network of male doctors and psychologists, who accept the phenomenon as a legitimate matter of clinical importance which requires nosologies and instruments of verification, and whose professional reputation and public career are derived from it, diagnosing it where others fail, and who are identified publicly with it as authoritative experts through their newspaper articles, publicized case histories, and, in the recent wave, cinema dramatizations and television shows. And the epidemic furnishes evidence for philosophers and moralists whose conclusions in turn are used to authenticate the phenomenon.

While he himself was not particularly interested in multiple personality, Freud's role is significant, for the new wave, both as an observed phenomenon and in its explanation, returns us to his theoretical position before he abandoned the seduction hypothesis. Criticism of his apparent suppression of the evidence for incest has followed the recognition that sexual rape or seduction of children by adult males in America is far more common than previously realized; and with this recognition has appeared an expert therapeutic practice for the 'survivors' which, although partly influenced by psychoanalytical therapy, has resonances with an earlier emphasis on the individual's adaptation to a single traumatic event. Classical psychoanalysis has lost the pre-eminence it held in America from the 1930s to the 1960s, squeezed out between psychiatry's recent rapprochement with biomedical experimentalism and the competition from these, more focused, lay therapies with radically shorter and cheaper training.[28]

MPD is still rarely reported in Britain or elsewhere in Europe, and the recognition of child sexual abuse has generally not involved British doctors

---

[28] Reviewed in (Piper 1994). While post-abuse counselling, like therapies for rape and post-traumatic stress disorder, may accept the psychoanalytic understanding of an illness as a potential avoidance of other dilemmas, counsellors in the 'recovery movement' are trained to emphasize one particular trauma. To understand the process by which memories are banished from awareness they retain, however, like the Scientologists and other religio-therapeutic groups, the Freudian term 'repression' (on the popularization of which, see Moscovici 1976; Crews 1994; Loftus and Ketcham 1994). These therapies are open to the criticism made against social workers of too readily accepting the reality of reported incidents which may be exaggerated, imagined, fabricated, or induced (B. Campbell 1988; Loftus and Ketcham 1994). Repressed memories of sexual trauma are revealed to the expert by too soft or loud a voice, by starvation or by obesity, by avoidance of the dentist, by an increased interest in sex, or by a decreased interest (cited in Crews 1994): 'If you think you have been abused you probably have' (a therapist quoted in Horn 1993). Querying the veracity of one's memories is simply a denial of one's trauma, leaving the issue, like that of alternative medicine, in the usual circular debates on consensual reality—for the very justification of the therapy is that there has indeed been an observable trauma potentially accessible at some point to empirical validation.

in demonological quests. Why the British scepticism? That the sexual violation of children is less common in Britain seems unlikely. Is it experienced differently in the United States, or are we to locate MPD in some specific therapeutic intervention? There are far fewer psychiatrists per population in the United Kingdom (less than 3,000 for the whole country), and they have never had the popular and juridical influence of their North American colleagues. They remain within the public hospitals, committed to treatment of psychosis, and have not been subject to the enthusiastic paradigm shifts of American medicine now engaged with an extensive medical malpractice industry and biomedical ethicists (not to mention the new profession of medical anthropologists). British psychiatrists, like their other medical colleagues, argue a robust dichotomy between 'real' and 'imaginary' symptoms, placing less emphasis on implicit motivations. Their professional interest lies in solving clinical problems briskly rather than maintaining a lucrative clientele of chronic private patients—the preserve of the small number of British psychoanalysts who generally take an 'integrative' view of dissociative symptoms. Dramatic symptoms which engage others are discouraged, regarded, doubtless, as in rather poor taste, certainly as insincere or exaggerated.

Beyond this perhaps lie wider questions of a society's susceptibility to 'ideas in the air'—as Dostoevsky put it in the case of Raskolnikov. Why multiplicity? Ian Hacking argues that 'what we do see from time to time in European and American milieux are some very troubled people interacting with their cultural and medical surroundings . . . They cast, perhaps, a distorting image of what their communities think it is to be a person.'[29] Kenny characterizes multiple personalities as 'parodies of conventional social roles'.[30] We might invoke broader idioms for contemporary identity and self-transformation, and for the justification of distress and personal failure. It is certainly not difficult to offer homologies between individual and society, such that the experiencing self offers a microcosm of wider issues, the dissociation of the individual standing for the dis-sociation of the collectivity, now less an ordered hierarchy than a contractual network.[31] The nineteenth-century occurrence of double

---

[29] Hacking (1992).   [30] Kenny (1986).

[31] As in the Durkheimian approach of Mary Douglas, in which loosely organized polities (the United States?) parallel and somehow facilitate individual dissociation and spirit intrusion. Both psychologically orientated anthropologists and cultural critics (e.g. Kenny 1986; Lasch 1978) commonly take individual conflicts as the microcosm of wider social fragmentations. And thus an organism's fault lines illuminate the quotidian, whether in the justifications of cultural psychiatry (culture-bound syndromes), anthropology (social dramas), or neuropsychology (head injuries).

consciousness was regarded by its psychologists and cultural commentators as the mirror of a fragmenting society.[32]

It is less easy to show how such correspondences plausibly motivate personal experiences. That the self is a mirror of society is itself a local psychology: contemporary Europeans may experience matters that way, or they may not, or more likely they see it that way in certain situations. As Hacking notes, it is a particular local notion of the person that is significant, yet the individual may represent society less as its mirror than as the locus of social fault lines or as the recipient of quite various 'stresses'. Yet expert groups maintain their authority through the importance of their therapeutic intercessions, the illness becoming emblematic of current dilemmas, 'the national disease', 'the sickness of our age', 'our number-one mental health problem': a prototype to which other ills are referred or into which they are subsumed. To be successful, healers need to convince others not only that they cure the individual but that they are, to use La Barre's term, culture healers. The particular ambiguities of psychiatry's concerns with the medical and the moral allow it a privileged place in Western societies in resolving such moral dilemmas; its conceptions of the mind become popularized as normative models for the mind. Allan Young has argued that the new category of post-traumatic stress disorder—of which MPD has been seen as a variant—originally developed in American military hospitals as an exculpation for the personal guilt of Vietnam War veterans, transforming them from the aggressors into the victims in their turn,[33] a diagnosis that has now become available for taking on other vexed questions of the attribution of responsibility in a contractual society.

British class identity still provides some residual location for failure as outside the individual in political contingency, but in the United States, during the late nineteenth century as much as now, personal disappointment requires less some sense of bad luck than of competitive disadvantage or the malevolence of others—and hence recourse to legal redress or else to the sort of 'positive' transformation, eliding religious conversion, self-knowledge, and managerial presentation, exemplified by Dale Carnegie and Norman Vincent Peale. The United States has always taken itself as the site for strategic self-fashioning, by which diverse immigrant groups realize themselves as Americans as they move to higher-status jobs and improve their education, as they change their residence, neighbourhood, profession, friends, spouses, political affiliation, leisure activities,

---

[32] A Young (1995). See also Rivers (1923, ch. 3).   [33] A. Young (1995).

voluntary associations, and even their name and religion, with associated changes of presentation in mannerism, comportment, language, idiom, and dress. With dedication to manuals of kinaesthetics, personal communication, and handwriting, earlier selves and practices become incorporated or even forgotten. American identity is achieved in the very process of transformation, in fulfilling some apparently inherent potential, both as the normative expectation of what it is to become genuinely American and as a practical possibility, articulated for men in self-monitoring manuals of salesmanship and entrepreneurial psychology, for women through remodelling their bodies by dieting and plastic surgery: realizing one's personality in the marketing of it, through self-help groups and civil associations which emphasize the achievement of a 'real' or 'positive identity' for minorities and stigmatized groups, currently articulated through a politico-therapeutic language of communication, growth, personal space, realization and authenticity. America is a psychologized society, not just in that psychology is the most popular supplementary subject for its university students, but in that psychology is the national idiom which, reading social power as personal performance, argues for autonomy and self-scrutiny, for consumer choice and therapeutic transformation.

The late nineteenth and earlier twentieth century were characterized by a proliferation of technologies by which a number of objective and replicable characteristics came to constitute the individual—callisthenics, graphology, intelligence and personality testing, photometrics, and somatotyping, the polygraph. Such characteristics could, to an extent, be achieved: to alter your handwriting under professional supervision would change your personality and thus your financial mobility. Whether they should be regarded as therapeutic or transformative seems arbitrary: the police psychologist's lie detector (galvanometer) emerges as the 'e-meter' of the Church of Scientology, through which repressed traumatic memories, often of past lives, are identified and 'cleared'. What might be regarded elsewhere as an extreme response to current dissatisfaction with personal circumstances—voluntarily disappearing from one's present neighbourhood and family to emerge elsewhere with a new name and personal identity—is now facilitated by a publishing house which has produced over thirty manuals to direct something British psychiatrists would recognize as a hysterical fugue.[34]

I am aware that this is a European's image of the United States, one which since Trollope and Tocqueville has seen that country as anomic

---

[34] *The Times*, 11 Sept. 1993; e.g. Martin (1993).

and neotenic, its emphasis on personal self-transformation as the concealment of class conflict, its institutions maintained through periodic moral panics and social dramas, its citizens unable to agree on what constitutes reality without recourse to legal or medical authority. Yet America's 'obsession with self-awareness', what Louis Hartz in *The Liberal Tradition in America* terms the 'peculiar quality of America's hysteria', is well recognized by its own cultural critics.[35] Self-realization through pulling on one's bootstraps has always been central to what it is to be an American—from the frontier regeneration of the Great Awakening and its transformation of self and nature, to universalism, transcendentalism, New Thought, Christian Science, pragmatism, 'little man' populism, to boosterism, soroptimism, and the search for university tenure: a quest for achieved rather than ascribed status, a fundamentally optimistic view that time and space still lie unlimited before one. Relocation, upward social mobility, self-reliance, and perfectionism are hardly limited to America;[36] and it is easy to identify in any society a concern with rapid social transformations, the breakdown of family life, and traditional interpersonal ties (as did the European pessimism of Herder, Gissing, Pater, and Musil), but it has seemed integral to American exceptionalism to regard incompleteness as the appropriate state of affairs. Nor am I necessarily critical of an optimism which reframes disabilities through 'normalization', which reasserts the moral integrity of stigmatized minorities and the chronically ill in 'the politics of identity', and which can translate misfortune into achievement. Yet we might take an ironically European view and question whether the search for authenticity does not preclude its own goal; that to develop a hundred personalities is perhaps to have none.[37]

In any period of perceived change or creolization, both society and self may be experienced as hollow, fragmented, or double, as estranged from a past unity to enter an indeterminant future.[38] If George Gissing

[35] Kenny (1986: 2). And Lasch (1978); Rieff (1966); Bellah *et al.* (1985).

[36] Cf. Renaissance self-fashioning or the 18th-century 'project'.

[37] A common modernist image is the empty self (Lasch 1978). The American poet Anne Sexton developed a second personality, Elizabeth, in the course of her psychoanalysis, whose appearance was discouraged by her therapist, to whom Sexton then wrote plaintively, 'I suspect I have no self so I produce a different one for different people' (Ross 1994).

[38] Cf. German and Russian 19th-century literary concerns with the *Doppelgänger* (J. Hawthorn 1983;, Miller 1985; Showalter 1990; Tanner 1993): James Thompson's *City of Dreadful Night*—'I was twain, two selves distinct that cannot join again'; Dickens's *Edwin Drood*—'two states of consciousness which never clash, but each of which pursues his separate ways as though it were continuous instead of broken'; Stevenson's *Dr Jekyll and Mr Hyde*—'man is not truly one but truly two'; or Poe's *William Wilson*. Inspired by the

bemoaned the end of the nineteenth century as 'decades of sexual anarchy . . . with the laws governing human identity, friendships and sexual behaviour breaking down', now our 'radical democratisation of the personal', as Antony Giddens calls it,[39] our fragmented and commodified assimilation of alternative selves, may be argued to be especially part of a late modern condition where the ascription of risk becomes more significant than the ascription of value. With the decline of Calvinist moral imperatives, American individualism has become, as Jackson Lears puts it, 'weightless and unreal'.[40]

Is there anything more specific about contemporary *fin de siècle* America, endlessly self-creating, polyphonic, ludic, and multiplex,[41] which suggests closer parallels with the site of the last outbreak of double consciousness in late nineteenth-century France—that other daughter of the Enlightenment, which also perceived itself as preoccupied with artifice and representation, which recognized the commodification of sex and marriage, and was confused about civil divorce and public religion, about the sexual exploitation of children and female emancipation: an increasingly contractual and legalistic society characterized by the detachment of the voyeuristic boulevard *flâneur* posing in the rootless spleen of the anonymous crowd; with immersion in new and impersonal *grands magasins*, and increased opportunities for social mobility and travel; enthusiasms for bodily transformation and athletic spectacle; with the intermittent emergence of variant sexualities, and the loss of traditional clerical authority under the governments of the Third Republic: public concerns ambivalently countered by a response which Ellenberger has aptly described as 'Neo-Romantic'—irrational, narcissistic, decadent, and primitivist, with positivism's project of boundless technical progress and limitless material prosperity now foreclosed, shot through with pessimism and a sense that time was running out with the century, the race exhausted, its vigour dissipated, threatened by its incorporation of aliens, with a quest for secular myths and new heroes, or else for mystical continuities with a natural world that at times seemed exhausted too, with a return to religious orthodoxy or else to domesticated variants of Asian

---

literature on hypnotism, modernism developed a more fractured individual (Dostoevsky) whose apparent linear consciousness either congealed into temporary consistencies (Joyce, Woolf) or was accessible to an enduring self (Pirandello). Descartes's proposition that one cannot think there is no 'I' has become increasingly implausible.

[39] Giddens (1992).　　　　　　　　　　　　　　　　[40] Lears (1983).

[41] Warhol's ('I want to be a machine') and Oldenberg's multiples, body counts and mass disaster statistics, serial killers, serial monogamy, embryo banks, and multiple births: the sheer absurdity of multiplication, as Walter Benjamin put it.

religions ? In the United States the resurgence of Protestant fundamentalism in the 1980s required public figures to acknowledge that they had
been 'born again'—as having spontaneously achieved a new moral identity.[42] Recalling the fate of double consciousness, this demand for testi-
monies of spontaneity collapsed in religious scandals and accusations of
feigning; we might wonder if the demands for 'born again' experiences
should be taken as a response to the perceived fragmentation of personal
identity (a spiritual and psychological healing, as argued by its protagonists) or simply a manifestation of it.

It would be easy to delineate parallels between the end of the French
nineteenth century and the end of the American twentieth. More specif-
ically we might prefer to note a similar shift in the location of the self, less
a dissociation than a deterritorialization of it; the external physical fron-
tiers of a now mechanized nature becoming congested and foreshort-
ened so that our bodies turn in on themselves, self-sufficient through
dietetics and 'body consciousness'. Muscle-building as a parody of
labour; the perfectible body less the housing of the self than the very
self; social controls and standardized rituals becoming internalized as
'self-expression' and 'choice' in transformations attained through potentially unlimited consumption. We have both become lesser than we
thought, as simply elements in a natural world which is indifferent to
human interests; and greater, in that we recognize that this world is
refracted and remade in our cognitions and actions.

Cybernetic Suggestions

Multiple personality was attributed last century to such reshapings of the
self in lived time as the photograph, the phonograph, the telephone, and
the X-ray.[43] Where then did the new telephone conversation take place?
We might argue in the emerging world of what we now term 'cyberspace':

[42] Authenticity rather than sincerity; experience not action. And there were born-again
Catholics and Jews in the New Right as public officials, and Presidents Reagan and Bush
rather unconvincingly attested to born-again experience. Strozier (1994) notes the conver-
gence between the alien abductions and the Christian Right's 'rapture' (faithful individuals
plucked from the earth before the 'end time tribulation' to meet Christ in the air: following
1 Thess. 4:17). Some doctors propose that the satanic and UFO breeding programmes are
the same experiment (e.g. Ross 1994)—what cyberaesthetics plausibly lauds as technology's
'harvesting of humans' (Kroker 1992).

[43] Ellenberger (1970); Ronell (1989). The phonograph was a common model for the
unconscious (Campbell *et al.* 1925: 318), the telegraph for the medium (Kenny 1986). Clinical engagement with the elusive secondary personalities recalls the practice not only of the
medium but of the telephone operator: 'Later in the course of the same interview Chris

in the virtual architecture of electronically, now electronically generated, accessed, and sustained memory which we enter through our personal computer or notebook, in interactive television (and more recently virtual reality and other prosthetic embodiments), in electronic mail, the Internet, multidimensional graphical user interfaces and hypertext, in the recorded space of portable stereos, in 'personality profiles' generated by our credit card transactions, in satellite television channels and electronic conferencing, teledildonics ('telephone sex') and cybererotics: an increasingly global modularity which questions individual time, proximity, work, value, and ownership, and whose shift from material production to information and representation radically resituates the location of our taken-for-granted physical experience and interactions in a post-industrial and post-corporeal global space, our embodied experience fragmented and commodified. As do the replaceable parts of our biomedical body shop—sperm, egg, and embryo banks, fertility drugs and multiple births, cerebral implants of foetal tissue and computer chips, life support machines to harvest organs from the brain-dead, market-ready tissue-typed kidneys, electronic prostheses, and gene-splicing. For women these are particularly significant in the 'life versus choice' debate on foetal personhood—the salient schema for two beings housed in one body. And with this has gone a decay of linear or determinist theory, whether as prose, progress, or biography, in favour of fragmented, multiple, iterative, and creolized imagery, a dissatisfaction with ascribed hierarchies and a preference for market vicissitudes over command economies, a loosely associated milieu of ideas which we might remark in post-colonial aesthetics, social constructivism, evolutionary epistemology, biosociality, non-linear chaos models, fractal mathematics, and dissipative systems theory. A similar idiom of multiplicity emerges in 'the new biology', which argues that our early ancestors once incorporated other bacteria which have become our bodies' organelles and tissues.

In 1986 Bolter proposed that the computer, like the medieval mechanical clock, had become our 'defining technology', an instrumental extension of the body but which was taken as the model for a self in an idiom of inputs and outputs, the body as hardware with consciousness as

---

[another personality] was obtained. The same questions were put to her' (Prince 1905: 32). Telephones, X-rays, and, more recently, 'sound systems' and computers have generally replaced intruding spirits, 'influencing machines', and the voice of God as the defining technologies for alien dislocations of the self. My colleague Maurice Lipsedge asks a young man diagnosed with schizophrenia how he can hear through his ears a voice that originates from inside his head; the patient explains it is like the doctor using his stereo headphones.

software. If they have any identifiable locus at all, human minds are now serial virtual machines implemented on parallel hardware, and MPD is just a different program run on this same hardware.[44] But computers are not just a fashionable and accessible metaphor, our latest edition of *l'homme machine*, for the computer network actually embodies rather than merely represents symbolic logic in a virtual space which in each generation seeks to grow ever larger in relation to the physical limitations of its linear circuits and available telephone bandwidth. The computational theories of the 1960s proposed that human mentation, like digital computers, operated in accordance with logic-based manipulations of symbols; practically unsuccessful in such tasks as natural language translation, recent connectionist revisions now evoke the mind as a distributed network of elementary subsystems that work by trial and error rather than from unified design. Cyberpunk novels and ecotechnology, like the not dissimilar 'hard AI' and artificial life arguments, offer more than a fantasied model of the self—rather an ad hoc, virtual, but potentially immortal, multiplex self which has no inevitable locus in the physical body.[45] 'Cyberspace becomes another venue for consciousness itself . . . Animism is not only possible, it is implicit . . . To the body in cyberspace we are the mind. By a strange reversal of our cultural expectations, however, it is the body in cyberspace that is immortal, while the animating soul, housed in a body outside cyberspace, faces mortality.'[46] Customary distinction between nature, agency, and technology are elided in robotics, in our recognition of self-organizing inorganic chemical reactions, and in information-based biological procedures such as DNA replication. Proponents of artificial life argue that it collapses our categories of matter, life, and artefact, the whole universe being a 'cellular automaton'. 'There is no "I" for a person, for a beehive, for a corporation, for an animal, for a nation, for any living thing.'[47]

---

[44] Hans Moravec (1989), the director of the Carnegie Mellon University robotics centre, proposes a twenty-year programme of transferring human personalities onto hard disks in preparation for our ultimate dissolution as biological beings. Dennett (1991: 430) appears mildly sympathetic to not dissimilar possibilities. In the hard AI view (function equals purpose), thermostats 'think' in that they are 'goal-directed', and mentation is no longer limited to biological organisms; similar to the hylozoic interpretation by deep ecologists of Lovelock's Gaia hypothesis or to Sheldrake's deity as an 'evolving morphogenic field'. Haraway (1991) argues that biology as the study of material organisms has 'ceased to exist' in favour of the cybernetics of ecosystems and population genetics.

[45] Kelly (1994); Emmerche (1994); Levy (1994). The physicist Stephen Hawking claimed in a lecture in 1994 that malevolent computer viruses fulfil all the criteria for life (cf. Schrödinger 1944). [46] Benedict (1991: 124, 140, 141); cf. Martin (1992).

[47] Kelly (1994). Dawkins has proposed that our embodied selves are simply the mechanical replicators for genes, 'survival machines'.

I do not want to make too much of cyberspace as a fundamental rupture with previous locations of the self. Parallel processing and virtual reality, like the new reproductive technologies, are the latest relocation of our embodied agency in a biosocial history marked by the development of clothes, spear throwers, figurative representation, property, silent reading, autobiography, linear perspective, printing, coordinate geometry, the novel, mechanized transport, military brothels, limited liability, cosmetic surgery, and cultural relativism. Each progression may be experienced as a 'dissociation of sensibility' [48] yet taken as the model for ourselves. But if the problem for nineteenth-century philosophers lay in the disintegration of a unitary self given in nature, current interest lies in the opposite—in the surprising synthesis of our subpersonal modules. It is not altered states of consciousness that are now problematic but our illusive experience of unitary consciousness in a data-based collectivization of the human sensorium.

The self as a contesting network of separate modules is found not just in Riemannian space, AIDS and auto-immune disease, in recent cognitive psychology, linguistics, and neurophilosophy,[49] but, significantly for the immediate development of MPD, in the more practical 'human potential' therapies (derived from the 'ego-centred' psychoanalysis of the United States through the object relations school, primal therapy, and transactional analysis)—clinical practices and self-help techniques which promote the realization of all our 'selves' aptly recognized under an extraordinary multiplicity of terms: psychological models for the self rather than models of the self. The ego-state school recognizes a 'federal government over all',[50] while in other American therapies no single state may hold ascendancy. The decisive therapeutic step in concretizing these serial potentials into competing selves 'hiding from each other',[51] and thus into MPD, seems to be in therapist and client personalizing them with a proper name, as in the implausibly named technique of psychosynthesis.[52] Akin

---

[48] (Although Eliot chose to locate that in the 16th century.) An alienation from our agency leading to what Jameson (1991: 44) terms postmodern hyperspace—an 'alarming disjunction between the body and its built environment'.

[49] Martindale, Chomsky, Fodor, Pinker, Sperry, Minsky, Gardner, Dennett, Edelman. And in the cybernetic and field models of 'systemic family therapy' which replace selves with flexible control systems akin to those of contemporary 'matrix management', 're-engineering', and 'total human resource management'.

[50] Rowan (1990: 89).   [51] Ibid. 44.

[52] From Number Six and the Stranger Within to the more personalized Little Monica and Charlene, etc. (Ross 1994). (Compare the earlier Jungian archetypes: the Shadow, the Trickster, the Wise Old Woman.)

to the earlier guides to self-perfectioning and managerial efficiency, such expert technologies employ a popularized psychoanalytical idiom of unrealized levels of individuation, as in est, Scientology, and transcendental meditation potential selves which are to be sequentially realized through a no longer self-sufficient body, in which transformations of identity can have fruitful economic implications; in which our variant identities are neither transitory masks nor imaginary novelties but rather the achievement of something which is authentically there, of which we rest unfulfilled until therapeutically liberated from our repressions, purged of our historical sincerities, lower stages, and naive or hypocritical social obligations. 'Be yourself.' As the philosopher Charles Taylor puts it, making 'what was hidden manifest for both myself and others'. One might argue that such a practice rather downplays the radical novelty of any new self while at the same time encouraging us to acquire it— less the Puritan struggle for arduous refashioning than freedom for something already there to assume its natural place. Slippery and elusive though a new persona may be, it works as it is taken by others for an authentic self.

Multiple personality as experience and practice is not just a reflection of the popular psychology or fiction. As Mark Micale noted of the pervasive idiom of hysteria in the nineteenth century,

once a disease concept enters the domain of public discussion, it effectively becomes impossible to chart its lines of cultural origin, influence and evolution with any accuracy. Rather, visual, dramatic, and medical theories and images become inextricably caught up with one another. Eventually, this criss-cross of ideas, information and associations forms a single sociocultural milieu from which all authors—professional and popular, scientific and literary—may draw.[53]

And patients: if individuals spontaneously develop multiple personality it is not only as they participate in a pervasive representation of serial multiplicity through cinema, television, newspaper reports, and popular texts. We know as yet little of the relationship that develops between the

---

[53] Micale (1995: 238). He favours 'a model of influence that is neither one– nor two–directional but *circular*. In France during the 19th century in particular, the three primary cultures of hysteria were medical, literary, and religious. To stress the isolation and exclusion of these cultures in the public sphere is to ignore deeper, underlying cultural and discursive continuities . . . ' (ibid. 238–9). Not merely did decadent and positivist literature both draw on the pervasive image of the hysteric in the Salpêtrière, but the current biomedical category of the hysterical personality owes less to empirical observation than to *Madame Bovary*, in which Flaubert explored his own identification with 'male hysteria', the diagnosis he had been offered by his physicians for his physical complaints (ibid.).

multiple and her therapist except that the therapist vigorously endorses the integrity of the patient's struggles and her 'unchained memories'. And when the integrity of the therapist is attacked by sceptics, the patient angrily rallies to the defence. Such formative theories emerge out of more widespread cultural preoccupations through the collaboration of a committed young doctor with an intelligent and engaging patient. Together they elaborate a mutually agreeable script which encompasses both the woman's distress and the intellectual ambitions of the doctor, a paradigmatic new illness whose manifestation shapes and confirms the emerging theory, and which then becomes standardized both as a new technology and as a legitimate research programme.[54]

The cyborgs of the cosmologies of technovisionary bionics and the 'distributed conversation' of the Net, like the sub-personalities of the human potential therapies and the animism of deep ecology, provide techniques for self-transformation into alternative identities which are no longer embodied in the taken-for-granted way. Potential selves are 'accessed' serially through everyday cultural potentials legitimized and enhanced by computer games and medical technologies. Undesirable future selves are to be identified through 'risk factors' and then averted through self-monitoring techniques such as stress management. Despite its affinity with the pluripotent roles demanded by post-industrial managerialism, multiple personality is not a phenomenon which somehow emerges as an index of cultural life but is rather one elaborated in certain expert practices; and now validated in a medico-legal commerce which places the sources of affliction beyond a unitary body which seeks to repossess some 'personal space'. Computer-simulated worlds like Habitat and MUDS structure the 'internal landscape' of the self: psychiatrists are taught to enter cyberspace to advise and direct their patients' alters, escape from dungeons, or launch into 'mission[s] to rescue other alters, destroy castle walls, disarm internal computers, rebuild architecture, create safe places.'[55] If nineteenth-century double consciousness was recognized as a repression of physical energy, then our current cosmological representations are those of replication and iteration, of intrusive embodiments alien to our still perduring subjectivities.

[54] Ellenberger (1993: 239–305).   [55] Ross (1994: 148).

8

Naturalistic and Personalistic
Models of Thought

Natural Cosmologies

The human sources of religious experience and belief have been debated
since the eighteenth century. To what extent may cosmologies and moral
order be derived from—or modelled on—natural phenomena? May we
argue that they originate in our experience of the physical world, whether
through phenomenological apperception of that world—or else directly
through psychophysiology? I am concerned here not with the extent to
which religious cosmologies inevitably reproduce certain naturally given
psychological capacities—the recent work of Scott Atran and Pascal
Boyer—but with the extent to which these constraints themselves are
derived from natural models.

In these lectures, I have variously looked at those extreme personal
experiences we characterize as madness; and at the experiences of pregnancy and childbirth, and at sexual violation, and at female sexuality more
generally, all as a model for cosmological speculation; and I have considered what may be taken as a later stage, the matching of the experiencing
sick body against such a cosmology once established. In the last lecture I
considered how a contemporary analogue of spirit possession has recently
appeared in Western societies, and how it has become socially organized.
Now I shall conclude by edging further into our two poles, as it were—
embodiment and representation—and at the two modes of thought they
may be considered to manifest: the naturalistic and the personalistic.

Multiple Spirits and Selves

Much of anthropology's debate on 'primitive mentality' as one possible
origin for religious speculation need not be repeated here, except to note
our shift from such an empirical psychology of competences and states
given in nature to a sociological reading in which 'consciousness' and

'psychology' themselves represent particular cultural sentiments and memories through local categories of personhood, character, autonomy, moral agency, responsibility, and the like. And that these public categories are variably deployed in certain situations, tensions between social sectors becoming salient in the personal experience of socially vulnerable or pivotal individuals—experience then shaped by immediate context and procedures for managing distress whether medical, lay, or religious.

Students of spirit possession (to follow on from the last lecture) have noted similarities between the contexts of possession ritual, the nineteenth-century American seance, and the contemporary clinic—in particular shared idioms of distress which remove moral accountability from the afflicted individual; the manifestation of these idioms through spontaneous or sought (or induced) altered states of consciousness; with a charismatic shaman, medium, or doctor directing the proceedings; the altered experience being personified as the entry of a named spirit, control, or secondary personality; with a variable surrender of volition and agency to this external power; the local response elaborating and validating the altered state, integrating and resolving the presumed psychological split explicitly (in the goals of psychotherapy) or in our analysis (anthropology's explanation of a local healer's efficacy). The theoretical language now adopted is less clinical and of a higher order of generality, allowing incorporation of less obviously medical concerns: affliction or invidia rather than psychological trauma, alternative phases of consciousness rather than hysteria or possession states, indeed creativity rather than pathology.

The 'standard model' of this splitting of selfhood—the mechanism of spirit possession, euhemerism, and multiple personality, to take these as examples—however, remains not unlike that elaborated by Ribot and Janet in the 1890s: that these patterns could be specified by physiology alone. Humans have the ability to dissociate their mental processes and do so the whole time—through changing moods, selective attention, and putting unpleasant issues out of mind, through fantasy and dreaming—for the potential contents of our awareness are hardly accessible simultaneously. And some experiences are not easily remembered, because they are hardly significant enough to remark for more than a few seconds, because memories of them have not been periodically recalled and thus have faded, or else because they are unpleasant or painful in some way, for forgetting can be active and motivated. And the immediacy of our bodies and surroundings fluctuates, depending on what we can recognize as intended perception; the quality of our will being variable, depending on our current interests and customary procedures. You can eat an apple while riding your bicycle, but you are not equally 'in' each activity at any one moment, nor are you generally aware of switching from one to the other deliberately, for your stream of awareness appears a seamless web. To be 'conscious' is to know you are aware of something, bestowing reality through perception: an adaptive disposition located in the neo-cortex, selected in evolution, which enables the human organism to engage flexibly but attentively with different situations. Your ability to dissociate is adaptive in switching attention when necessary, in avoiding sensory overload in severe pain or terrifying and conflictual situations of cognitive dissonance where all your available responses seem inadequate. Severe tiredness, fear, pain, or startling can result in the experience of numbing ('depersonal-ization') whose behavioural concomitant ('freezing') might, like the tem-porary analgesia of accident or battle, once have had some survival value.

Dissociation is thus the necessary flip side of consciousness: it allows detachment of awareness from the immediate passage of events, part of the evolutionary development of 'self-consciousness' as an internal system of representation and self-monitoring, where the individual's awareness can then objectivize their own cognitions ('my senses deceived me', 'I was overcome by emotion', 'God spoke through me'), allowing self-recognition, anticipation, introspection, creative imagination, recognition of another's motives and possible identification with them, disbelief, deceit, and acting: all requirements for our complex programmes of intersubjective action. Under certain conditions such as hypnosis, or standardized types of sensory patterning, deprivation, and overload, through an altered balance between sympathetic and parasympathetic neural activity, through hyperventilation or the ingestion of psychoactive substances, dissociation can be facilitated physiologically to enhance or diminish attention, to daydream or meditate, as a sense of shared communality or an out-of-body experience, as hallucination, anaesthesia, motor passivity, or paralysis. Through our cog-nitive schema of a bounded self as the usual locus of experience and voli-tion, whether given in biology or in the responses of others, we may recognize the distinctive bodily facilitation of these experiences as other to our volition:[1] like religious or artistic inspiration, they may be recog-

---

[1] As 'passiones' (Lienhardt 1961: 151): 'A diviner is a man in whom the division is per-manently present; a Power, or Powers, are always latent within him but he has the ability to dissociate them in himself at will, letting them manifest themselves in him. While thus dis-sociated, the diviner *is* a Power, for which his body is host' (see also Krippner 1987; Stoller 1989). And, if dissociation provides an available model for multiplicity, then also in psy-chosis—particularly where there seems a phasic shift of the 'whole personality' as in manic-depressive or toxic psychoses (Littlewood 1993). Less so with the fragmentation of psychological experience held to be characteristic of schizophrenia, where our bounded

nized as something alien, reinforcing our notions of external reality, causality, and personal subjectivity through standardized rituals which enable us to realize our particular schema in immediate situations. In what may be experienced as 'disturbances' of the everyday self—that is in situations of extensive dissociation—interrelated memories, sensations, and bodily actions may cease to be recognized as in any way our own, to become personified as human-like entities, whether these are benign or malevolent. Out of the alternative possibilities of human awareness a culture selects its 'ordinary consciousness', its 'characteristic and habitual patterning of mental functioning that adapts the individual, more or less consciously, to survive in his culture's consensual reality'.[2]

This rather Kantian but 'natural theological' model leaves certain problems. In arguing for an increasing historical split (yet one independent of any specific cultural history) between physical states and the cognizing actor, its dualism tends to emphasize the more salient aspects of dissociation, thus facilitating an apparently clear distinction between an autonomous physiological state and the local psychology which it generates and through which it is experienced: as in Durkheim's religious effervescences or Bourguignon's typology of altered states of consciousness.[3] In the generally unremarked fluctuations of our daily awareness it is difficult to make this distinction. Such dualism renders everyday embodied consciousness and moral selfhood relatively unproblematic and fixed, as if given by a constant natural physiology about which we need say no more.[4]

---

identity may become elusive, though doubling or spirit intrusion may still be an accessible explanatory model: indeed hospital psychiatrists repeatedly complain of the popular idea of schizophrenia as Jekyll and Hyde dualism. (A 1980s horror film, *Schizo*, was advertised by a poster showing two hands, one open, one clenching a knife, with the legend 'His right hand didn't know what his left hand was doing'; recalling the competing angels sitting on each shoulder of medieval ascetics or the self-tattooing on the knuckles of certain men—assumed to be suffering from psychopathy or Tourette's syndrome, or else members of a delinquent subculture—on the right hand HATE, on the left LOVE.) I recall as a young psychiatrist brushing aside a psychotic patient's tentative suggestion of his dual personality—'No, that's hysteria, you've got schizophrenia.'

[2] Tart (1980: 249).

[3] Bourguignon (1973) distinguishes between T (trance, altered state of consciousness), P (the local ascription of possession), and PT (both occurring together); thus recalling the binarism of physiology : concept :: *res extensa* : *res cogitans*. On the whole British anthropology with its suspicion of empirical psychology ducks the naturalistic approach to emphasize 'dissociation' as purely conceptual (as does, for example, Lienhardt, n. 1 above). The idea that the relationship between the moral and the physical is illustrated best where the physical dominates goes back at least to the Enlightenment physician Alibert, who urged the study of dreams, madness, and animal instinct as a route to understanding everyday mental processes.

[4] Needham (1981); Lakoff (1987); Littlewood (1993).

Nor does it allow for our less obviously cognitive but socially enacted modes of acquiring bodily schemata[5] for a divided self: particularly through the state of pregnancy, but also lactating, menstruating, masturbating, and coitus; in dancing, playing, exercising, pratfall, violence, crying, tickling and startling, grooming, gesturing, blushing, swallowing, excreting, soothing pain, sleeping, and dreaming.[6]

Affinities between the sub-personal elements of rather different local psychologies have often been remarked: Robin Horton has noted the resemblance of the psychoanalytical schema (ego, id, and super-ego processes) to certain West African psychologies (the individual demonstrating agencies deriving from a unique soul, from nature, and from lineage).[7] Such elements are not generally experienced or identified as separate centres of awareness, for something like a superordinate 'self'[8] has an enduring existence unified in self-awareness, will, action, and memory. By and large, everyday identity does seem fairly unitary, with the development in early life of an internally consistent awareness as the locus of biographical experience, and which is recognized by others as a distinct entity continuing through time which is accountable for its past actions: a single centre of narrative gravity, as Daniel Dennett puts it.[9] Both psychoanalytic and West African schemata are accounts which reconcile our

---

[5] *Habitus* (Mauss 1979*a*, pt. III); similarly Johnson (1987); Bloch (1991). Cognitive psychologists have generally accepted that perception is enacted in a sensorimotor process, an engagement in the world which creates its objects.   [6] See Lecture 2.

[7] I am grossly simplifying Horton's instances, for which McDougall's 'animism' offers an academic psychology closer than Freud's hierarchy, the components each having a greater personified autonomy: more of a 'vertical' split recalling Plato's distinction between appetite, spirit, and reason as fairly autonomous agencies (Price 1995).

[8] Mauss (1979*a*: 61). Mauss restricted the term *moi*, conventionally translated as 'self' (or 'person'), to the social and moral representation, not as I have done here to the operational and embodied 'I': cf. William James's 'empirical me', the 'private self' of Lienhardt, and the 'biological individual' of La Fontaine (both in Carrithers *et al.* 1986), or the 'individual body' of Scheper-Hughes and Lock (1987). Yet in cognized experience these must generally be fairly isomorphic, or at least not too disconsonant, with the representation of the self. Patients in psychoanalysis are not encouraged to personify the analytic mechanisms (which are anyway objectified more in the professional literature than in the consultation), nor does the contemporary psychologist generally wonder if someone at any one moment should be distinguished as either a cognitive or an affective being. In Creole Trinidad, where different individuals may describe themselves as comprising a physical body to which are added quite various combinations of a soul, a spirit, a mind, a shadow, and a guardian angel, they do not recognize themselves as fragmented except in certain crises where everyday unity is called into question (generally moral responsibility for otherwise unintelligible or antisocial actions) or during personal cogitations on how to diminish physical pain or discard undesirable vices (Littlewood 1993). No more does the European Christian generally worry about whether her mind or her soul is in charge, except for moments of temptation, guilt, religious doubt, or conversion.   [9] Laughlin *et al.* (1993); Dennett (1987).

understanding that we are unique, self-aware, and volitional agents, yet we each share aspects of our identity with animals and with our close fellows. In circumstances where everyday identity does not hang together in the expected way, when our taken-for-granted boundary between action and contingency is radically disrupted by dispute, disaster, or sickness, we may emphasize such available distinctions and give the elements a greater degree of personified autonomy such that human-like action between them serves for a more plausible understanding.

Yet our everyday social experience as an enduring self is multifaceted. We are not completely here, now, always, in quite the same way. The self 'occupies' a variety of roles, titles, offices, and statuses—as woman, adult, member of clan or age set, as patient, parent, or prophetic master—without these obscuring some continuing personal identity.[10] We are not distinct individuals in each, and usually these identities do not conflict too much, yet we enact a different comportment and social character (persona) in each, context-dependent yet drawn from and representing an enduring individual, even if in certain circumstances we identify ourselves more fully with one or other. The available alternative selves of multiple personalities or possessing spirits may advertise a particular social status, often one to which we do not otherwise have access.[11] For, against the neurologists, we might argue that alternative personalities are not simply an existing part of us which is then split off, but rather new social potentials, ambitions, stratagems, perversities, and imagined identities which we try on to see how they fit, whether aspiring to adopt them permanently, perhaps to become them, or just in game-playing masquerade or private fantasy (for an individual is frequently their own principal audience). And there are all sorts of options and uncertainties along different continua: play-acting, glossolalia, and deceit with personae nominalized not just as ad hoc interpretations of some physiological shift but in social standardization as representing personified values or as historical and cosmological figures. We might recall the medieval morality play where European virtues and vices were each represented on the stage as personified beings—Lust, Charity, Envy, and so on—without the play as a whole being intended for a human anatomy rather than as an allegory for humankind.

---

[10] Schutz (1976). Or more modestly, the self at dinner, at war, making love.

[11] Such as a male (for women), or colonial officer, foreigner, or enemy: an idea emphasized in the so-called strategic and deprivation theories of spirit mediumship (I. M. Lewis 1969; P. J. Wilson 1967; cf. Boddy 1989).

An Inescapable Antinomy

What might constitute a biological 'reality' for religious possession, godhood, or multiple personality? Presumably that it exists independently of willed intention and that it can be objectively demonstrated as a distinct state prior to any local recognition, understanding, or therapeutic intervention. As with certain contentious Euro-American syndromes (post-traumatic stress disorder, premenstrual tension, myalgic encephalomyelitis, Munchausen's syndrome, hyperactivity syndrome, total allergy syndrome), the debate on, for instance, multiple personality mobilizes supporters and opponents who argue for and against its validity. Inauthenticity is recognized in such an illness if it is *already* recognized as an illness such as depression, or if it is induced by doctor or simulated by patient (this sliding into unconscious motivation), or less commonly if the whole phenomenon is a duplicitous joint fabrication which neither patient nor professional take for actuality. Patient self-help groups generally maintain that these illnesses are biologically specified and accuse doctors of implying they are 'only psychological'.[12]

It is obvious that the academic study of religion and the investigation of illness employ rather different approaches. The former generally aligns itself with the humanities, on occasion with social psychology, while the latter has usually preferred to seek an affinity with the biomedical sciences. We may characterize the procedures of religious studies as personalistic: as concerned with the intentions and experiences of individuals in particular cultural contexts, to be understood through the same empathetic and critical procedures as those we employ when interpreting literature or history. By contrast, medicine and psychology endeavour to follow the procedures of contemporary science in ascertaining cause-and-effect relationships in a naturalistic world which is usually opaque to

[12] Alcoholics Anonymous and ME groups argue that alcoholism and myalgic encephalomyelitis are biological events whose causation is independent of moral agency. (Indeed aboulia is recommended in the various 'twelve–step programmes' such as AA in which past actions are exposed as compelled by the addictive power: the first step acknowledges one's complete powerlessness over the disease, the second affirms the existence of an external Higher Power, the third turns your will over to him: a psychology which is effective through denying it is a psychology.) The rigid dualism of self-help therapies cuts across the psychodynamic recognition of unconscious motivations, and thus rather offends therapists who work with 'psychosomatic' illness; but it is probably acceptable to most hospital doctors for whom psychological explanations come close to a personalistic explanation of frank 'malingering' or at least some slightly more sympathetic but still perjorative notion of 'hysteria', 'functional overlay', 'supratentorial', 'subjective', 'self-deception', or even—since medical students now study sociology—'abnormal illness behaviour'. In any event, not real in that the phenomenon cannot be naturalistically specified.

human awareness, but which is rule-governed and predictable, and potentially accessible to direct and unmediated observation.

Personalistic and naturalistic paradigms are not altogether contradictory. At certain points they slide into each other, certainly providing many of the ironies and ambiguities of Western everyday medical practice. Is the depressed person who takes an overdose acting as a moral agent, perhaps intending certain consequences, and thus conventionally to be held responsible for their actions? Or do we take the act as the symptoms of an underlying disease for which they cannot, in any everyday sense, be held accountable? Even with mental illnesses where psychiatry presumes some biological disease process as causal, as with my examples of Sabbatai Sevi or Mother Earth, the patient is hardly regarded as passive matter, for practical clinical and legal assumptions are made about their particular degree of volition and moral accountability. Similar ambiguities occur with such illnesses as the chronic pain syndromes: Do we take the patient as 'malingering'? Do they have a 'real' illness? When dealing with religious experiences and ideas in the course of illness, psychiatrists place priority on an underlying pathology which simply employs any cultural values as the material through which abnormal beliefs are elaborated or which are the 'normal' responses anyone might have to such an extraordinary experience.

This conventional distinction between the naturalistic and the personalistic has been eroded in twentieth-century physics and cognitive science, while the epistemological claims of natural science to reflect reality directly have been challenged as themselves culturally constructed. From their side, social theorists have argued that a full account of human life requires not only an understanding of how we act to create social institutions, but an explanation of how these institutions may be said to determine us through providing the necessary, indeed possible, limits through which our lives are lived. Understanding and explaining: neither is completely true, nor false. Yet as practised academic knowledge they generally remain distinct.

A number of twentieth-century disciplines have attempted to reconcile the naturalistic and the personalistic, notably psychoanalysis, phenomenology, cybernetics, and sociobiology. Psychoanalysis has some claim to our interest here for Freud argued that novel social institutions, particularly religious innovations, are simply individual psychopathology writ large, and that this pathology would ultimately be understood in naturalistic terms. Psychoanalysts, as well as those historians and literary critics influenced by psychoanalysis, have produced a number of accounts of religious change by examining the personal lives of their innovators (Chapter 1), a procedure more popular in North American scholarship than elsewhere, and which has come to be called psychohistory or psychobiography.

My concern here is rather different. We may fault psychoanalysis for failing to keep both naturalistic and personalistic knowledge in play. It has abandoned its claims to naturalistic explanation, and now employs the idioms of descriptive psychiatry—paranoid, manic, and so forth—simply as moral metaphors for everyday life. Whatever its earlier claims, psychoanalysis has become hermeneutics—an interpretive procedure which seems to uncover meaning rather than provide a causal explanation of disease. Any attempt to keep in play a descriptive psychology which ultimately situates its claims to knowledge in biology, simultaneously with an understanding of religious experience and institutions, needs to proceed on both our two levels; inevitably, it will be dialogic in attempting to do justice to both types of knowledge rather than seeking an elision which in practice reduces the one to the other. Illness is not just a literary trope, nor can human experience be predicated on neurophysiology alone.

As with hypnosis or hysteria,[13] claims to the plausibility of experiences like MPD or religious possession can be considered from three positions:

Biological. There certainly seem to be consistent physiological distinctions associated with the different personalities. But biological variation does not in itself conventionally constitute a disease entity any more than consistent changes in our galvanic skin response during moments of anger would allow us to characterize this mood as pathological or indeed as any more real than non-angry experience.

Phenomenological. Does the reported pattern correspond with its protagonists' experience? There seems little doubt that most instances of religious conversion or divine identification are recognized at the time as genuine and spontaneous new selves, although instances of motivated invention do occur.

Dramaturgical. If in a particular case we recognize the influence of a theory upon the existence of things which it is held to explain,[14]

---

[13] Or indeed spirit possession if we favour a robust materialism, although here, until the 1980s, claims to physical reality were seldom advanced except by biblical fundamentalists and some enthusiasts for extra-sensory perception. Hypnosis and other altered states of consciousness cannot be specified (Needham 1981) by any characteristic physiological pattern, although there appear some consistent changes in cortical and subcortical activity and in endorphin regulation. Physical and sexual abuse have both been associated with fairly non-specific changes in endocrine response (Brown 1991).   [14] As Kenny (1981) puts it.

claims to their independent reality and subjective truth then seem to evaporate, for the individual now has access to the expected scenario through the procedures common to everyday social life—learning, mimesis, strategic role-playing, compliance. (Requesting experimental subjects to explicitly 'simulate' hypnosis and multiple personality leads to the desired phenomena: the extent to which the individuals report the experience to observers controlling the experiment as 'real' depends on the degree of encouragement.[15])

Thus Kenny, like Needham, prefers to talk here of social metaphor.[16] That empirical observations occur within a social context in which they take on more extended meanings and power is not, however, a criterion for denying their claims to provide context-independent truth about the world;[17] and if multiple personality or hysteria seem phenomena dependent on the act of informed observation, then the private individual is always their own observer, nor can any psychological state be empirically 'real'.[18]

Protagonists and critics of the independent reality of multiple personality or religious novelty agree on an essential dualism: either it just happens to you or else you deliberately do it. Each 'it' is a rather different sort of thing: disease entity versus masquerade. In a number of recent papers and books I have argued rather for a procedural dualism: we can understand ourselves and the world as a consequence of cause and effect processes, generally independent of, but potentially accessible to, human awareness—the naturalistic mode of thought; yet we can also understand the same matters personalistically—as the motivated actions of volitional agents employing such characteristically human attributes as intention, representation, narration, self-awareness, intersubjectivity, identification, deceit, and shame. And while Euro-Americans conventionally allocate one or other area of interest to the naturalistic or the personalistic, perhaps objectifying them as separate domains (nature : culture :: brain : mind :: godhood : illness), we can apply either mode of thought to any phenomenon. The self may be a machine, the natural world may be personified.[19] Psychiatric considerations of such phenomena as self-harm (symptom of depressive illness? intention to die?) or myalgic encephalomyelitis (disease process? malingering?), like medico-legal debates on criminal responsibility (mad? bad?), continually slip between one and the other, for only

---

[15] Reviewed in Spanos (1989).　　　　　[16] Kenny (1986); Needham (1981).
[17] The 'strong programme' in the sociology of science; but see Bloor's position.
[18] Wittgenstein (1958).
[19] And society may be either an organism or just a convenient grouping of human subjects.

one mode can be correct at any one time. Neither can be demonstrated as completely true, nor false: we always live with the two options.[20] As Plato put it in the *Timaeus*, 'the world came about as a combination of reason and necessity'. But combined how? In certain areas—anthropology, psychiatry, medical jurisprudence, cognitive science, ethology, and the sociology of knowledge—the practical problems of reconciling causation and volition become especially salient. As in the Hegelian or Marxist emergence of mind, in phrenology, phenomenology, and psychoanalysis, in sociobiology, and in current neuropsychology and the philosophy of mind, these generally reduce one position to the other as prior and essential: whether in ontology, in epistemology, or, usually, in both.

Baconian and eighteenth-century medicine proposed fluid reciprocity or 'rapports' between the physical and the moral:[21] what Mauss[22] called 'connecting cogs', Searle's[23] 'gap-filling efforts'; currently towards one side, Dennett's[24] multiple drafts, Edelman's[25] neuronal group selection, Churchland's eliminative materialism, or Crick's recent claim to locate free will in the anterior cingulate sulcus; towards the other, perhaps Fodor's[26] intentional realism, Penrose, Davidson, Lakoff, Hacking, McGinn, Searle, Nagel, and Eccles. The monistic claims of 'embodiment' by moral philosophers and phenomenologists in practice follow a personalistic line; as do feminist assertions of a potential affinity between the new information technologies and women's lives. There is no shortage of gushing popular religious or philosophical claims to transcend what is taken as an arid Western dichotomy (such as the proposed 'unity of *technē* and *logos*' in the cyber-aesthetics of Kroker[27]) but intertheoretical reductionism has proved unconvincing here except perhaps in the field of artificial life. Similarly, anthropological objections to dialectic and interactionist solutions tend to replicate something very similar;[28] as do critiques of a biomedical rationality opposed to the 'life worlds' of patients. Rather, I would argue that both biomedicine and the idiom of 'experience' currently favoured in anthropology are simply systematizations

---

[20] An ironic dualism (Littlewood 1993); the very distinction may be seen as naturalistic (the distinction in our experience and actions between the involuntary and voluntary nervous system, as Merleau-Ponty noted, or in rather different cognitive domains distinguishing animate from inanimate) or as personalistic (given by cultural history as, for example, the dualism of Judaeo-Christianity refined in the mechanical science of the Renaissance). The antinomy in the form I have expressed it may be traced to Kant (or indeed to Descartes's First Meditation).

[21] E. A. Williams (1994).   [22] Mauss (1979a: 121).   [23] Searle (1984: 4).
[24] Dennett (1991).   [25] Edelman (1992).   [26] Fodor (1992).
[27] Kroker (1992).   [28] e.g. Toren (1993: 462).

of our two everyday modes of thought; whether these are to be considered 'additive' or discrepant remains a continuing problem for anthropology and psychiatry, as for Western jurisprudence.

This is not a lecture on scientific method and I do not wish to detail current attempts to resolve the antinomy but rather to take it as an inescapable ambiguity in everyday life and thence in expert practice. Psychoanalysis once attempted to reconcile the opposition through a sub-personal psychology which showed how the possibility of intention emerges dynamically from naturalistic sub-personal structures. Its resulting notion of fantasy (not empirically true, yet not exactly fabricated) elided for multiple personality or religious identification the contraries of physiologically autonomous or personally contrived. That the professional acceptance of psychoanalysis now seems inversely related to the recognition of multiple personality argues against reading the current wave of multiple personality disorder (MPD) simply as our postmodern consciousness, for its enthusiasts insist on the objective reality both of the syndrome as biologically specified and of its invariant cause, child sexual abuse, a signifier with an all-too-real signified.[29] And opponents too generally revert to a pre-Freudian empiricism in denying its existence: no reality to MPD because no causal trauma. This goes along with a shift in the moral economy of our two modes of thought in the last twenty years in both Britain and the United States, in an apparently more personalistic and contractual direction—towards an emphasis on individual responsibility for sickness, unemployment, and poverty, and on the rights and responsibilities of the mentally ill;[30] with diminished space available in a now contracted natural world transformed by self-sufficient individuals for 'accidents'—which remain observable events yet have now become violating traumata occasioned by the mischief or negligence of others, responsible agents whom we hold morally and legally accountable for the 'management' of our risks.

Paul Heelas has argued on the basis of 'locus of control' experiments by psychologists that when there is such a strong emphasis on an

---

[29] Cf. Jameson (1991). And recently on the physical reality of possessing spirits and extra-terrestrial life forms (Ross 1994; Mack 1994), although some enthusiasts have now retreated to an idea of psychological truth (Ross 1995).

[30] And on the rights (if not yet responsibilities) of children, animals, and the natural world (Littlewood 1993). Andrea Dworkin has recently proposed that sexually abused women should sue pornographers for damages. A unitary and contractual individual taken as the given entity is one without an inherent social identity (Etzioni 1994), and empirical psychology has of course pursued its contrary project of delineating a Nature that exists independently of immediate sense perception.

autonomous self, we attribute undesired deviations to some discrete agency external to this self, whether a personal or technological conspiracy or a cannibalistic spirit:[31] recalling what the critic Hofstadter has recently called America's 'paranoid political style', the anthropologist Mulhern's[32] 'conspiracy thinking', or Kenny's[33] 'paradoxes of liberty' (presaged in Augustinian psychology's opening to the reality of witchcraft[34]). Enhanced competitive individualism is the bedfellow of paranoia, whether we understand this competition in terms of psychology (Kluckholn, Field) or social action (Lienhardt, Macfarlane). Underlying this is the phenomenologists' pursuit of how the flux of pre-objective experience becomes congealed into hypostasized entities—a process surprisingly ignored by anthropologists interested in cognition but which has been variously addressed by Marxists, Kleinians, and Buddhists through the idea that nominal categories are less ambiguous than experiencing, and under problematic circumstances we essentialize a fetishized world following our own objectification of ourselves as physical entities.[35] Early in life we start to perceive the world as nominalized—as composed of entities of recurrent invariance[36] whose interaction then inevitably becomes problematic (Lukács); such reification is fundamental to social categorization, giving ontological status to the experienced world.[37] And, in the same way, since Kant we reify our awareness and action in the world as consciousness, as something like an entity. Biographies of the Christian Right's apocalyptics indicate that they reattribute everyday agency from their traumatized self to an Antichrist who manifests himself through human malevolence or liberal government policies, final restitution being deferred to the 'end time'.[38]

---

[31] (Or one's own body as other; Heelas 1981: 50.) Similarly from feminism (Haraway 1991) and computer simulations of the development of hierarchical social institutions (Doran *et al.* 1994). The alter of MPD seems to have shifted from an external to an increasingly internal locus, yet Brazilian psychiatrists sympathetic to Kardecism treat MPD with exorcism (as do some American psychiatrists: e.g. Ross 1994) or even by encouraging the individual to become a spirit medium (Krippner 1987). American alters may on occasion gain some sort of concrete existence as separate physical beings yet *within* the host body: 'several times Jed [an alter] was beaten up inside by the Evil One [another alter], and told us that his face was bruised and swollen' (Ross 1994: 129). We might map these shifting locations along the parameters of aboulia versus intentional agency, and self versus other (cf. Heelas 1981); and plot contemporary medical evaluation of the traumatic memory along the aetiological dimensions of naturalistic–personalistic and internal–external.

[32] Mulhern (1994).   [33] Kenny (1986: 24).   [34] Mathews (1992).
[35] Mead (1934).   [36] Schutz (1976); Laughlin *et al.* (1993).   [37] Lakoff (1987).
[38] Strozier (1994).

Social and Engendered Embodiments

Access to an experience we might gloss as a severe diminution or even a dissolution of everyday agency has appeared in rather different cultural and political contexts, available to certain individuals through alterations in their brain physiology (naturalistically)[39] and through their enacted situation (personalistically); and this can be occasioned by experienced conflicts and sickness understood through conventional bodily techniques and notions of the self—'this isn't happening to me, this is happening to someone else'—and by its immediate consequences (recognition by the individual and others, expert encouragement, and legitimization).

Despite continued subjective dissociations, the everyday locus of experience and action is a generally unitary and internally consistent individual, bounded, autonomous, and fairly undifferentiated, coextensive with a physical body and with that body's history: whether we assume that such unity is given in our body's neural make-up, or else that the idiom of a single rather than a double or multiplex self has proved rather more successful in our biological and cultural history. Such a unitary individual may recognize his or her self as losing will, coherence, and responsibility, whether in emergencies or at times of radical social change, through diseases of the brain, or in situations standardized as illness, dance, violence, and sorcery, or as ecstasy, glossolalia, spirit mediumship, hypnosis, hysteria, and multiple personality: occasions when our local representations of a self may provide operational models for multiplicity through mind–body distinctions, psychological faculties or energies, consciousness, humours, emotions, addictions, winds and faces, evolutionary and topographical levels, dream selves, multiple souls, spirit familiars, powers, hidden doubles, guardian angels, many-personed and consubstantial deities, mythical transformations, the identity or otherwise of twins and other products of unnatural fecundity,[40] the differentiation of kin, through onomastics and the avoidance of homonyms, in personifications

---

[39] And there are a number of psychophysiological studies which demonstrate consistent differences in 'suggestible hypnotic subjects' in their predisposing personality, cerebral evoked potentials, proneness to sleepwalking, daydreaming, fantasy-induced orgasm, and so on (Wilson and Barber 1981; Brown 1991). Trance and other altered states of consciousness have been likened to temporal lobe epilepsy, with similar alterations in limbic and adrenal function (Erwin *et al.* 1988).

[40] Who may have the same (late dynastic Egypt) or very similar (contemporary Afro-Caribbean) names. As Dennett (1991: 422) puts it, a situation of one mind in two bodies: like incest or nationalism, an elision of personal identities, the inverse of multiple personality. As the structuralist might observe, incest (not enough differentiation) is the classic trauma for multiple personality (too much differentiation).

of the foetus, the dead, and the dreamer,[41] through metempsychosis, the sub-personalities of West African psychologies and the human potential movement, and the cyborgs and extraterrestrials of the computer techno-visionaries. The loss of volition and control may be recognized as temporary or permanent, as partial or total (the Christian exorcist's distinction between *obsessio* and *possessio*), as a conflict or as a penetration, as loss, rape, or theft (*latah*, *zombi*, *susto*); or we may recognize our moral agency in the intruding other, simultaneously or serially, whether aware of seeking such an identification or just finding it happen—as 'voluntary' or 'involuntary' godhood or possession.[42] (As in those not uncommon situations in which we reflect on some past act and wonder if it really was this same 'I' that performed it.[43]) Context, expectation, access to a particular schema, and the example and response of others organize a variety of standardized narratives, tentative essays, partial stages, elisions, and the like, which in turn demonstrate the experiential reality of our local cosmology. Social location facilitates access to particular patterns; thus I would propose that dissociative states, like shamanic or cyberspace vision quests, masking, and 'central possession cults', are just more available to men, consistent with male access to a more extensive geographical and social space with anticipated movement into a new social persona; in the same societies 'static' dissociations, involuntary and 'peripheral' possession, latah, hysteria, and multiple personality follow from women's restricted mobility or from their experience of pregnancy and something like a sick role.[44]

[41] Boureau (1991) (cited in Mulhern 1994) argues that 14th-century witch-finding enthusiasms were facilitated by a theological debate on somnambulism which favoured a post-Thomist idea of something like moral dissociation—and thus a potential vulnerability to daytime displacement of aspects of the self in frank possession.

[42] Akin to the projective identification of psychoanalysis. Bloch (1993), employing Lienhardt's (1961) Dinka material, argues that an initial experience of penetration may be followed by an attempt at catharsis which, if unsuccessful, then leads to identification with the intrusion as 'possession' or assimilation.

[43] Parfit (1984). Or whether the American convict executed for a murder after twenty years in prison is the 'same person'.

[44] Well illustrated in Firth's (1961) account of Tikopian responses to solitary canoe trips: heroic self-transformations by men, dangerous cries for help by women. We might argue more embodied analogies between subjectivity and experienced 'space' and 'constraint': Bourguignon (1973, introd.) describes trance and vision quests as more plausible for nomadic societies, possession trance for settled communities; and the cognitions of female sexuality and pregnancy make possible idioms of spirit penetration and an unfolding cosmology (Littlewood 1996). Compare cyberspace: male surfing but female occupation of MUDs and other habitats (Ess 1996).

To take these patterns simply as motivated strategies which the participants themselves prefer to recognize as involuntary assumes that the very articulation of the two modes is voluntary. The recently fashionable personalism of aesthetics, role play, and performance in anthropological theory, however, recapitulates the public assumptions through which hypnosis and godhood emerge: the particularly Western idea of an achieving self. Reading them, however, in the earlier 'bottom–up' way still favoured by psychologists and physiologists—and some participants—leaves us with the contrary problem: that our loss of volition is necessarily non-volitional. The naturalistic idiom is limiting, not just because this is the immediate biomedical context which legitimizes such patterns in Western societies as pathologies but because of the difficulty in making here the customary distinction between aetiology, pathology, symptoms, and treatment.

Why women? You will perhaps have been struck by my number of subdominant religious protagonists who are female. At a high level of generality, the pattern identified as the significant novelty may be interpreted as a reconfiguring of the position already ascribed to subdominant individuals; if the female is sickly and fearful, vulnerable to demons, controlled by others or lacking in moral will, enacting rather than transforming, carrying another being within her, with relatively free access to her body by others, then her 'illness' or 'godhood' will be an affirmation of these characteristics. And illness or religiosity are perhaps an extreme variant of those other patterns by which women can negotiate through the characteristics ascribed to them by men; for to be ill is to identify with an image of oneself as being open and vulnerable.[45] Last century the neurologist Benedikt wondered if women were more prone to hysteria because they had more to hide; and in the sense that women's 'muted voice', to use the Ardeners' terminology,[46] argues for a double-voiced tradition, simultaneously inside and against the public way of seeing things, double consciousness seems an apt representation (and practical deployment) of their situation. Like the intruding spirit, a disease is something which limits our moral agency; and shared recognition of an external cause, whether spirit or disease, compels others to legitimization

---

[45] I have never seen a patient with Munchausen's syndrome (when the individual is recognized by others as deliberately inducing illness through self-mutilation, opening scabs, swallowing metal objects) who in some way was not 'genuinely hurt' at being accused of malingering; and contrawise in every patient with a non-psychotic illness, the illness comes over to me as, in a sense, 'motivated'.   [46] Ardener (1975).

and restitution. It is in the inescapable slippage between naturalistic and personalistic that alien penetration and godhood emerge.

Critics of new religious cults and the multiple movement have likened them to the late medieval European witch-hunts, and it will be evident that in the last lectures I have recommended analogies between multiple personality in particular and certain Africanist categorizations of spirit possession and witchcraft: peripheral possession, introspective witchcraft, the direction of accusation, witch-finding, strategic advantage, and so on. Without pushing the parallel too far, I find Ioan Lewis's scheme for the relations between possession and witchcraft a potential map.[47] Nineteenth-century double consciousness recalls involuntary trance possession with its emphasis on only partial displacement of the victim's identity, with restitution rather than public redress, while with contemporary MPD we approach something recalling witchcraft accusation, greater significance now being attached to a reckoning with a human or human-like perpetrator who is to confess before being (perhaps) absolved. Lewis proposes that both patterns may occur in the same society: trance possession attributed to spirits 'expresses insubordination, but not to the point where it is desired to sever the relationship', whereas witchcraft accusations are frequently associated with themes of incest 'representing as they do a much more direct line of attack, express[ing] hostility between equal rivals, or between superior and subordinate . . . and often seek[ing] to sunder an unbearably tense relationship'. If witchcraft accusations are indeed frequently directed against coevals in situations of publicly expected amity (but actual animosity, competition, and incipient rupturing of domestic obligations or co-residence), then the directions of accusation in MPD—typically daughter to father, or vulnerable young woman to powerful male—suggest increasingly uncertain markings of power and sexuality between childhood and adulthood, female and male.[48] The not uncommon characterization of the jealous refusal of the American mother to protect her abused daughter as a theft of that daughter's identity[49]

---

[47] I. M. Lewis (1970).

[48] Of the sort suggested in Giddens (1992). The litigiousness of both protagonists and antagonists in the MPD drama seems to have prevented any serious ethnography. Beyond the therapists' own reports we know little of the clinical encounter, the everyday life of the patient, their changes in domestic or social circumstances, in the sort of detail so well presented for women's possession in Northern Sudan by Boddy (1989).

[49] Walker (1993); Ross (1994); Wright (1993); Wyllie (1973). I forget who first proposed the canard that the history of Western psychotherapy is that of the increasing attribution of malevolence to parents.

recalls the 'involuntary' malevolence of the cannibalistic witch mother to her daughter in which she devours the vital essence of her own child.

If illnesses are to be taken as mirrors of their age, then MPD, for example, seems to acknowledge the loss of once accepted gender complementarity in a rawer manifestation of male domination, opening up our society's terrible secrets,[50] yet it challenges this through an ambivalent assertion of the rights of the young female to her body. If the spirits of vodu and sar present standardized historical memories,[51] and the secondary personalities of the nineteenth-century hysterics were taken by their psychiatrists for factitious neurological signs, for unacceptable sexual desire, or for an earlier level of evolutionary development,[52] then the fragmented alters of the current MPD epidemic offer a secularized West an unstable multiplicity of now doubtfully welcome children, incorporated aliens, fantasized selves, and wounded healers.[53]

MPD is simultaneously a psychophysiological state, a moral identity, a medical technology, a disease, a theory of the mind, an allegory of late capitalism, and an expressive aesthetic. It is also a political drama. As with certain other illnesses in Western societies, women who demonstrate

[50] e.g. Walker (1993). A common justification of MPD is that any sort of sexual abuse was once disbelieved, yet the phenomenon is now clinically accepted: therefore satanic abuse similarly (e.g. Sinason 1994). 'The study of trauma in sexual and domestic life becomes legitimate only in a context that challenges the subordination of women and children. Advances in the field occur only when they are supported by a political movement powerful enough to legitimate an alliance between investigators and patients and to counteract the ordinary social processes of silencing and denial' (the American protagonist of 'recovered memories' Judith Herman in 1993, quoted by Crews 1994: 54). The accusations of the MPD therapists are directed not only at the sexual abuser but at any denier of the act: as with witchcraft accusations, restitution necessitates public repentance by the perpetrator who must be named by the victim to ensure full recovery (e.g. Herman 1992).

[51] Larose (1977); Boddy (1989); similarly Stoller (1989).

[52] Ellenberger (1970). Nineteenth-century double consciousness—the bland innocent girl revealing her capricious secondary personality—recalls Romantic moral dualism. (Reading clinical accounts such as those of Prince suggests that it was only in the course of extended hypnotic interventions that the vaguer third or fourth personalities began to emerge as the doctor tried to isolate the real self.) By contrast, Ross notes approvingly that 29% of North American alters are now immediately diagnosed as demons, this in a society where more than 2% of the population currently report that they have been demonically possessed, half accept the existence of angels, and a third anticipate being raptured by Jesus into the skies (Ross 1994: 124; Strozier 1994: 5).

[53] Recognized by MPD therapists as 'polyfragmentation' (Ross 1994). As if, pursuing our overinterpretation, with the 'self as a reflexive project' (Giddens 1992), late modernity cannot sustain the attempt to unify time, place, and action, yet cannot cope with flux alone, and retreats to concretized but inconstant simulacra of an embodied individual: akin to what Felix Guattari terms the 'reterritorializations' of post-colonial consciousness. Participants in electronic conferencing still tend to act as if in Cartesian space, and place considerable importance on establishing the sex and other physical characteristics of their fellow participants.

MPD have now joined together in survivors' groups which play down the idea of treatment: sororities through which the symptom is accommodated as a testimony to oppression, but at the cost of continuing propriation.[54] After 1948 opium addiction in China was reframed from an individual psychopathology into a testimony of a colonial domination dating from the Opium Wars, and contemporary feminist therapists have similarly reinscribed a number of women's pathologies as an ambivalent resistance to male power.[55] As in the non-Western analogues (anthropology's cults of affliction)—such as the sar cults of Somalia and Ethiopia or the hernia chiefships of Zaire—sufferers in Alcoholics Anonymous or Speaking for Our Selves come together to affirm their illness, to strike a contract with it, and dedicate themselves to its power, often to gain a

[54] In their terms, no longer as sufferers or even victims but as witnesses: cf. the politics of survivor syndrome in Israel, or of therapy groups for the survivors of torture, or of the post-Soviet group Memorial. Similarly, in the literature of a number of survivors' groups the problem is presented as real but falsely 'contained' by powerful interests, including medicine, and the group's task is to enable the survivor to 'find a voice'—public expression and accusation. (The now common term 'survivor' was popularized in psychotherapy by Bruno Bettelheim to refer to people liberated from Nazi concentration camps.)

[55] On Western sickness as counter-hegemonic see Littlewood (1991*c*). Showalter (1993) details our strange 'modern marriage of hysteria and feminism', hysteria now affirmed as a proto-feminism, a bodily and linguistic resistance to male power: an image perhaps not so dissimilar from that offered by 19th-century medicine itself (and, later, surrealism: Breton 1964), which took the hysteric as the quintessential female, neurasthenia being the consequence of, if not the impetus for, female emancipation (Kenny 1986: 136; see also Micale 1995: 66–88). Bryan Turner (1984) argues that hysteria provided the Victorian bourgeoisie with a 'solution' for the sexuality of their unmarried women in a period of delayed marriage: as with MPD, I think a deprivation model which takes women's bodies simply as objects of (and resistance to) male commodification is inadequate, but we might consider the very material consequences of serial monogamy for contemporary working-class women in America. Boddy (1989) notes that to read northern Sudanese possession trance simply as women's symbolic 'resistance' to men misses very real bodily insults which are readily recognized by the women, yet their trancing is primarily an ambiguous accommodation and a self-sustaining aesthetic. Her account of the sar spirits entering a body 'sealed' earlier through the scarring of infibulation recalls MPD's interesting elision of Christian fundamentalism with feminist politics in affirming American women's control over their body entrances and margins ('Our Bodies, Our Selves'). Double consciousness and hysteria have certainly been portrayed as a battle between woman and doctor, both in the military metaphors of the clinician and in recent feminist revisions. The doctor triumphed only partially with the triumph of psychoanalysis: as hysteria's elusive mimesis of physical disease was banished to a realm of unconscious fantasy, the patient was left to string out her 'resistances' for as extended a period of combative therapy as possible. On the gender conflict model the recovery of lost memories of abusive power, now validated by courts and scientists, seems to reframe and challenge the terrain towards a closer mimesis of the actual dominance itself. Mulhern, however, has argued that MPD initially represented a depoliticization of feminist social work in which during the 1980s socialism was discarded in favour of therapy.

sense of heightened control. Not so much a restitution as an accommodation, through which the sodality can then take on less evidently 'therapeutic' roles, in which affected individuals market their experience as emblematic, their suffering as achievement, their recovery as expert knowledge.[56]

The weapons of the weak, to use Victor Turner's well-known expression,[57] not only compel the dominant to restitutive action but may—strategically or otherwise—provide a new identity and material resources for the protagonists, and thence for others. Nineteenth-century women reworked the existing relationship between medical hypnotist and suggestible female to affirm their weakness as a privileged access to higher knowledge, the medium establishing for herself a professional career which claimed wider solutions to the problems of others,[58] and for the social reformers of the period offered a demystified and natural religion. As contemporary multiples affirm the legitimacy of their several personalities, they too have aligned themselves with contemporary movements for 'the politics of identity' and for women's ownership of their bodies; the stigmata of rape becoming the means of transcending their origin, the ascribed now translated into the achieved, the pathological becoming a marketable realm of political authenticity. And in that, they have become something we might not inappropriately gloss as a new if secular cosmology.

---

[56] Compare I. M. Lewis (1969); Janzen (1982); Sharp (1993). And who then attract recruits who had not previously regarded themselves as sufferers but who now revise their biographies. I recall Trinidadian doctors' complaints that Alcoholics Anonymous in Port of Spain was an Asian business fraternity whose members had no drink problems (similarly Britain: anon. 1994).

[57] Taken from Wilde via Eliot's *The Family Reunion*.

[58] Owen (1989). Cf. the current term for a New Age medium whose profession emerges out of her affliction with MPD—*trance channeller*; similarly among contemporary groups for survivors of civil disasters or for relatives of the victims, who transcend their suffering through advocating greater safety controls and public accountability.

REFERENCES

ABRAHAMS, R. G. (1986). Ordinary and Extraordinary Experience. In V. Turner and E. Bruner (eds.), *The Anthropology of Experience*. Urbana: Illinois University Press.

ACKERNECHT, E. (1943). Psychopathology, Primitive Medicine and Primitive Culture. *Bulletin of the History of Medicine*. 14: 30–68.

ADELMAN, J. (1992). *Suffocating Mothers: Fantasies of Maternal Origin in Shakespeare's Plays*. London: Routledge.

ADLER, M. (1986). *Drawing down the Moon*. 2nd edn., rev. Boston: Beacon Press.

AHERN, E. M. (1979). The Problem of Efficacy: Strong and Weak Illocutionary Acts. *Man* (NS), 14, 1–17.

ALBANESE, C. L. (1990). *Nature Religion in America: From the Algonkian Indians to the New Age*. Chicago: Chicago University Press.

ALEXANDER, F. (1939). Psychoanalytic Study of a Case of Essential Hypertension. *Psychosomatic Medicine*, 1: 139–52.

ALEXANDER, J. (1977). The Culture of Race in Middle-Class Kingston. *American Ethnologist*, 4: 413–35.

ANDREWS, E. D. (1953). *The People Called Shakers*. Oxford: Oxford University Press.

ANON. (1994). AA's Potent Network. *The Times*, suppl., 5 Feb., 1.

ANSEL, A. (1982). *Judaism and Psychology*. 3rd edn. New York: Felshelm.

ARDENER, E. (1980). Some Outstanding Problems in the Analysis of Events. In Foster and Brandes (1980).

ARDENER, S. (ed.) (1975). *Perceiving Women*. London: Dent.

ARDOSSI, J., and EPSTEIN, L. (1975). The Saintly Madmen of Tibet. Abstracted in *Transcultural Psychiatric Research Review*, 12: 21–22.

ARDT, K. J. R. (1965). *George Rapp's Harmony Society*. Philadelphia: University of Pennsylvania Press.

ARMYTAGE, W. H. G. (1961). *Heavens Below: Utopian Experiments in England 1560–1960*. London: Routledge & Kegan Paul.

ASSOCIATION OF PSYCHIATRISTS IN TRAINING (1977). *Newsletter*, Sept., 1.

AUSTIN-BROOS, D. J. (1997). *Jamaica Genesis: Religion and the Politics of Moral Order*. Chicago: Chicago University Press.

BABCOCK, B. (ed.) (1978). *The Reversible World: Symbolic Inversion in Art and Society*. Ithaca, NY: Cornell University Press.

BAIER, A. (1994). *Moral Prejudice: Essays on Ethics*. Cambridge: Cambridge University Press.

BAKAN, D. (1958). *Sigmund Freud and the Jewish Mystical Tradition*. Princeton: Princeton University Press.

BALLARD, R. (1973). An interview with Thomas Szasz. *Penthouse*, Oct.

BARRETT, R. J. J., and LUCAS, R. H. (1993). The Skulls are Cold, the House is Hot: Interpreting Depths of Meaning in Iban Therapy. *Man* (NS), 28: 573–96.

BECKFORD, J. A. (1975). *The Trumpet of Prophecy: A Sociological Study of Jehovah's Witnesses*. Oxford: Blackwell.

—— (1985). The World Images of New Religious and Healing Movements. In R. K. Jones (ed.), *Sickness and Sectarianism: Exploratory Studies in Medical and Religious Sectarianism*. Aldershot: Gower.

BEESTON, R. (1992). 'Messiah' Arouses Rival Rabbi's Wrath. *The Times*, 29 Feb.

BELLAH, R. N., MADSEN, R., SULLIVAN, W. M., SWIDLER, A., and TIPTON, S. M. (1985). *Habits of the Heart: Individualism and Commitment in American Life*. Berkeley: California University Press.

BEN-AMOS, D., and MINTZ, J. R. (eds. and trans.) (1970). *In Praise of the Ba'al Shem Tov (Shivhei ha-Besht)*. Bloomington: Indiana University Press.

BENEDICT, M. (ed.) (1991). *Cyberspace: First Steps*. Cambridge, Mass.: MIT Press.

BEN SHIMON HALEVI, Z. (1974). *Adam and the Kabbalistic Tree*. London: Rider.

BERGER, P. L., and LUCKMAN, T. (1966). *The Social Construction of Reality*. New York: Doubleday.

BILU, Y., WITZTUM, E., and VAN DER HART, O. (1990). Paradise Regained: 'Miraculous Healing' in an Israeli Psychiatric Clinic. *Culture, Medicine and Psychiatry*, 14: 105–27.

BLACKING, J. (ed.) (1977). *The Anthropology of the Body*. London: Academic Press.

BLOCH, M. (1991). Language, Anthropology and Cognitive Science. *Man* (NS), 26: 183–98.

—— (1993). *Prey into Hunter: The Politics of Religious Experience*. Cambridge: Cambridge University Press.

BLOCH, S., and REDDAWAY, P. (1975). *Russia's Political Hospitals*. London: Gollancz.

BLOOM, H. (1984). *Kabbalah and Criticism*. New York: Continuum.

BODDY, J. (1989). *Wombs and Alien Spirits: Women, Men and the Zār Cult in Northern Sudan*. Madison: University of Wisconsin Press.

BOLINGER, D. (1980). Intonation and 'Nature'. In Foster and Brandes (1980).

BOLTER, J. D. (1986). *Turing's Man: Western Culture in the Computer Age*. Harmondsworth: Penguin.

BOTTOMLEY, F. (1980). Ideas of the Body in the Old Testament. In Bottomley, *Attitudes to the Body in Western Christendom*. London: Lepus.

BOURDIEU, P. (1977). *Outline of a Theory of Practice*. Cambridge: Cambridge University Press.

BOUREAU, A. (1991). Satan et le domeur: une construction de l'inconscient au Moyen Âge. *Chimère*, 14: 41–61.

BOURGUIGNON, E. (ed.) (1973). *Religion, Altered States of Consciousness and Social Change*. Colombus: Ohio State University Press.

BOYER, P. (1986). The 'Empty' Concepts of Traditional Thinking: A Semantic and Pragmatic Description. *Man* (NS), 21: 50–64.

—— (ed.) (1993). *Cognitive Aspects of Religious Symbolism*. Cambridge: Cambridge University Press.

—— (1997). *The Naturalness of Religious Ideas: A Cognitive Theory of Religion*. Berkeley: University of California Press.

BRAUDE, S. (1991). *First-Person Plural: Multiple Personality and the Philosophy of Mind*. London: Routledge.

BRETON, A. (1964). *Nadja*. (Rev. edn.) Paris: Gallimard.

—— (1969). *Manifestes de Surréalisme*. Paris: Gallimard.

British Medical Journal (1971). Suicide Attempts. 11: 483.

BROOKE, J. L. (1994). *The Refiner's Fire: The Making of Mormon Cosmology 1644–1844*. Cambridge: Cambridge University Press.

BROWN, P. (1991). *The Hypnotic Brain: Hypnotherapy and Social Communication*. New Haven: Yale University Press.

BROWN, PETER (1982). *Society and the Holy in Late Antiquity*. Berkeley: University of California Press.

—— (1989). *The Body and Society: Men, Women and Sexual Renunciation in Early Christianity*. London: Faber & Faber.

BRYAN, C. D. (1995). *Close Encounters of the 4th Kind: Alien Abduction and UFOs: Witnesses and Scientists Report*. London: Weidenfeld & Nicolson.

BUBER, M. (1948). *Tales of the Hasidim*. 2 vols. New York: Schocken Books.

BULKA, R. P. (ed.) (1979). *Mystics and Medics: A Comparison of Mystical and Psychotherapeutic Encounters*. New York: Human Sciences Press.

BURKE, K. (1970). *The Rhetoric of Religion: Studies in Logology*. Berkeley: University of California Press.

BURNE, J. (1993). One Person, Many People. *The Times*, 4 Mar.

BYNUM, C. W. (1982). *Jesus as Mother: Studies in the Spirituality of the High Middle Ages*. Berkeley: University of California Press.

—— (1991). *Fragmentation and Redemption: Essays on Gender and the Human Body in Medieval Religion*. New York: Zone.

CABANNE, P. (1961). *Van Gogh*. Paris: Aimery Somogy.

CALDECOTT, L., and LELAND, S. (1983). *Reclaim the Earth: Women Speak out for Life on Earth*. London: Women's Press.

CALLOWAY, H. (1978). 'The Most Essentially Female Function of All': Giving Birth. In S. Ardener (ed.), *Defining Females: The Nature of Women in Society*. New York: Wiley.

CAMPBELL, B. (1988). *Unofficial Secrets: Child Sexual Abuse—the Cleveland Case*. London: Virago.

CAMPBELL, C. M., LANGFIELD, H. S., McDOUGALL, W., ROBACK, A. A. and TAYLOR, E. W. (eds.) (1925). *Problems of Personality: Studies Presented to Dr. Morton Prince*. London: Kegan Paul, Trench & Trubner.

CARRITHERS, M., COLLINS, S., and LUKES, S. (eds.) (1986). *The Category of the Person*. Cambridge: Cambridge University Press.

CAWS, P. (1974). Operational, Representational and Explanatory Models. *American Anthropologist*. 76, 1–10.

CLIFFORD, J. (1988). *The Predicament of Culture: Twentieth Century Ethnography, Literature and Art.* Cambridge, Mass.: Harvard University Press.

COREA, G. (1988). *The Mother Machine: Reproductive Technologies from Artificial Insemination to Artificial Womb.* London: Women's Press.

CRAMER, P. (1993). *Baptism and Change in the Early Middle Ages c.200–c.1150.* Cambridge: Cambridge University Press.

CRAPANZANO, V. (1992). *Hermes' Dilemma and Hamlet's Desire: On the Epistemology of Interpretation.* Cambridge, Mass.: Harvard University Press.

CRARY, J., and KWINTER, S. (1992). *Zone 6: Incorporations.* Boston: MIT Press.

CREWS, F. (1994). The Revenge of the Repressed. *New York Review of Books,* 17 Nov., 54–60; 1 Dec., 49–58; corr. 12 Jan. 1995, 44–8.

CRUMP, T. (1990). *The Anthropology of Numbers.* Cambridge: Cambridge University Press.

CSORDAS, T. J. (1983). The Rhetoric of Transformation in Ritual Healing. *Culture, Medicine and Psychiatry,* 7: 333–75.

—— (1988). Elements of Charismatic Persuasion and Healing. *Medical Anthropology Quarterly,* 2: 445–69.

—— (1992). The Affliction of Martin: Religious, Clinical and Phenomenological Meaning in a Case of Demonic Oppression. In A. D. Gaines (ed.), *Ethnopsychiatry: The Cultural Construction of Professional and Folk Psychiatries.* New York: SUNY Press.

—— (1994*a*). *The Sacred Self: A Cultural Phenomenology of Charistmatic Healing.* Berkeley: University of California Press.

—— (1994*b*). Introduction. In Csordas (ed.), *Embodiment and Experience: The Existential Ground of Culture and Self.* Cambridge: Cambridge University Press.

—— (1994*c*). Words from the Holy People: A Case Study in Cultural Phenomenology. In Csordas (ed.), *Embodiment and Experience.* Cambridge: Cambridge University Press.

DA CUNHA, E. (1947). *Revolt in the Backlands* (1902). London: Gollancz.

DANN, G. (1987). *The Barbadian Male: Sexual Attitudes and Practice.* London: Macmillan.

DAVIS, B. D. (1966). *The Problem of Slavery in Western Culture.* Ithaca, NY: Cornell University Press.

DEIN, S. (1992). Millennialism, Messianism and Medicine. *International Journal of Social Psychiatry,* 18: 262–7.

—— (1999). Religion and Healing among the Lubavitch of Stamford Hill. Ph. D. thesis, University College London.

DELANEY, C. (1986). The Meaning of Paternity and the Virgin Birth Debate. *Man* (NS), 21: 494–513.

DENNETT, D. C. (1987). *The Intentional Stance.* Cambridge, Mass.: MIT Press.

—— (1991). *Consciousness Explained.* New York: Little, Brown.

—— (1991). Multiple Personality. Corr. *London Review of Books,* 9 July, 4.

DEVEREUX, G. (1956). Normal and Abnormal: The Key Problem in Psychiatric Anthropology. In *Some Uses of Psychopathology, Theoretical and Applied,* ed.

J. Gladwin and T. Gladwin. Washington, DC: Anthropological Society of Washington.

DEVOS, G. A. (1972). The Inter-Relationship of Social and Psychological Structures in Transcultural Psychiatry. In *Transcultural Research in Mental Health*, ed. W. P. Lebra. Honolulu: Hawaii University Press.

DORAN, J., PALMER, M., GILBERT, N., and MELLORS, P. (1994). The EOS Project: Modelling Upper Palaeolithic Social Change. In N. Gilbert and J. Doran (eds.), *Simulating Societies*. London: UCL Press.

DOUGLAS, M. (1970). *Purity and Danger: An Analysis of Concepts of Pollution and Taboo* (1966). Harmondsworth: Penguin.

—— (1973). *Natural Symbols: Explorations in Cosmology*. Harmondsworth: Penguin.

DOW, J. (1986). Universal Aspects of Symbolic Healing: A Theoretical Synthesis. *American Anthropologist*, 88: 56–69.

DRESNER, S. H. (1974). *The Zaddick*. New York: Schocken Books.

DURKHEIM, E. (1976). *The Elementary Form of the Religious Life* (1912). London: Allen & Unwin.

—— and MAUSS, M. (1963). *Primitive Classification* (1901–2). London: Cohen & West.

EARLY, E. A. (1982). The Logic of Well-Being: Therapeutic Narratives in Cairo, Egypt. *Social Science and Medicine*, 16: 1491–7.

EASTHOPE, G. (1986). *Healers and Alternative Medicine: A Sociological Examination*. London: Gower.

ECO, U. (1993). *La ricerca della lingua perfetta*. Rome: Laterza.

EDELMAN, G. M. (1992). *Bright Air, Brilliant Sun: On the Matter of the Mind*. New York: Basic Books.

EHRENWALD, J. (1979). Precognition and the Prophetic Tradition: From ESP to the Effective Myth. In Bulka (1979).

EILBERG-SCHWARTZ, H. (1992). *People of the Body: Jews and Judaism from an Embodied Perspective*. New York: SUNY Press.

—— (1994). *God's Phallus and Other Problems for Men and Monotheism*. Boston: Beacon Press.

ELIADE, M. (1964). *Shamanism: Archaic Techniques of Ecstasy*. New York: Plenum.

—— (1965). *Rites and Symbols of Initiation: The Mysteries of Birth and Rebirth*. New York: Harper and Row.

ELLEN, R. (1977). Anatomical Classification and the Semiotics of the Body. In Blacking (1977).

ELLENBERGER, H. F. (1970). *The Discovery of the Unconscious: The History and Evolution of Dynamic Psychiatry*. London: Allen Lane.

—— (1993). *Beyond the Unconscious: Essays*. Princeton: Princeton University Press.

EMMERCHE, C. (1994). *The Garden in the Machine: The Emerging Science of Artificial Life*. Princeton: Princeton University Press.

ERIKSON, E. (1958). *Young Man Luther*. New York: Norton.

ERWIN, F. R., PALMOUR, R. M., MURPHY, B. E. P., PRINCE, R., and SIMONS, R. C.

(1988). The Psychobiology of Trance: Physiological and Endocrine Correlates. *Transcultural Psychiatric Research Review*, 25: 267–84.

Ess, C. (ed.) (1996). *Philosophical Perspectives on Computer-Mediated Communication*. New York: SUNY Press.

Esslin, M. (1976). *Artaud*. London: Fontana.

Etzioni, A. (1994). *The Spirit of the Community: Rights, Responsibilities and the Communitarian Agenda*. New York: Crown.

Evans-Pritchard, E. E. (1977). *Theories of Primitive Religion* (1965). Oxford: Clarendon Press.

Fanon, F. (1952). *Peau Noire, Masques Blancs*. Paris: Seuil.

Featherstone, M. (ed.) (1990). *Global Culture: Nationalism, Globalisation and Modernity*. London: Sage.

Feder, L. (1980). *Madness and Literature*. Princeton: Princeton University Press.

Feinberg, R. (1990). Spiritual and Natural Etiologies on a Polynesian Outlier in Papua New Guinea. *Social Science and Medicine*, 30: 311–23.

Field, M. (1960). *Search for Security*. London: Faber & Faber.

Firth, R. (1961). Suicide and Risk-Taking in Tikopian Society. *Psychiatry*, 2: 1–17.

Fodor, J. A. (1992). *A Theory of Content and Other Essays*. Cambridge, Mass.: MIT Press.

Fortes, M. (1937). Review of W. Perry, *The Primordial Ocean*. *Man*, 37: 70–1.

Foster, M. L., and Brandes, S. H. (eds.) (1980). *Symbol and Sense: New Approaches to the Analysis of Meaning*. New York: Academic Press.

Foucault, M. (1970). *The Order of Things: An Archaeology of the Human Sciences*. London: Tavistock.

Fox, G. (1694). *Journals*. Repr. 1952. Cambridge: Cambridge University Press.

Freud, S. (1928). *The Future of an Illusion*. London: Hogarth Press.

Fustel De Coulanges, N. D. (1864). *La Cité antique*. Trans. as *The Ancient City* by W. Small. New York: Doubleday, n.d.

Gellner, E. (1992). *Postmodernism, Reason and Religion*. London: Routledge.

Giddens, A. (1992). *The Transformation of Intimacy: Sexuality, Love and Eroticism in Modern Societies*. Cambridge: Polity Press.

Gilligan, C. (1982). *In a Different Voice: Psychological Theory and Women's Development*. Cambridge, Mass.: Harvard University Press.

Gilman, S. (1992). *The Jew's Body*. New York: Routledge.

Godelier, M. (1986). *The Mental and the Material: Thought, Economy and Society*. London: Verso.

Good, B. (1994). *Medicine, Rationality and Experience: An Anthropological Perspective*. Cambridge: Cambridge University Press.

—— and Good, M. (1986). The Cultural Context of Diagnosis and Therapy: A View from Medical Anthropology. In M. Miranda and H. Kitano (eds.), *Mental Health Research Practice in Minority Communities: Development of Culturally Sensitive Training Programmes*. Washington, DC: Department of Health and Human Services.

GRADEK, M. (1976). Le concept de fou et ses implications dans la littérature talmudique. *Annales Médico-Psychologiques*, 134: 17–36.

GRUENBERG, E. (1957). Socially Shared Psychopathology. In *Explorations in Social Psychiatry*, ed. A. H. Leighton. New York: Basic Books.

GRUNBAUM, A. (1984). *The Foundations of Psychoanalysis: A Philosophical Critique*. Berkeley: University of California Press.

HACKING, I. (1992). Severals. Review of Braude (1991). *London Review of Books*, 22 June, 21–2.

—— (1995). *Rewriting the Soul: Multiple Personality and the Sciences of Memory*. Princeton: Princeton University Press.

HAGE, P., and HARARY, F. (1983). *Structural Models in Anthropology*. Cambridge: Cambridge University Press.

HALEVI, Z. BEN S. (1980). *Kabbalah and Exodus*. Bath: Gateway.

HALL, M. P. (1962). *An Encyclopedic Outline of Masonic, Hermetic, Qabbalistic and Rosicrucian Symbolic Philosophy: Being an Interpretation of the Secret Teachings Concealed within the Rituals, Allegories and Mysteries of All Ages*. Los Angeles: Philosophical Research Society.

HANDWERKER, W. P. (1989). *Women's Power and Social Revolution: Fertility Transition in the West Indies*. California: Sage.

HARAWAY, D. (1989). *Primate Visions: Gender, Race and Nature in the World of Modern Science*. New York: Routledge.

—— (1991). *Simians, Cyborgs and Women: The Reinvention of Nature*. London: Free Association Books.

HARRIS, G. (1957). Possession 'Hysteria' in a Kenyan Tribe. *American Anthropologist*, 59: 1046–66.

HARRIS, S. (1955). *The Incredible Father Divine*. London: Allen.

HARRISON, J. E. C. (1979). *The Second Coming: Popular Millenarianism 1780–1850*. London: Routledge & Kegan Paul.

HARRISON, M. (1922). Mental Instability as a Factor in Progress. *The Monist*, 32: 189–199.

HAWTHORN, H. (1955). *The Doukhobors of British Colombia*. London: Dent.

HAWTHORN, J. (1983). *Multiple Personality and the Disintegration of Literary Character*. New York: St Martin's Press.

HAYTER, A. (1968). *Opium and the Romantic Imigation*. London: Faber.

HEELAS, P. (1981). The Model Applied: Anthropology and Indigenous Psychologies. In P. Heelas and A. Lock (eds.), *Indigenous Psychologies: The Anthropology of the Self*. London: Academic Press.

—— and HAGLUND-HEELAS, A. M. (1988). The Inadequacy of 'Deprivation' as a Theory of Conversion. In W. James and D. H. Johnson (eds.), *Vernacular Christianity: Essays in the Social Anthropology of Religion Presented to Godfrey Lienhardt*. Oxford: JASO.

HERMAN, J. L. (1992). *Trauma and Recovery*. New York: Basic Books.

HERSHMANN, D. J., and LIEB, J. (1988). *The Key to Genius: Manic-Depression and the Creative Life*. New York: Prometheus.

HILL, C. (1975). *The World Turned Upside Down: Radical Ideas during the English Revolution*. Harmondsworth: Penguin.

HOBART, M. (1982). Meaning or moaning? An Ethnographic Note on a Little Understood Tribe. In Parkin (1982).

HOFFMAN, E. (1981). *The Way of Splendor: Jewish Mysticism and Modern Psychology*. New York: Shambala Press.

HOGAN, L. (1995). *From Women's Experience to Feminist Theology*. Sheffield: Sheffield Academic Press.

HOLLOWAY, M. (1966). *Heavens on Earth: Utopian Communities in America 1680–1880*. New York: Dover.

HOLLYWOOD, A. (1995). *The Soul as Virgin Wife: Mechthild of Magdeburg, Marguerite Porete, and Meister Eckhart*. New York: University of Notre Dame Press.

HOLY, L., and STUCHLIK, M. (eds.) (1981). *The Structure of Folk Models*. London: Academic Press.

HOPKINS, J. K. (1982). *A Woman to Deliver her People: Joanna Southcott and English Millenarianism in an Era of Revolution*. Austin: University of Texas Press.

HORN, M. (1993). Memories Lost and Found. *US News and World Report*, 19 Nov., 52–63.

HORTON, R. (1983). Afterword. In M. Fortes, *Oedipus and Job in West African Religion*. Cambridge: Cambridge University Press.

HOSKINS, J. (1967). Epilepsy and Guria. *Social Science and Medicine*, 3: 39–48.

HUNTER, A. (1959). *The Last Days*. London: Blond.

JACKSON, M. (1979). Prevented Succession: A Commentary upon a Kuranko Narrative. In R. H. Hook (ed.), *Fantasy and Symbol: Essays in Anthropological Interpretation*. London: Academic Press.

—— (1983). Knowledge of the Body. *Man* (NS), 18: 327–45.

JACOBS, L. (1973). *Hasidic Prayer*. New York: Schocken Books.

JAMES, W. (1958). *The Varieties of Religious Experience* (1902). New York: Mentor.

JAMESON, F. (1991). *Postmodernism; Or, The Cultural Logic of Late Capitalism*. London: Verso.

JANET, P. (1925). *Psychological Healing*. London: Allen & Unwin.

JANZEN, J. M. (1982). Drums Anonymous: Towards an Understanding of Structures of Therapeutic Maintenance. In M. W. De Vries, R. L. Berg, and M. Lipkin, (eds.), *The Use and Abuse of Medicine*. New York: Praeger.

JAROFF, L. (1993). Lies of the Mind. *Time*, 29 Nov., 56–61.

JARVIE, I. C. (1964). *The Revolution in Anthropology*. London: Routledge & Kegan Paul.

JOHNSON, M. (1987). *The Body in the Mind: The Bodily Basis of Meaning, Imagination and Reason*. Chicago: Chicago University Press.

—— (1993). *The Moral Imagination: Implications of Cognitive Science for Ethics*. Chicago: Chicago University Press.

JONTE-PACE, D. (1987). Object Relations Theory, Mothering and Religion. *Horizons*, 14: 310–27.

JULIAN OF NORWICH (1978). *Showings*. New York: Paulist Press.

KAPFERER, B. (1993). *A Celebration of Demons: Exorcism and the Aesthetics of Healing in Sri Lanka* (1983). Oxford: Berg.

KARLSSON, L. (1974). Schizophrenia and Creativity. *Acta Psychiatrica Scandinavica*, 247: suppl., 76.

KATZ, J. (1961). *Tradition and Crisis: Jewish Society at the End of the Middle Ages*. New York: Free Press.

KEHOT PUBLICATION SOCIETY (1981). *Likutei Amarim-Tanya*. Bilingual edn. Stamford Hill: Kehot.

KELLY, K. (1994). *Out of Control: The New Biology of Machines*. London: Fourth Estate.

KEMPE, M. (1994). *The Book of Margery Kempe*. Harmondsworth: Penguin.

KENNISTON, K. (1974). Psychological Development and Historical Change. In *Exploration in Psychohistory*, ed. R. J. Lifton. New York: Simon & Schuster.

KENNY, M. G. (1981). Multiple Personality and Spirit Possession. *Psychiatry*, 44: 337–58.

—— (1986). *The Passion of Ansel Bourne: Multiple Personality in American Culture*. Washington: Smithsonian Institution Press.

KERNS, V. (1983). *Women and the Ancestors: Black Carib Kinship and Ritual*. Urbana: University of Illinois Press.

KIRMAYER, L. (1993). Healing and the Invention of Metaphor: The Effectiveness of Symbols Revisited. *Culture, Medicine and Psychiatry*, 17: 161–95.

KITZINGER, S. (1978). *Women as Mothers*. London: Fontana.

—— (1982). The Social Context of Birth: Some Comparisons between Childbirth in Jamaica and Britain. In C. P. MacCormack (ed.), *Ethnography of Fertility and Birth*. London: Academic Press.

KLEINMAN, A., and SUNG, L. H. (1979). Why do Indigenous Practitioners Successfully Heal? *Social Science and Medicine*, 13: 7–26.

KNOX, R. A. (1950). *Enthusiasm: A Chapter in the History of Religion*. Oxford: Clarendon Press.

KOCH, K. E. (1972). *Christian Counselling and Occultism: The Counselling of the Psychically Disturbed and those Oppressed through Involvement in Occultism*. Grand Rapids, Mich.: Kregel.

KRIPPNER, S. (1987). Cross-Cultural Approaches to Multiple Personality Disorder: Practices in Brazilian Spiritism. *Ethos*, 15: 273–95.

KROEBER, A. L. (1952). Psychosis or Social Sanction. In Kroeber, *The Nature of Culture*. Chicago: Chicago University Press.

KROKER, A. (1992). *The Possessed Individual: Technology and Postmodernity*. London: Macmillan.

KROLL, O., and DE GANK, O. (1986). The Adolescence of a Thirteenth Century Visionary Nun. *Psychological Medicine*, 16: 745–56.

KUPFERMAN, A. J. (1976). The Lubavitch Hasidim of Stamford Hill. M. Phil. thesis, University of London.

KURELLA, H. (1911). *Cesare Lombroso*. London: Rebman.

KURTZ, P. D. (1988). Mary of Oignies, Christine the Marvellous and Medieval Heresy. *Mystics Quarterly*, 14: 186–96.

LA BARRE, W. (1969). *They shall Take up Serpents*. New York: Schocken Books.

—— (1970). *The Ghost Dance*. New York: Doubleday.

LADERMAN, C. (1987). The Ambiguity of Symbols in the Structure of Healing. *Social Science and Medicine*, 24: 293–301.

LA FONTAINE, J. S. (1994). *The Extent and Nature of Organised and Ritual Abuse*. London: HMSO.

LAING, R. D. (1965). *The Divided Self* (1959). Harmondsworth: Penguin.

LAKOFF, G. (1987). *Women, Fire and Dangerous Things: What Categories Reveal about the Mind*. Chicago: Chicago University Press.

LAMBEK, M. (1981). *Human Spirits: A Cultural Account of Trance in Mayotte*. Cambridge: Cambridge University Press.

LANG, A. (1884). *Custom and Myth*. London: Longmans, Green.

LAROSE, S. (1977). The Meaning of Africa in Haitian Vodu. In I. M. Lewis (ed.), *Symbols and Sentiments: Cross-Cultural Studies in Symbolism*. London: Academic Press.

LASCH, C. (1978). *The Culture of Narcissim: American Life in an Age of Diminishing Expectations*. New York: Norton.

LAST, M. (1981). The Importance of Knowing about not Knowing. *Social Science and Medicine*, 15: 387–92.

LAUGHLIN, C. D., and STEPHENS, C. D. (1980). Symbolisation, Canalisation and P-Structure. In Foster and Brandes (1980).

—— MCMANUS, J., and D'AQUILI (1993). *Brain, Symbol and Experience: Towards a Neurophenomenology of Human Consciousness*. New York: Columbia University Press.

LAW, J. M. (ed.) (1995). *Religious Reflections on the Human Body*. Bloomington: Indiana University Press.

LAWSON, E. T., and MCCAULEY, R. N. (1993). *Rethinking Religion: Connecting Cognition and Culture*. Cambridge: Cambridge University Press.

LEACH, E. (1976). *Culture and Communication*. Cambridge: Cambridge University Press.

LEARS, T. J. (1983). From Salvation to Self-Realisation: Advertising and the Therapeutic Roots of the Consumer Culture, 1880–1930. In R. W. Fox and T. J. Lears (eds.), *The Culture of Consumption*. New York: Random House.

LÉVI-STRAUSS, C. (1949). L'Efficacité symbolique, Trans. as The Effectiveness of Symbols. In Lévi-Strauss. *Structural Anthropology—1*. Harmondsworth: Penguin, 1968.

—— (1970). *The Raw and the Cooked: Introduction to a Science of Mythology—1*. London: Cape.

LEVY, S. (1994). *Artificial Life: The Quest for a New Creation*. London: Cape.

LEWIS, G. (1987). A Lesson from Leviticus: Leprosy. *Man*, NS, 22: 593–612.

LEWIS, I. M. (1969). Spirit Possession in Northern Somaliland. In J. Beattie and

J. Middletone (eds.), *Spirit Mediumship and Society in Africa*. London: Routledge & Kegan Paul.

—— (1970). A Structural Approach to Witchcraft and Spirit Possession. In M. Douglas (ed.), *Witchcraft Confessions and Accusations*. London: Tavistock.

LIENHARDT, G. (1961). *Divinity and Experience: The Religion of the Dinka*. Oxford: Oxford University Press.

—— (1964). *Social Anthropology*. Oxford: Oxford University Press.

LIFTON, R. J. (1974). *Exploration in Psychohistory*. New York: Simon & Schuster.

LINCOLN, E. (1961). *The Black Muslims in America*. Boston: Beacon Press.

LINTON, R. (1943). Nativist Movements. *American Anthropologist*, 45: 230–40.

LITTLEWOOD, R. (1983). The Antinomian Hasid. *British Journal of Medical Psychology*, 56: 67–78.

—— (1984). The Individual Articulation of Shared Symbols. *Journal of Operational Psychiatry*, 15: 17–24.

—— (1991a). Artichokes and Entities; or, How New is 'the New Cross-Cultural Psychiatry?'. *Transcultural Psychiatric Research Review*, 28: 343–56.

—— (1991b) Gender, Role and Sickness: The Ritual Psychopathologies of the Nurse. In P. Holden and J. Littlewood (eds.), *Anthropology and Nursing*. London: Routledge.

—— (1991c) Against Pathology: The 'New Cross-Cultural Psychiatry' and its Critics. *British Journal of Psychiatry*, 159: 696–702.

—— (1993). *Pathology and Identity: The Work of Mother Earth in Trinidad*. Cambridge: Cambridge University Press.

—— (1994). Verticality as the Idiom for Mood and Disorder: A Note on an Eighteenth Century Representation. *British Medical Anthropology Review*, (NS) 2/1: 44–8.

—— (1995a). Psychopathology and Personal Agency: Modernity, Culture-Change and Eating Disorders in South Asia. *British Journal of Medical Psychology*, 68: 45–63.

—— (1995b). Psychopathology and Religious Innovation: An Historical Instance. In D. Bhugra (ed.), *Psychiatry and Religion*. London: Routledge.

—— (1996). *Reason and Necessity in the Specification of the Multiple Self*. Royal Anthropological Institute Occasional Paper 42. London: RAI.

—— and DEIN, S. (1995). The Effectiveness of Words: Religion and Healing among the Lubavitch. *Culture, Medicine and Psychiatry*, 19: 339–83.

LLOYD, G. E. R. (1990). *Demystifying Mentalities*. Cambridge: Cambridge University Press.

LOCK, M., and GORDON, D. R. (1988). Relationships between Society, Culture and Biomedicine. In Lock and Gordon (eds.), *Biomedicine Examined*. Dordrecht: Kluwer.

—— and SCHEPER-HUGHES, N. (1990). A Critical Interpretative Approach in Medical Anthropology: Rituals and Routines of Discipline and Dissent. In T. Johnson and C. Sargent (eds.), *Medical Anthropology: A Handbook of Theory and Practice*. Westport, Conn.: Greenwood Press.

162 *References*

LOFLAND, J., and STARK, R. (1965). Becoming a World Saver: A Theory of Conversion to a Deviant Perspective. *American Sociological Review*, 30: 862–75.

LOFTUS, E., and KETCHAM, K. (1994). *The Myth of Repressed Memory: False Memories and Allegations of Sexual Abuse*. New York: St Martin's Press.

LOVEJOY, D. (1985). *Religious Enthusiasm in the New World: Heresy to Revolution*. Cambridge, Mass.: Harvard University Press.

LUBAVITCH PUBLICATIONS (1992). *A Collection of Stories on the Lubavitcher Rebbe*. New York: Lubavitch Printing House.

LUTZKY, H. (1989). Reparation and Tikkun: A Comparison of the Kleinian and Kabbalistic Concepts. *International Review of Psycho-Analysis*, 16: 449–58.

LYON, M. L., and BARBALET, J. B. (1994). Society's Body: Emotion and the 'Somatisation' of Social Theory. In T. J. Csordas (ed.), *Embodiment and Experience*. Cambridge: Cambridge University Press.

MACCORMACK, C. P. (1982). Biological, Cultural and Social Adaptation in Human Fertility and Birth. In MacCormack (ed.), *Ethnography of Fertility and Birth*. London: Academic Press.

MCDANIEL, J. (1989). *The Madness of the Saints: Ecstatic Religion in Bengal*. Chicago: Chicago University Press.

MCDOUGALL, L. (1977). Symbols and Somatic Structures. In Blacking (1977).

MCGUIRE, M. B. (1983). Words of Power: Personal Empowerment and Healing. *Culture, Medicine and Psychiatry*, 7: 221–40.

MCMULLIN, E. (1978). Structural Explanation. *American Philosophical Quarterly*, 15: 139–47.

MACK, J. (1994). *Abductions: Human Encounters with Aliens*. New York: Simon & Schuster.

MAGOLIN, J., and WITZTUM, E. (1989). Supernatural Impotence: Historical Review with Anthropological and Clinical Implications. *British Journal of Medical Psychology*, 62: 333–42.

MANDELBROT, B. B. (1977). *Fractals: Form, Chance and Dimension*. New York.

MARETT, R. R. (1909). *The Threshold of Religion*. London: Methuen.

MARTIN, E. (1987). *The Woman in the Body: A Cultural Analysis of Reproduction*. Boston: Beacon Press.

—— (1992). The End of the Body? *American Ethnologist*, 19: 121–40.

MARTIN, J. (1993). *Scram: Relocating under a New Identity*. Washington: Loompanics Unlimited. Cited in *The Times*, 9 Sept. 1993.

MATHEWS, G. B. (1992). *Thought's Ego in Augustine and Descartes*. Ithaca, NY: Cornell University Press.

MAUSS, M. (1979a). *Sociology and Psychology*. Trans. B. Brewster. London: Routledge & Kegan Paul.

—— (1979b). Body Techniques (1934). In Mauss (1979a).

MEAD, G. H. (1934). *Mind, Self and Society*. Chicago: Chicago University Press.

MERLEAU-PONTY, M. (1962). *Phenomenology of Perception*, Trans. C. Smith London: Routledge & Kegan Paul.

MERSKEY, H. M. (1992). The Manufacture of Personalities: The Production of Multiple Personality Disorder. *British Journal of Psychiatry*, 160: 327–40.

MICALE, M. S. (1995). *Approaching Hysteria: Disease and its Interpretations.* Princeton: Princeton University Press.

MILLER, K. (1985). *Doubles: Studies in Literary History.* Oxford: Oxford University Press.

MINDEL, N. (1974). *Philosophy of Chabad.* New York: Kehot Publication Society.

MINTZ, J. R. (1968). *Legends of the Hasidim.* Chicago: Chicago University Press.

—— (1992). *Hasidic People: A Place in the New World.* Cambridge, Mass.: Harvard University Press.

MOERMAN, N. (1979). Anthropology of Symbolic Healing. *Current Anthropology*, 20: 59–80.

MORAVEC, H. (1989). *Mind Children: The Future of Robot and Human Intelligence.* Cambridge: Mass.: Harvard University Press.

MORRIS, A. (1985). Sanctified Madness: The God-Intoxicated Saints of Bengal. *Social Science and Medicine*, 21: 221–35.

MOSCOVICI, S. (1976). *La Psychoanalyse, son image et son public.* Paris: Presses Universitaires de France.

MULHERN, S. (1994). Satanism, Ritual Abuse, and Multiple Personality Disorder: A Sociohistorical Perspective. *International Journal of Clinical and Experimental Hypnosis*, 42: 265–88.

MUNN, N. (1973). Symbolism in a Ritual Context: Aspects of Symbolic Action. In J. Honigmann (ed.), *Handbook of Social and Cultural Anthropology.* Chicago: Rand.

MURPHY, H. B. M. (1967). Cultural Aspects of the Delusion. *Studium Generale*, 2: 684–92.

MURPHY, J. (1964). Psychotherapeutic Aspects of Shamanism on St. Lawrence Island. In *Magic, Faith and Healing*, ed. A. Kiev. New York: Free Press.

NAIPAUL, S. (1980). *Black and White.* London: Sphere Edition, Hamish Hamilton.

NEEDHAM, R. (1980*a*). *Reconnaissances.* Toronto: University of Toronto Press.

—— (1980*b*). 'Reversals', Henry Myers Lecture, Royal Anthropological Institute.

—— (1981). Inner States as Universals: Sceptical Reflections on Human Nature. In P. Heelas and A. Lock (eds.), *Indigenous Psychologies: The Anthropology of the Self.* London: Academic Press.

NELSON, K. (1979). *The Origin: An Investigation into Primitive Matriarchal Societies, the Patriarchal Takeover and its Effect on Society Today, and the Building of a Just and Egalitarian Post-Patriarchal Society.* San Francisco: Venusian Propaganda.

NETTLEFORD, R. (1970). *Mirror, Mirror: Identity, Race and Protest in Jamaica.* Kingston: Collins.

NEUMANN, E. (1963). *The Great Mother: An Analysis of the Archetype.* Princeton: Princeton University Press.

NORDOFF, C. (1875). *The Communistic Societies of the United States from Personal Observations.* New York: Harper & Brothers.

OBEYESEKERE, G. (1981). *Medusa's Hair: An Essay on Personal Symbols and Religious Experience*. Chicago: Chicago University Press.

O'DWYER, J. M., and FRIEDMAN, T. (1993). Multiple Personality Following Childbirth. *British Journal of Psychiatry*, 162: 831–3.

OLIVIER, C. (1989). *Jocasta's Children: The Imprint of the Mother* (1980). London: Routledge.

ORTNER, S. (1973). On Key Symbols. *American Anthropologist*, 75: 1338–46.

OTTO, R. (1958). *The Idea of the Holy*. New York: Oxford University Press.

OWEN, A. (1989). *The Darkened Room: Women, Power and Spiritualism in Late Victorian England*. London: Virago.

PAGELS, E. (1982). *The Gnostic Gospels*. Harmondsworth: Penguin.

PARFIT, D. (1984). *Reasons and Persons*. Oxford: Clarendon Press.

PARKIN, D. (ed.) (1982). *Semantic Anthropology*. London: Academic Press.

—— (ed.) (1985). *The Anthropology of Evil*. Oxford: Blackwell.

—— (1995). Latticed Knowledge: Eradication and Dispersal of the Unpalatable in Islam, Medicine and Anthropological Theory. In R. Farndon (ed.), *Counterworks: Managing the Diversity of Knowledge*. London: Routledge.

PERKINS, P. (1995). Creation of the Body in Gnosticism. In Law (1995).

PIAGET, J. (1968). *Le Structuralisme*. Paris: Presses Universitaires de France.

PIPER, A. (1994). Multiple Personality Disorder. *British Journal of Psychiatry*, 164: 600–12.

PLATO (1965). *Timaeus*. Harmondsworth: Penguin.

PREIS, K. (1928). Die Medizin im Zohar. *Monatsschrift für Geschichte und Wissenschaft des Judentums*, 72: 241–60.

PRESTON, J. L. (1982). Introduction. In Preston (ed.), *Mother Worship: Theme and Variation*. Chapel Hill: University of North Carolina Press.

PREUSS, J. (1978). *Biblical and Talmudic Medicine*. New York: Hebrew Publishing.

PRICE, A. W. (1995). *Mental Conflict*. London: Routledge.

PRICE, J. S., and STEVENS, A. (1996). The Human Male Socialisation Strategy Set: Cooperation, Defection, Individualism and Schizotypy. *Evolution and Human Biology*, 19: 57–70.

PRINCE, M. (1905). *The Dissociation of a Personality: The Hunt for the Real Miss Beauchamp*. Repub. 1978 with an introduction by C. Rycroft. Oxford: Oxford University Press.

RABUZZI, K. A. (1994). *Mother with Child: Transformations through Childbirth*. Bloomington: Indiana University Press.

RADIN, P. (1953). *The World of Primitive Man*. New York: Schuman.

RAPHAEL, M. (1996). *Theology and Embodiment: The Post-Patriarchal Reconstruction of Female Sacrality*. Sheffield: Sheffield Academic Press.

REYNOLDS, V., and TANNER, R. (1983). *The Biology of Religion*. London: Longman.

RIEFF, P. (1966). *The Triumph of the Therapeutic*. London: Chatto & Windus.

RIVERS, W. H. R. (1920). *Instinct and the Unconscious*. Cambridge: Cambridge University Press.

—— (1923). *Psychology and Politics*. London: Kegan Paul, Trench & Trubner.

—— (1924). *Medicine, Magic and Religion*. London: Kegan Paul, Trench & Trubner.

ROBERTSON-SMITH, J. S. R. (1927). *Lectures on The Religion of the Semites: The Fundamental Institutions*. 3rd edn. London: A. & C. Black.

ROHEIM, G. (1950). *Psychoanalysis and Anthropology*. New York: International Universities Press.

RONELL, A. (1989). *The Telephone Book: Technology, Schizophrenia, Electric Speech*. Lincoln: University of Nebraska Press.

RORTY, R. (1980). *Philosophy and the Mirror of Nature*. Oxford: Blackwell.

ROSEN, G. (1968). *Madness in Society*. London: Routledge & Kegan Paul.

ROSS, C. A. (1994). *The Osiris Complex: Case Studies in Multiple Personality Disorder*. Toronto: University of Toronto Press.

—— (1995). *Satanic Ritual Abuse: Principles of Treatment*. Toronto: University of Toronto Press.

ROWAN, J. (1990). *Subpersonalities: The People inside Us*. London: Routledge.

RUBIN, N. (1988). Body and Soul in Talmudic and Mishnaic Sources. *Koroth*, 9: 151–64.

SAHLINS, M. (1976). *Culture and Practical Reason*. Chicago: University of Chicago Press.

SAMUEL, G. (1990). *Mind, Body and Culture: Anthropology and the Biological Interface*. Cambridge: Cambridge University Press.

SCHACHTER, Z. M. (1979). The Dynamics of the Yehidut Transaction. In Bulka (1979).

SCHEPER-HUGHES, N., and LOCK, M. (1987). The Mindful Body: A Prolegomenon to Future Work in Medical Anthropology. *Medical Anthropology Quarterly*, 1: 6–39.

SCHIEFFELIN, E. L. (1985). Performance and the Cultural Construction of Reality. *American Ethnologist*, 12: 707–24.

SCHNABEL, J. (1994). *Dark White: Aliens, Abductions and the UFO Obsession*. London: Hamish Hamilton.

SCHOCHET, J. (1979). *Mystical Concepts in Hasidism*. New York: Kehot Publication Society.

SCHOLEM, G. C. (1954). *Major Trends in Jewish Mysticism*. 3rd edn. New York: Schocken Books.

—— (1965). *On the Kabbalah and its Symbolism*. New York: Schocken Books.

—— (1971). *The Messianic Idea in Judaism and Other Essays in Jewish Spirituality*. New York: Schocken Books.

—— (1973). *Sabbatai Sevi*. London: Routledge.

SCHREIBER, F. R. (1973). *Sybil*. Chicago: Regnery.

SCHRÖDINGER, E. (1944). *What is Life?* Cambridge: Cambridge University Press.

SCHUTZ, A. (1976). *The Phenomenology of the Social World*. Rev. edn. London: Heinemann.

SCHWARTZ, T. (1976). The Cargo Cult: A Melanesian Type-Response to Change. In G. A. Devos (ed.), *Responses to Change*. New York: Van Norstrand.

SEAGER, W. (1991). *Metaphysics of Consciousness*. London: Routledge.

SEARLE, J. (1984). *Minds, Brain, Science.* Harmondsworth: Penguin.

SERED, S. S. (1994). *Priestess, Mother, Sacred Sister.* New York: Oxford University Press.

SHAFFIR, W. (1974). *Life in a Religious Community: The Lubavitcher Chassidim in Montreal.* Toronto: Toronto University Press.

SHAROT, S. (1982). *Messianism, Mysticism and Magic: A Sociological Account of Jewish Religious Movements.* Chapel Hill: University of North Carolina Press.

—— (1991). Hasidism in Modern Society. In G. Avroekt (ed.), *Essential Papers in Hasidism.* New York: SUNY Press.

SHARP, L. A. (1993). *The Possessed and the Dispossessed: Spirits, Identity and Power in a Madagascar Migrant Town.* Berkeley: California University Press.

SHOWALTER, E. (1990). *Sexual Anarchy: Gender and Culture at the Fin de Siècle.* New York: Viking.

—— (1993). Hysteria, Feminism and Gender. In S. L. Gilman, H. King, R. Porter, G. S. Rousseau, and E. Showalter, *Hysteria beyond Freud.* Berkeley: California University Press.

SIMONS, R. C., and Hughes, C. C. (eds.) (1985). *Culture-Bound Syndromes: Folk Illnesses of Psychiatric and Anthropological Interest.* Dordrecht: Reidel.

SIMPSON, G. (1955). Jamaican Revivalist Cults. *Social and Economic Studies,* 4: 133–49.

SINASON, V. (ed.) (1994). *Treating Survivors of Satanist Abuse.* London: Routledge.

SMITH, G. E. (1932). *In the Beginning.* London: Watts & Co.

SMITH, R. T. (1988). *Kinship and Class in the West Indies.* Cambridge: Cambridge University Press.

SMITH-ROSENBERG, C. (1972). The Hysterical Woman: Sex Roles and Conflict in 19th Century America. *Social Research,* 39: 652–78.

SOBO, E. (1993). *One Blood: The Jamaican Body.* New York: SUNY Press.

SONTAG, S. (1979). *Illness as Metaphor.* London: Allen Lane.

SOUTHCOTT, J. (1995). *A Dispute between the Woman and the Powers of Darkness* (1802). Oxford: Woodstock.

SPANOS, N. P. (1989). Hypnosis, Demonic Possession and Multiple Personality: Strategic Enactments and Disavowals of Responsibility for Actions. In C. A. Ward (ed.), *Altered States of Consciousness and Mental Health: A Cross-Cultural Perspective.* Newbury Park: Sage.

—— and GOTTLIEB, J. (1979). Demonic Possession, Mesmerism and Hysteria: A Social Psychological Perspective on their Historical Interrelationship. *Journal of Abnormal Psychology,* 88: 527–46.

SPENCER, H. (1876). *The Principles of Sociology,* i. London: Williams & Norgate.

SPERBER, D. (1975). *Rethinking Symbolism.* Cambridge: Cambridge University Press.

—— (1980). Is Symbolic Thought Pre-Rational? In Foster and Brandes (1980).

—— (1985). *On Anthropological Knowledge.* Cambridge: Cambridge University Press.

SPERO, M. H. (1979). On the Nature of the Therapeutic Encounter between Hasid and Master. In Bulka (1979).

STIRRAT, R. L. (1984). Sacred Models. *Man* (NS), 19: 199–215.

STOCKING, G. W. (1996). *After Tylor: British Social Anthropology 1888–1951*. London: Athlone Press.

STOLLER, P. (1984). Sound in Songay Cultural Experience. *American Ethnologist*, 11: 559–70.

—— (1989). *Fusion of the Worlds: An Ethnography of Possession among the Songhay of Niger*. Chicago: Chicago University Press.

STORR, A. (1972). *The Dynamics of Creation*. London: Secker & Warburg.

STROZIER, C. B. (1994). Apocalypse: On the Psychology of Fundamentalism in America. Boston: Beacon Press.

SULLIVAN, L. (1987). Healing. In M. Eliade (ed.), *Encyclopaedia of Religion*. Macmillan/Free Press.

TAMBIAH, S. J. (1968). The Magical Power of Words. *Man* (NS), 3: 175–208.

—— (1990). *Magic, Science, Religion and the Scope of Rationality*. Cambridge: Cambridge University Press.

TANNER, T. (1993). In Two Voices. *Times Literary Supplement*, July, 12.

TART, C. (1980). A Systems Approach to Altered States of Consciousness. In J. M. Davidson and R. J. Davidson (eds.), *The Psychobiology of Consciousness*. New York: Plenum.

TAUSSIG, M. (1993). *Mimesis and Alterity: A Particular History of the Senses*. New York: Routledge.

THIGPEN, C. H., and CLECKLEY, H. M. (1957). *The Three Faces of Eve*. New York: McGraw-Hill.

TOREN, C. (1983). Thinking Symbols: A Critique of Sperber 1979. *Man* (NS), 18: 260–8.

—— (1993). Making History: The Significance of Childhood Cognition for a Comparative Anthropology of Mind. *Man* (NS), 28: 461–78.

TORREY, E. F. (1971). *The Mind Game: Witchdoctors and Psychiatrists*. New York: Emerson Hall.

TRACHTENBERG, J. (1977). *Jewish Magic and Superstition* (1939). New York: Atheneum.

TURNER, B. (1984). *The Body and Society: Explorations in Social Theory*. Oxford: Blackwell.

TURNER, V. (1974). *Dramas, Fields and Metaphors*. Ithaca, NY: Cornell University Press.

TYLOR, E. B. (1904). *Anthropology*. London: Macmillan.

VICTOR, J. S. (1993). *Satanic Panic: The Creation of a Contemporary Legend*. London: Open Court.

VONNEGUT, M. (1976). *The Eden Express*. London: Cape.

WAGNER, R. (1986). *Symbols that Stand for Themselves*. Chicago: Chicago University Press.

WALKER, M. (1993). *Surviving Secrets*. Buckingham: Open University Press.

WALLACE, A. F. C. (1958). *Revitalisation Movements*. New York: Random House.

168 *References*

WALLACH, M. (1977). The Chassidism of Stamford Hill, London. *Jewish Chronicle Magazine*, 27 May, 11–19.

WARNER, M. (1983). *Joan of Arc: The Image of Female Heroism*. Harmondsworth: Penguin.

WEBER, M. (1947*a*). *The Theory of Social and Economic Organisations* (1923). New York: Free Press.

—— (1947*b*). The Sociology of Charismatic Authority. In Weber, *Essays in Sociology*. London: Routledge.

WEDENOJA, W. (1989). Mothering and the Practice of 'Balm' in Jamaica. In C. S. McClain (ed.), *Women as Healers: Cross-Cultural Perspectives*. New Brunswick: Rutgers University Press.

WEIGLE, M. (1989). *Creation and Procreation: Feminist Reflections on Mythologies of Cosmogony and Parturition*. Philadelphia: University of Pennsylvania Press.

WEISEL, E. (1978). *Four Hasidic Masters and their Struggle against Melancholy*. London: Notre Dame.

WIENER, H. (1969) *9½ Mystics: The Kabbala Today*. New York: Collier.

WILLIAMS, E. A. (1994). *The Physical and the Moral: Anthropology, Physiology and Philosophical Medicine in France, 1750–1850*. Cambridge: Cambridge University Press.

WILLIAMS, F. M. (1934). The Vaihala Madness in Retrospect. In E. E. Evans-Pritchard (ed.), *Essays Presented to C. G. Seligman*. London: Kegan Paul.

WILSON, B. (1973). *Magic and the Millennium*. London: Heinemann.

—— (1975). *Noble Savages: The Primitive Origins of Charisma*. Berkeley: California University Press.

WILSON, P. J. (1967). Status Ambiguity and Spirit Possession. *Man* (NS), 2: 366–78.

WILSON, S., and BARBER, T. (1981). Vivid Fantasy and Hallucinatory Abilities in the Life Histories of Excellent Hypnotic Subjects. In E. Klinger (ed.), *Imagery: Concepts, Results and Applications*. New York: Plenum.

WINTER, J. A. (1973). The Metaphoric Parallelist Approach to the Sociology of Theistic Beliefs: Themes, Variations and Implications. *Sociological Analysis*, 34: 212–29.

WITTGENSTEIN, L. (1958). *Philosophical Investigations*. Oxford: Blackwell.

WITZTUM, E., and GREENBERG, D. (1990). Mental Illness and Religious Change. *British Journal of Medical Psychology*, 63: 33–41.

WOLMAN, B. (ed.) (1973). Sense and Nonsense in History. In *The Psychoanalytic Interpretation of History*. London: Harper.

WOOCHER, J. S. (1979). The Kabbalah, Hasidism and the Life of Unification. In Bulka (1979).

WOODCOCK, G., and AVAKUMAIC, J. (1968). *The Doukhobors*. London: Faber.

WORSLEY, P. (1970). *The Trumpet shall Sound*. London: Paladin.

WRIGHT, L. (1993). *Remembering Satan*. New York: Knopf.

WYLLIE, R. W. (1973). Introspective Witchcraft among the Effutu of Southern Ghana. *Man* (NS), 8: 74–9.

YAP, P. M. (1954). The Mental Illness of Hung Hsiu Chu'an, Leader of the Taiping Rebellion. *Far East Quarterly*, 13: 287–304.

YOUNG, A. (1976). Some Implications of Medical Beliefs and Practices for Social Anthropology. *American Anthropologist*, 78: 5–24.

—— (1995). *The Harmony of Illusions: Inventing Post-Traumatic Stress Disorder*. Princeton: Princeton University Press.

YOUNG, I. M. (1984). Pregnant Embodiment: Subjectivity and Alienation. *Journal of Medicine and Philosophy*, 9: 45–62.

ZBOROWSKI, M., and HERZOG, E. (1962). *Life is with People: The Culture of the Shtetl*. New York: Schocken Books.

ZOHAR (1934). *Selections translated by H. Sperling, M. Simon and P. Levertoff*. London: Soncino.

INDEX